Ninja Foodi
Smart XL Grill
Cookbook for Beginners

1500-Day Easy & Tasty Ninja Foodi Grill Recipes
for Your Ninja Foodi XL Grill

Loreen Swanson

CONTENT

Introduction

When it comes to grilling, Ninja Foodi Smart XL Grill is in a league of its own. This incredible machine offers the perfect combination of features and performance, making it the ideal choice for any grilling enthusiast. With its large grilling surface, even heat distribution, and easy-to-use controls, Ninja Foodi Smart XL Grill lets you grill like a pro. But what really sets this Grill apart is its ability to lock in flavors. Thanks to its specially designed sear plates, Ninja Foodi Smart XL Grill seals in juices and moisture, resulting in juicy, flavorful food every time. So, whether you're cooking for a crowd or just yourself, Ninja Foodi Smart XL Grill is sure to make your next grilling adventure a success.

Ninja Foodi Smart XL Grill Cookbook is the perfect guide for anyone who wants to get the most out of their Grill. The included recipes are designed to help you make mouth-watering meals to impress your friends and family. Whether you're cooking for a crowd or just yourself, Ninja Foodi Smart XL Grill Cookbook has everything you need to make delicious grilled food. From simple burgers and hot dogs to chicken and steak, Ninja Foodi Smart XL Grill Cookbook has everything you need to make mouth-watering meals to suit anyone and everyone. So, fire up your Grill and get cooking!

What is Ninja Foodi Smart XL Grill?

Are you ready to take your grilling game to the next level? Look no further than Ninja Foodi Smart XL Grill. This state-of-the-art appliance combines the convenience of indoor grilling with outdoor flavor, thanks to its unique Cyclonic Grilling Technology. In just a few effortless steps, you can set the desired temperature and cook time on the Smart Cook System, then let the Grill work its magic. Not only does this powerful appliance reach high searing temperatures, but you can also use it to reheat your food without drying it out. So go ahead and try out that new grilled salmon recipe or experiment with veggie kabobs—Ninja Foodi Smart XL Grill takes all the guesswork out of cooking. Plus, with its easy cleanup feature and PTFE/PFOA-free non-stick coating, you can enjoy delicious grilled food without any hassle. The possibilities are endless with this unique and modern appliance.

Ninja Foodi Smart XL Grill is a 6-in-1 indoor grill that can act as an air fryer, roaster, baker, and dehydrator. It circulates hot air around food for even cooking. The grill also has a 500°F air fryer and a 500°F grill for perfectly cooked food done your way. Ninja Foodi Smart XL Grill is equipped with a Smart Cook System that allows you to choose from 6 cooking functions and multiple temperature settings.

The Smart XL Grill is a new-fashioned piece of kitchen equipment, and it features ample cooking space, making it perfect for entertaining. Additionally, the Grill comes with a Foodi Smart Thermometer and an automatic shut-off feature, ensuring that food is cooked evenly and safely. Ninja Foodi Smart XL Grill has Intelligent Cooking Technology, allowing it to adjust cooking times and temperatures based on the type of food being cooked. As a result, the Grill can produce restaurant-quality meals with ease. Whether you're hosting a backyard barbecue or cooking for a large family, Ninja Foodi Smart XL Grill is sure to make your life easier.

Features

Whether you're a beginner or a pro when it comes to grilling, Ninja Foodi Smart XL Grill is a great choice. This appliance has all the features you need to cook delicious meals, including two independent temperature zones, Smart Cook Technology that automatically adjusts cooking times, and a 6-in-1 design that allows you to grill, air fry, roast, bake, and more. Plus, Ninja Foodi Smart XL Grill is designed to be used indoors so that you can enjoy grilled foods all year long. Here

are some of the other key features of this appliance:

6–in–1 design
Ninja Foodi Smart XL Grill can be used as a grill, air fryer, roaster, baker, broiler, and sear station.

Two temperature zones
The grill features two temperature zones that allow you to cook multiple items at once or keep food warm until it's time to eat.

Smart Cook Technology
This feature automatically adjusts cooking times based on the type of food you're cooking.

Removable drip pan
The drip pan catches excess fat and juices for easy cleanup.

Nonstick grill plate
The non-stick grill plate ensures your food doesn't stick to the surface.

Dishwasher–safe parts
The removable parts of the Grill are dishwasher-safe for easy cleanup. With all these features, it's no wonder Ninja Foodi Smart XL Grill is a popular choice for both beginners and experienced home cooks. This appliance is the perfect option if you're looking for a versatile and easy-to-use indoor grill.

Benefits of Using Ninja Foodi Smart XL Grill

Ninja Foodi Smart XL Grill is a trendy kitchen gadget that can help you create healthy, delicious meals. Here are 20 benefits of using a Ninja Foodi Smart XL Grill:

- It can grill, air fry, bake, roast, and dehydrate food.
- With its cyclonic grilling system, it evenly distributes heat for precision cooking.
- It has 500°F air fry and 500°F grill capabilities.
- It has a 6-in-1 intelligent cooking system that automatically adjusts the temperature and cooking time for different foods.
- The smart temperature control system prevents food from overcooking or drying out.
- The digital display makes it easy to see and set the temperature.
- The unit comes with a 6-quart ceramic-coated grill pan and a 4-quart

ceramic-coated Crisper Basket.

- It has a non-stick surface for easy cleanup.
- Ninja Foodi Smart XL Grill has a sear function that can lock in juices and flavor.
- The removable drip pan catches excess fat and juices for healthier meals.

- Many of the parts and accessories are dishwasher-safe.
- Ninja Foodi Smart XL Grill comes with a recipe book with delicious recipes to get you started.
- It also has an air frying basket divider allowing you to cook multiple items at once.
- The unit has a built-in fan for circulating hot air for even cooking results.
- It has a built-in digital display that shows the current temperature and time remaining.
- It has cool-touch side handles for easier handling.
- Its 1400-watt heating element ensures evenly-cooked food every time.
- Additionally, Ninja Foodi Smart XL Grill is ETL certified and is backed by a 1-year limited warranty.

Step-By-Step Use

Ninja Foodi Smart XL Grill is one of the most versatile and easy-to-use kitchen appliances on the market. Whether you're grilling, smoking, roasting, or even baking, Ninja Foodi Smart XL Grill can help you get the perfect result every time. Here's a quick guide to using your Ninja Foodi Smart XL Grill:

Power Button

The Grill's power button is located on the front of the unit, and it's easy to press. Once the unit is plugged in, simply press POWER to turn on Ninja Foodi Smart XL Grill. If you need to stop cooking for any reason, just press this button again, and the current cooking function will stop. The Grill will also turn off. That's all there is to it! So, when you're ready to start grilling, remember to press the power button. And when you're finished cooking, press it again to turn off the unit.

Arrow Buttons

The Ninja Foodi has many great features, but one of the best is the ability to adjust the cooking temperature and cooking time. The left and right arrows on the left and right of the display make it easy to adjust the settings, including the cooking temperature. To set the cooking temperature, use the up and down arrows next to the left side of the display. For the cooking time, use the arrows to the right of the display. You can also use these arrows to set the internal doneness when using the PRESET or MANUAL button. So, whether you're cooking with the Foodi Smart Thermometer or not, you can easily adjust the settings to get your food just right.

Manual Setting

The MANUAL function switches the display screen so you can manually set the thermometer's internal doneness. This feature is great when you want to cook something to a specific temperature or use a recipe that requires a particular cooking time/temperature. To use this function, simply select the MANUAL option on the touchscreen display and then use the + and - buttons to set the desired cooking time and temperature. Once you've set the timer and temp, simply press START, and the grill will begin cooking your food to perfection!

Preset Setting

The preset button on your food thermometer is a great way to get the perfect temperature for whatever you're cooking. Whether you're trying to achieve a certain internal doneness for your steak or making sure your chicken is cooked all the way through, the preset button can help you get it just right. And since the internal temperature of food can vary depending on the type of meat or vegetable, PRESET makes it easy to adjust for different ingredients.

Start/Stop Button

After you've selected your desired cooking temperature and time, the final step is to press START/STOP. Once you've done that, your appliance will begin preheating to the chosen temperature. Depending on the model, you may also see a light or other indicator that lets you know when the preheating stage has been reached. Once preheating is complete, your food will start cooking, and the timer will begin counting down. When the timer reaches zero, your food will be done, and the oven will shut off automatically.

Thermometer

Press the button on the left side of the grill to activate the built-in thermometer.

Grill

① Before you begin cooking, setting up your unit correctly is essential. First, place the Cooking Pot in the unit with the indent on the Pot aligned with the bump on the main unit. Then, place the Grill Grate in the Pot with the handles facing up. Ensure that the Splatter Shield is in place, then close the Hood.

② Just press GRILL and the default temperature will be displayed. If you want to adjust the temperature, just use the arrows next to the display to raise or lower the temperature.

③ The arrows on the display make it easy to adjust the cooking time in 1-minute increments, up to 30 minutes. Or, if you're using a thermometer, you can refer to the relevant instructions.

④ Press START/STOP to begin the preheating process. You'll know it's working because the progress bar will start to illuminate. In about 10 minutes, the unit will be fully preheated and ready for cooking.

⑤ When the appliance is done preheating, the display will show "ADD FOOD." At that point, you can add your food.

⑥ Before you begin cooking, it's important to prepare your ingredients. For best results, open the Hood and place the food directly on the Grill Grate. This will help to sear the food and lock in flavor. Once the Hood is closed, the cooking process will begin, and the timer will start counting down. You may need to adjust the time or temperature depending on what you're cooking.

Air Crisp

① Before you begin, it's important to ensure that your Pot is properly positioned on the unit. The indent on the Pot should be aligned with the bump on the main unit, and the Pot should be placed inside the Crisper Basket. Once everything is in place, you'll need to close the Hood. Make sure that the Splatter Shield is in place before you do so, as this will help to prevent any accidental spills.

② Just press AIR CRISP, and the default temperature will be displayed. Use the set of arrows to the left of the display to adjust the temperate up to 400°F.

③ To adjust the cooking time, simply use the set of arrows to the right of the display. You can increment the cooking time in 1-minute intervals up to 1 hour. So if you need to cook your food for a little longer or for a full hour, this function makes it easy.

Roast

① Press ROAST. The display will show the default temperature setting, which you can adjust using the arrows to the left of the screen. If you want to change the temperature, just scroll up or down until you find the perfect setting. For most meats, the ideal temperature is 425°F.

② To adjust the cooking time, use the set of arrows to the right of the display. You can adjust the cooking time in 1-minute increments up to 1 hour or 5-minute increments from 1 to 4 hours.

③ Before you can start cooking, your unit will need to preheat. Press START/STOP to begin the preheating process. You'll see a progress bar that starts to illuminate. After a few minutes, the unit will beep to let you know it's finished preheating and it's ready to use.

④ Once it's reached the correct temperature, it will beep, and the display will read "ADD FOOD." At that point, you can open the Hood and add your ingredients to the Pot. Once the Hood is closed, cooking will begin, and the timer will start counting down.

Dehydrate

① Place your Cooking Pot on the main unit. The indent on the Pot should be aligned with the bump on the unit. Next, you'll add a single layer of ingredients to the Pot. Then, you'll place the Crisper Basket on top of the ingredients in the Pot and add another layer of ingredients to the Basket. Ensure that the Splatter Shield is in place before closing the Hood. This will help to prevent any food from splattering and making a mess.

② The default temperature setting will display when you press DEHYDRATE. To adjust the temperature, simply use the arrows to the left of the display. The temperature can be increased up to 195°F. To adjust the dehydration time, use the arrows to the right of the display. The time can be increased in 15-minute increments, up to 12 hours.

③ To begin dehydrating your food, press START/STOP. The unit will not preheat in DEHYDRATE mode. Once the dehydration time is complete, the unit will beep, and END will appear on the display.

Broil

① First, place your Cooking Pot in the oven with the indent aligned with the bump on the main unit to use the broil function. Next, add your desired ingredients to the Pot. Make sure to put the Splatter Shield in place, then close the Hood. To start the broil function, simply press BROIL. The default temperature setting will display. If you want to adjust the temperature, use the set of arrows to the left of the display to select your desired temperature, up to 500°F.

② Use the set of arrows to the right of the display to adjust the cooking time in 1-minute increments up to 30 minutes.

③ Press START/STOP. The unit will begin cooking immediately and will not need to preheat first. When the cooking time is up, the unit will beep, and END will appear on the display.

How to Use the Thermometer

The leave-in Foodi Smart Thermometer is an excellent tool for any griller who wants to make sure their food is cooked perfectly every time. The Thermometer continuously monitors the internal temperature of food in two places, so you can be sure that your food is cooked evenly throughout. The Smart Cook System also lets you know when it's time to take your food off and let it rest, so you can avoid overcooking or undercooking your food. With the Foodi Smart Thermometer, you can grill with confidence, knowing that your food will come out perfectly cooked every time.

The Ninja Foodi Smart Thermometer is a kitchen tool that can make cooking easier and more enjoyable. Here are some tips on how to use it:

■ Before cooking, calibrate the Thermometer by placing it in ice water. This will ensure accurate readings.

■ When cooking meat, insert the Thermometer into the thickest part of the meat, away from bone or fat. Cook to your desired doneness.

■ The Thermometer can also be used to check the temperature of liquids, such as soups and sauces. Simply insert the probe into the liquid and wait for the reading to stabilize.

■ After cooking, clean the probe with soap and water. The stainless steel probe is dishwasher safe for easy cleanup.

With these tips, you can make the most of your Ninja Foodi Smart Thermometer and enjoy perfect results every time.

Straight from the Store

If you're new to Ninja Foodi Smart XL Grill, this quick guide will help you get started.

■ Before using your new Ninja Foodi Smart XL Grill for the first time, be sure to remove all packaging material, promotional labels, and tape. These can interfere with the Grill's performance and may cause damage. To remove the packaging material, simply lift up the Grill's lid and remove any packing material that may be inside. Use a damp cloth to rub away any adhesive residue caused by promotional labels. Finally, use a sharp knife to carefully remove any tape from the Grill's surface. With the Grill now clean and ready to use, you can enjoy delicious grilled meals all summer long!

■ Before using your new purchase, it's always a good idea to remove all accessories from the package and read the manual carefully.

This helps ensure you're familiar with your new item's features and safety information. In addition, it's important to pay attention to any operational instructions, warnings, or necessary safeguards to avoid any injury or damage. By taking a few moments to review this information before using your new purchase, you can help to ensure a safe and enjoyable experience.

■ Before you start cooking, it's essential to make sure your Grill is clean. Start by washing the Grill Grate, Splatter Shield, Crisper Basket, Thermometer, Cleaning Brush, and Cooking Pot in warm, soapy water. Then rinse and dry them thoroughly. All accessories, except the Thermometer, are dishwasher-safe. NEVER clean the main unit or Thermometer in the dishwasher. By taking a few minutes to clean your Grill before you start cooking, you'll ensure that your food tastes great and that your Grill lasts for many grilling seasons to come!

Cleaning for Ninja Foodi Smart XL Grill

Ninja Foodi Smart XL Grill is a modern and easy-to-use appliance that can help you cook a delicious meal. However, it's essential to clean the grill thoroughly after every use. Otherwise, food particles and grease can build up, making it more difficult to clean the next time. Always let the appliance cool before cleaning it.

■ First, remove any food debris from the grilling surface. Then, use a soft brush or cloth to remove any grease or residue. Unplug the unit from the wall outlet and open the Hood. This will help the unit to cool quicker so that you can avoid any burns. Be sure to use a non-abrasive cleaner on all surfaces to avoid scratching the finish.

■ Wipe up any spills immediately to prevent them from hardening and becoming difficult to remove.

■ The Cooking Pot, Grill Grate, Crisper Basket, Splatter Shield, Cleaning Brush, and any other included accessories are dishwasher-safe, except the Thermometer.

■ DO NOT place the Thermometer in the dishwasher.

■ The best way to clean the Thermometer is to wipe it down with a damp cloth after each use. You can also use a mild soap and water solution for stubborn dirt or residue.

■ Be sure to rinse the Thermometer well after cleaning and dry it thoroughly before using it again.

■ Rinse your Grill Grate, Crisper Basket, Splatter Shield, and any other accessories with warm water before placing them in the dishwasher. This will help remove any food particles or grease that could cause the dishwasher to work less effectively.

- Be sure to check the manufacturer's instructions to ensure that all of your dishwasher's accessories are safe to clean in this way.
- If you choose to hand-wash your dish, we recommend using the included Cleaning Brush. The Brush will help scrub off debris, and the opposite end can be used as a scraper to release baked-on sauces or cheese.

- If food residue or grease is stuck on the Grill Grate, Splatter Shield, or any other removable part, soak them in warm soapy water before cleaning. This will help to loosen the dirt and make it easier to wipe away.
- Soaking the Shield overnight will help soften any baked-on grease, making it easier to remove with the Cleaning Brush.
- Be sure also to clean the stainless steel frame and front tabs.
- Try deep-cleaning the Splatter Shield by boiling it in a pot of water for 10 minutes. This will kill off any harmful bacteria and germs clinging to its surface. After boiling, rinse with room temperature water and allow the Shield to dry completely before using it again.
- The Thermometer and holder should only be hand-washed and never submerged in water or any other liquid. We recommend using a damp cloth to wipe them down after use. Taking these precautions will ensure you get the most out of your Thermometer for as long as possible.

Caring for Ninja Foodi Smart XL Grill

If you're the proud owner of a Ninja Foodi Smart XL Grill, congratulations! You're in for some delicious meals. But like any piece of equipment, it's important to give your Grill some TLC to ensure it lasts for many grilling seasons to come. Here are my top 10 tips for caring for your Ninja Foodi Smart XL Grill:

Before each use, brush off any food residue from the grates with a wire grill brush.

Using cooking oil on the grates before and after each use will help prevent food from sticking and retain their non-stick quality.

After cooking, let your Grill cool before cleaning it to avoid warping or damage.

Never use harsh chemicals or metal scrubbers on the grates—stick with nylon or plastic scrubbing pads instead.

Clean the drip tray after each use to prevent grease buildup and potential fire hazards.

Keep your Grill covered when not in use to protect it from the elements.

Periodically check for rust and replace the grates as necessary.

Replace damaged components (such as burner covers) immediately.

Refer to your owner's manual for recommended maintenance schedules and procedures.

Be sure to properly winterize your Grill if you plan on storing it during colder months.

Taking care of your Ninja Foodi Smart XL Grill may seem like a lot of work, but trust me, it's worth it in the end! Happy grilling!

Grilling Tips

It's grilling season, and Ninja Foodi Smart XL Grill is the perfect tool to make your BBQs stand out. From prepping to cleaning, here are our top tips for using this multi-purpose cooking appliance. First and foremost, always make sure to preheat your Grill before adding any food. This will ensure even cooking and prevent sticking. Next, don't overcrowd the grilling surface; leave some room between each piece of food to allow air circulation and promote browning. It's also important to pay attention to temperature; use a meat thermometer for larger cuts of meat or check for doneness with a fork for vegetables and smaller pieces of protein. During cooking, resist the urge to constantly flip your food; let it sit on each side for a few minutes before turning to achieve those beautiful char marks. And finally, when you're finished, let the Grill cool down before giving it a good scrub with soapy water and a grill brush. Happy grilling!

To get the most out of your Grill, here are our top grilling tips:

1) Preheat the Grill for at least 15–20 minutes before cooking to ensure proper and even cooking.

2) Use paper towels or a brush to lightly oil the grates before placing food on them to prevent sticking.

3) Keep a spray bottle handy for flare-ups or to add moisture to foods like vegetables.

4) Cook thicker cuts of meat or dense vegetables over direct heat, then move them to indirect heat until they reach the desired doneness.

5) For tender, juicy burgers, make an indentation in the center with your thumb before placing them on the Grill; this prevents them from puffing up while cooking.

6) Place chicken on the Grill skin-side down first to crisp up the skin before flipping it over to finish cooking through.

7) Toast buns directly on one side of the Grill for added flavor and texture.

8)Flip meat only once during cooking to prevent any loss of juices.

9)Use a meat thermometer to check for doneness rather than cutting into the meat while cooking.

10)Let cooked meats rest for 5–10 minutes before serving to allow juices to redistribute throughout the meat.

11)Keep vegetables whole or in large chunks for easier flipping and shorter cook times on the Grill.

12)If using wooden skewers, soak them in water for 15–30 minutes before threading on food to prevent burning on the Grill.

13)When adding BBQ sauce, do so towards the end of cooking time rather than at the beginning to prevent any burning or charring.

14)Marinate meats overnight for optimal flavor infusion before grilling.

15)Place foil packets filled with thinly sliced veggies onto the hot Grill for perfectly cooked veggies without having to flip or stir them constantly.

16)Use indirect heat when smoking meats at low temperatures over several hours for tender and juicy results.

17)Trim excess fat off meats before grilling, as it can cause excessive flare-ups and uneven cooking

18)Placing aromatics like sliced onions directly under chicken or fish helps infuse flavor while also preventing sticking.

19)Make kabob skewers by alternating different types of meats and veggies on each skewer for a well-rounded meal.

FAQs

Whether you're a seasoned grill master or just getting started, Ninja Foodi Smart XL Grill is the perfect tool for outdoor cooking. Here are answers to some of the most frequently asked questions about this top-notch Grill.

① Can it cook frozen food without having to defrost it first?
Yes! The Grill's Cyclonic Grilling Technology will air crisp frozen foods to give them a crispy outside and a tender inside.

② Is the Grill non-stick?
The Grill Grate and Crisper Basket are ceramic coated and PTFE/PFOA-free for easy cleaning.

③ Can it be used as a smoker?
Absolutely! With its smoke control settings, you can turn your Grill into a smoker to infuse rich smoky flavors into your meats and veggies.

④ How big is the cooking space?
The grill has 450 square inches of grilling space, enough to fit 6 steaks or up to 9 burgers at once.

⑤ Does it come with a temperature probe?
Yes, there is a probe included that can measure temperatures up to 450°F.

⑥ How do I clean the removable parts?
The removable parts of the Grill are dishwasher-safe for easy cleaning.

⑦ Does it come with any recipe ideas or guides?
Yes, there is a recipe book included with many delicious options for meals and snacks.

⑧ Does it have multiple cooking functions?
Indeed it does; in addition to grilling, the Ninja Foodi can also air crisp, roast, bake, and dehydrate.

⑨ How does it compare to traditional grills?
Not only does it offer the same grilling options as traditional grills, but it also provides more versatility with additional cooking methods.

⑩ Is cleanup easy?
With its removable, non-stick Grill Grate and integrated drip tray, cleanup is a breeze.

⑪ Is there a way to check on the temperature of my food while cooking?
Absolutely; just use the probe function to monitor your food's internal temperature without having to open the lid and interrupt cooking.

⑫ Can I make desserts on this Grill?
Definitely! Try using the baking function for everything from cakes to pies.

⑬ Can I cook a whole chicken on this Grill?
Absolutely! The XL size gives you plenty of room to fit whole chickens or even large cuts of meat like brisket or ribs.

⑭ How do I clean it?
The removable parts are dishwasher-safe, and the Grill surface can be easily wiped down with warm water and soap after use.

⑮ Is there an app or online community for sharing recipes and tips with other Ninja Foodi users?
There's an online Ninja Foodi community where members can share recipes, ask questions, and connect with fellow foodies.

• 4-Week Diet Plan •

Week 1

Day 1:
Breakfast: Breakfast Potato Casserole
Lunch: Grilled Potato Rounds
Snack: Tarragon Asparagus
Dinner: Ninja Foodi Herbed Beef Steak
Dessert: Grilled Apples a la Mode

Day 2:
Breakfast: Mushroom Pepper
Lunch: Tomato Salsa
Snack: Tasty Cauliflower Tots
Dinner: Chicken and Tomatoes
Dessert: Marshmallow Roll-Up

Day 3:
Breakfast: Banana Oat Muffins
Lunch: Baked Mushrooms
Snack: Bacon Hot Dogs
Dinner: Raspberry Pork Chops
Dessert: Easy Scalloped Pineapple

Day 4:
Breakfast: Ninja Foodi Breakfast Sausages
Lunch: Cool Rosemary Potatoes
Snack: Cheesy Chicken Dip
Dinner: Ninja Foodi Southern Catfish
Dessert: Strawberry Cobbler

Day 5:
Breakfast: Ninja Foodi Breakfast Frittata
Lunch: Grilled Veggies with Vinaigrette
Snack: Lemon Herb Carrots
Dinner: Greek Lamb Meatballs
Dessert: Chocolate Cheesecake

Day 6:
Breakfast: Coffee Glazed Bagels
Lunch: Vegetable Orzo Salad
Snack: Cob with Pepper Butter
Dinner: Grilled Red Curry Chicken
Dessert: Ninja Foodi Vanilla Donuts

Day 7:
Breakfast: Grilled Chicken Tacos
Lunch: Ninja Foodi Potato Gratin
Snack: Grilled Butternut Squash
Dinner: Lemon Basil Pork Chops
Dessert: Grilled Pound Cake

Week 2

Day 1:
Breakfast: Homely Zucchini Muffin
Lunch: Ninja Foodi Spicy Cauliflower
Snack: Grilled Oysters with Chorizo Butter
Dinner: Easy BBQ Roast Shrimp
Dessert: Grilled Pineapple Pizza

Day 2:
Breakfast: Veggie Packed Egg Muffin
Lunch: Honey Dressed Asparagus
Snack: Ninja Foodi Potato Croquettes
Dinner: Ninja Foodi Beef Satay
Dessert: Banana Muffins

Day 3:
Breakfast: Campfire Hash
Lunch: Italian Squash Meal
Snack: Savory Roasted Almonds
Dinner: Chicken Thigh Yakitori
Dessert: Banana Skewers

Day 4:
Breakfast: Simple Zucchini Egg Muffins
Lunch: Cajun Green Beans
Snack: Crispy Brussels
Dinner: Balinese Pork Satay
Dessert: Grilled Fruit Skewers

Day 5:
Breakfast: Ninja Foodi Pumpkin Bread
Lunch: Rosemary Potatoes
Snack: Mammamia Banana Boats
Dinner: Dijon Fish Fillets
Dessert: Fudgy Brownie

Day 6:
Breakfast: Cinnamon Oatmeal
Lunch: Zucchini Carrot Patties
Snack: Grilled Potato Wedges
Dinner: Grilled Beef Skewers
Dessert: Lovely Rum Sundae

Day 7:
Breakfast: The Broccoli and Maple Mix
Lunch: Air Grilled Brussels
Snack: Bison Sliders
Dinner: Tomato Turkey Burgers
Dessert: Cute Marshmallow and Banana

Week 3

Day 1:

Breakfast: Energetic Bagel Platter
Lunch: Ninja Foodi Broccoli Chicken
Snack: Honey Glazed Bratwurst
Dinner: Crispy Pork Chops
Dessert: Dessert Nachos

Day 2:

Breakfast: Sausage with Eggs
Lunch: Baked Parmesan Zucchini
Snack: Ninja Foodi Lemon Tofu
Dinner: Ninja Foodi Crispy Salmon
Dessert: S'mores Pizza

Day 3:

Breakfast: Delicious Berry Oatmeal
Lunch: Baked Apple and Sweet Potatoes
Snack: Pesto Cheese Dip
Dinner: Beef Cheese Burgers
Dessert: Fruit Kabobs

Day 4:

Breakfast: Ninja Foodi Bacon Bombs
Lunch: Balsamic Vegetables
Snack: Grilled Honey Carrots
Dinner: Chicken Kebabs with Currants
Dessert: Chocolate Chip Bars

Day 5:

Breakfast: Epic Breakfast Burrito
Lunch: Cheddar Cauliflower Meal
Snack: Grilled Stuffed Mushrooms
Dinner: Curried Pork Skewers
Dessert: Moist Raspberry Muffins

Day 6:

Breakfast: Avocado Eggs
Lunch: Ninja Foodi Glazed Vegetables
Snack: Grilled Peach Salsa
Dinner: Grilled Salmon Packets
Dessert: Pumpkin Muffins

Day 7:

Breakfast: Grilled Bruschetta
Lunch: Ninja Foodi Mushroom Steak
Snack: Cheese-Stuffed Grilled Peppers
Dinner: Ninja Foodi Broiled Tilapia
Dessert: Rummy Pineapple Sunday

Week 4

Day 1:

Breakfast: Kale and Sausage Delight
Lunch: Baked Zucchini and Eggplant
Snack: Eggplant and Tomato Meal
Dinner: Korean Beef Steak
Dessert: Cinnamon Grilled Peaches

Day 2:

Breakfast: Ninja Foodi Bread and Bacon Cups
Lunch: Honey Carrot Dish
Snack: Creamy Chicken Dip
Dinner: Balinese Grilled Chicken
Dessert: Grill Pineapple Slices

Day 3:

Breakfast: Ninja Foodi Eggs with Ham
Lunch: Garlic Flavored Artichoke Meal
Snack: Figs Stuffed with Cheese
Dinner: Grilled Pork Chops with Plums
Dessert: Moist Lemon Cupcakes

Day 4:

Breakfast: Delicious Banana Bread
Lunch: Sweet Grilled Pickles
Snack: Lovely Seasonal Broccoli
Dinner: Ninja Foodi Tuna Patties
Dessert: Apricots with Brioche

Day 5:

Breakfast: Bacon-Herb Grit
Lunch: Crispy Cauliflower Florets
Snack: Delicious Corn Dip
Dinner: Beef Chimichurri Skewers
Dessert: Pecan Kabobs

Day 6:

Breakfast: Greek Egg Muffins
Lunch: Hearty Spinach Olive
Snack: Chicken Stuff Jalapenos
Dinner: Mexican Chicken
Dessert: Grilled Chocolate Sandwiches

Day 7:

Breakfast: Ninja Foodi Smart XL Grill Bean
Lunch: Ninja Foodi Seasoned Asparagus
Snack: Ninja Foodi Mac n' Cheese
Dinner: Ninja Foodi Cajun Salmon
Dessert: The Healthy Granola Bites

Chapter 1 Breakfast Recipes

Breakfast Skewers

Prep time: 15 minutes | Cook Time: 8 minutes | Serves: 4

Ingredients:

1 package (7 oz.) cooked sausage links, halved
1 can (20 oz.) pineapple chunks, drained
10 medium fresh mushrooms

2 tbsp. butter, melted
Maple syrup

Directions:

1. Toss sausages, pineapple, and mushrooms with butter and maple syrup in a bowl. 2. Thread these ingredients on the wooden skewers. 3. Select the "Grill" Mode, set the temperature to MED. 4. Use the arrow keys to set the cooking time to 8 minutes. 5. Press the START/STOP button to initiate preheating. 6. Once preheated, place the skewers in the Ninja Foodi Smart XL Grill. 7. Cover the hood and allow the grill to cook. 8. Flip the skewers once cooked halfway through. 9. Serve warm.

Serving Suggestion: Serve the skewers with bacon and keto bread.

Variation Tip: Drizzle red pepper flakes on top for a tangier taste.

Nutritional Information Per Serving: Calories 246 | Fat 20g |Sodium 114mg | Carbs 13g | Fiber 1g | Sugar 10g | Protein 7g

Breakfast Burger

Prep time: 15 minutes | Cook Time: 26 minutes | Serves: 4

Ingredients:

1 lb. ground beef
1 tbsp. Worcestershire sauce
1 tsp. Montreal steak seasoning
½ tsp. salt
½ tsp. pepper
3 tbsp. butter

8 Texas toast slices
2 tbsp. canola oil
2½ cups hash brown potatoes, shredded
4 American cheese slices
8 cooked bacon strips

Directions:

1. Mix beef with ¼ tsp. black pepper, ¼ tsp. salt, steak seasoning and Worcestershire sauce in a bowl. 2. Make 4-½ inch thick patties out of this beef mixture. 3. Select the "Grill" Mode, set the temperature to MED. 4. Press the START/STOP button to initiate preheating. 5. Once preheated, place the patties in the Ninja Foodi Smart XL Grill. 6. Cover the hood and allow the Ninja Foodi Smart XL Grill to cook. 7. Transfer the patties to a plate. 8. Brush the toast slices with butter and grill them for 2 minutes from both the sides. 9. Similarly, grill the hash browns for 6 minutes per side. 10. Divide the patties, hash brown, cheese, and bacon strip in the grilled toasts. 11. Serve.

Serving Suggestion: Serve the burgers with fried eggs.

Variation Tip: Add chopped parsley to the patty mixture.

Nutritional Information Per Serving: Calories 859 | Fat 49g |Sodium 595mg | Carbs 55g | Fiber 6g | Sugar 13g | Protein 45g

Campfire Hash

Prep time: 10 minutes | Cook Time: 31 minutes | Serves: 4

Ingredients:

1 large onion, chopped
2 tbsp. canola oil
2 garlic cloves, minced
4 large potatoes, peeled and cubed

1 lb. smoked kielbasa sausage, halved and sliced
1 can (4 oz.) green chillies, chopped
1 can (15¼ oz.) whole kernel corn, drained

Directions:

1. Sauté the onion with canola oil in a skillet for 5 minutes. 2. Stir in garlic and sauté for 1 minute then transfer to a baking pan. 3. Toss in potatoes and kielbasa then mix well. 4. Select the "Bake" Mode, set the temperature to 400°F/200°C. 5. Use the arrow keys to set the cooking time to 20 minutes. 6. Press the START/STOP button to initiate preheating. 7. Once preheated, place the baking pan in the Ninja Foodi Smart XL Grill. 8. Cover the hood and allow the grill to cook. 9. Serve warm.

Serving Suggestion: Serve the hash with crispy bread toasts.

Variation Tip: Add chopped tomatoes to the hash before baking.

Nutritional Information Per Serving: Calories 535 | Fat 26g |Sodium 1097g | Carbs 46g | Fiber 4g | Sugar 8g | Protein 17g

Spinach Tater Tot Casserole

Prep time: 10 minutes | Cook Time: 8 minutes | Serves: 8

Ingredients:

8 eggs

15 ounces frozen tater tots

1½ cup cheddar cheese, shredded

4 ounces fresh spinach, chopped & sautéed

1 cup roasted red peppers, chopped

Pepper

Salt

Directions:

1. In a bowl, whisk eggs with pepper and salt. Add cheese, roasted peppers and spinach, stir well. 2. Place the tater tots into the greased baking dish. Pour egg mixture over tater tots. 3. Inset the cooking pot and place your own baking dish in the pot. Select Bake mode, set the temperature to 350°F/175°C and time to 40 minutes. 4. Press START/STOP to begin preheating. 5. Once preheated, place the food in, cover the hood and let the appliance grill. 6. Serve.

Serving Suggestion: Serve warm.

Variation Tip: Add your choice of seasonings.

Nutritional Information per Serving: Calories 254 | Fat 16g |Sodium 680mg | Carbs 15g | Fiber 1g | Sugar 680g | Protein 12g

Sausage with Eggs

Prep time: 15 minutes | Cook Time: 10 minutes | Serves: 4

Ingredients:

4 sausage links

2 cups kale, chopped

1 sweet yellow onion, chopped

4 eggs

1 cup mushrooms

Olive oil

Directions:

1. Place the cooking pot in the Ninja Foodi Smart XL Grill then place the grill grate in the pot. 2. Place the sausages in the Ninja Foodi Smart XL Grill. 3. Cover the Ninja Foodi Smart XL Grill's Hood, select the Grill mode, set the temperature to Low and grill for 2 minutes. 4. Flip the sausages and continue grilling for another 3 minutes. 5. Now spread the onion, mushrooms, sausages, and kale in an iron skillet. 6. Crack the eggs in between the sausages. 7. BAKE this mixture for 5 minutes in the grill at 350°F/175°C. 8. Serve warm and fresh.

Serving Suggestion: Serve the sausages with crispy bread toasts.

Variation Tip: Add chopped tomatoes to the mixture before baking.

Nutritional Information per Serving: Calories 212 | Fat 12g | Sodium 321mg | Carbs 14.6g | Fiber 4g | Sugar 8g | Protein 17g

Grilled Bruschetta

Prep time: 15 minutes | Cook Time: 4 minutes | Serves: 4

Ingredients:

1 cup celery, chopped

1 pound tomatoes, seeded and chopped

3 tablespoons Balsamic vinegar

¼ cup basil, minced

Mustard Spread:

1 tablespoon green onion, chopped

¼ cup Dijon mustard

1 garlic clove, minced

3 tablespoons olive oil

½ teaspoon salt

2 garlic cloves, minced

3 tablespoons Dijon mustard

¾ teaspoon dried oregano

½ cup mayonnaise

1 French loaf bread, sliced

Directions:

1. Place the cooking pot in the Ninja Foodi Smart XL Grill then place the grill grate in the pot. 2. Take the first eight ingredients in a bowl and mix them together. 3. Cover this prepared topping and refrigerate for about 30 minutes. 4. Now take mayonnaise, onion, garlic, oregano and mustard in a bowl. 5. Mix them well and prepare the mayonnaise spread. 6. Select the "Grill" Mode, set the temperature to MED. 7. Use the arrow keys to set the time to 4 minutes. 8. Press the START/STOP button to initiate preheating. 9. Place the bread slices in the Ninja Foodi Smart XL Grill. 10. Cover the hood and allow the grill to cook. 11. Top the grilled bread with mayonnaise spread and tomato relish. 12. Serve fresh.

Serving Suggestion: Serve the Bruschetta with crispy bacon on the side.

Variation Tip: Add a layer of garlic mayonnaise to the bruschetta.

Nutritional Information per Serving: Calories 284 | Fat 7.9g | Sodium 704mg | Carbs 46g | Fiber 3.6g | Sugar 6g | Protein 18g

Coffee Glazed Bagels

Prep time: 15 minutes | Cook Time: 4 minutes | Serves: 4

Ingredients:

4 bagels split in half

¼ cup coconut milk

1 cup fine sugar

2 tablespoons black coffee

2 tablespoons coconut flakes

Directions:

1. Place the cooking pot in the Ninja Foodi Smart XL Grill then place the grill grate in the pot. 2. Place two bagels in the Ninja Foodi Smart XL Grill. 3. Cover the Ninja Foodi Smart XL Grill's Hood, select the Grill mode, select the Low setting and grill for 2 minutes. 4. Flip the bagel and continue grilling for another 2 minutes. 5. Grill the remaining bagels in a similar way. 6. Whisk the rest of the ingredients in a bowl well. 7. Drizzle this sauce over the grilled bagels. 8. Serve.

Serving Suggestion: Serve the bagels with chocolate syrup.

Variation Tip: Cut the bagels in half and layer them with cream cheese.

Nutritional Information per Serving: Calories 412 | Fat 25g | Sodium 132mg | Carbs 44g | Fiber 3.9g | Sugar 3g | Protein 18.9g

Grilled Honeydew

Prep time: 15 minutes | Cook Time: 6 minutes | Serves: 4

Ingredients:

¼ cup peach preserves

1 tbsp. lemon juice

1 tbsp. crystallized ginger, chopped

2 tsp. lemon zest, grated

⅛ tsp. ground cloves

1 medium honeydew melon, cut into cubes

Directions:

1. Mix peaches preserves with lemon juice, ginger, lemon zest, and cloves in a bowl. 2. Thread the honeydew melon on the wooden skewers. 3. Brush the prepared glaze over the skewers liberally. 4. Select the "Grill" Mode, set the temperature to MED. 5. Use the arrow keys to set the cooking time to 6 minutes. 6. Press the START/STOP button to initiate preheating. 7. Once preheated, place the skewers in the Ninja Foodi Smart XL Grill. 8. Cover the hood and allow the grill to cook. 9. Flip the skewers once cooked halfway through. 10. Serve.

Serving Suggestion: Serve the skewers with muffins on the side.

Variation Tip: Add some salt to season the honeydew.

Nutritional Information per Serving: Calories 101 | Fat 0g |Sodium 18mg | Carbs 26g | Fiber 3.6g | Sugar 6g | Protein 1g

Grilled Chicken Tacos

Prep time: 15 minutes | Cook Time: 18 minutes | Serves: 4

Ingredients:

2 teaspoons sugar

⅓ cup olive oil

⅓ cup lime juice

⅓ cup red wine vinegar

2 teaspoons salt

Taco Wraps:

8 flour tortillas

4 Poblano peppers

2 teaspoons pepper

1 cup fresh cilantro, chopped

2 tablespoons chipotle in Adobo sauce, chopped

2 pounds boneless skinless chicken thighs

1 tablespoon olive oil

2 cups shredded Jack cheese

Directions:

1. Place the cooking pot in the Ninja Foodi Smart XL Grill then place the grill grate in the pot. 2. Take the first six ingredients in a blender jug and blend them together. 3. Once blended, mix with chipotles and cilantro. 4. Mix chicken with this cilantro marinade and cover to refrigerate for eight hours. 5. Grease the Poblano peppers with cooking oil and keep them aside. 6. Select the "Grill" Mode, set the temperature to MED. 7. Press the START/STOP button to initiate preheating. 8. Place the peppers in the Ninja Foodi Smart XL Grill. 9. Cover the hood and allow the grill for 5 minutes. 10. Flip the peppers and then continue grilling for another 5 minutes. 11. Now peel and slice the peppers in half, then also slice the chicken. 12. Spread each tortilla and add half cup chicken, half peppers and ¼ cup cheese. 13. Fold the tortilla and carefully place it in the Ninja Foodi Smart XL Grill and cover its lid. 14. Grill each for 2 minutes per side on the MED temperature setting. 15. Serve.

Serving Suggestion: Serve the tacos with crumbled crispy bacon on top and warm bread on the side.

Variation Tip: Add chopped carrots and cabbage to the chicken filling.

Nutritional Information per Serving: Calories 134 | Fat 4.7g | Sodium 1mg | Carbs 54.1g | Fiber 7g | Sugar 3.3g | Protein 26g

Portobello Mushrooms Bruschetta

Prep time: 15 minutes | Cook Time: 8 minutes | Serves: 6

Ingredients:

2 cups cherry tomatoes, cut in half
3 tablespoons red onion, diced
3 tablespoons fresh basil, shredded
Balsamic Glaze:
2 teaspoons brown sugar

Salt and black pepper to taste
4 tablespoons butter
1 teaspoon dried oregano

¼ cup balsamic vinegar

6 Portobello mushrooms caps

Directions:

1. Place the cooking pot in the Ninja Foodi Smart XL Grill then place the grill grate in the pot. 2. Start by preparing the Balsamic glaze and take all its ingredients in a saucepan. 3. Stir, cook this mixture for 8 minutes on medium heat, then remove from the heat. 4. Take the mushrooms and brush them with the prepared glaze. 5. Stuff the remaining ingredients into the mushrooms. 6. Place the stuffed mushrooms in the Ninja Foodi Smart XL Grill with their cap side down. 7. Cover the Ninja Foodi Smart XL Grill's Hood, select the Grill mode, select the Low setting and grill for 8 minutes. 8. Serve.

Serving Suggestion: Serve the mushrooms with fried eggs and crispy bacon.
Variation Tip: Add chopped parsley to the mushrooms
Nutritional Information per Serving: Calories 331 | Fat 2.5g | Sodium 595mg | Carbs 19g | Fiber 12g | Sugar 12g | Protein 8.7g

Avocado Eggs

Prep time: 15 minutes | Cook Time: 5 minutes | Serves: 2

Ingredients:

2 eggs
1 ripe avocado

1 pinch of barbecue rub
Salt and pepper, to taste

Directions:

1. Place the cooking pot in the Ninja Foodi Smart XL Grill then place the grill grate in the pot. 2. Slice the avocado in half and remove its pit. 3. Remove some flesh from the center. 4. Drizzle barbecue rub, salt and black pepper on top. 5. Place the avocado in the Ninja Foodi Smart XL Grill with their skin side down. 6. Cover the Ninja Foodi Smart XL Grill's Hood, select the Grill mode, select the Low setting and grill for 8 minutes. 7. Flip the avocados once grilled half-way through. 8. Crack an egg into each half of the avocado. 9. Serve.

Serving Suggestion: Serve the avocado cups with crispy bacon on top.
Variation Tip: Top egg with chopped bell pepper and fresh herbs.
Nutritional Information per Serving: Calories 322 | Fat 12g | Sodium 202mg | Carbs 14.6g | Fiber 4g | Sugar 8g | Protein 17.3g

Bacon-Herb Grit

Prep time: 15 minutes | Cook Time: 10 minutes | Serves: 4

Ingredients:

2 teaspoons fresh parsley, chopped
½ teaspoon garlic powder
½ teaspoon black pepper

3 bacon slices, cooked and crumbled
½ cup Cheddar cheese, shredded
4 cups instant grits

Cooking spray

Directions:

1. Place the cooking pot in the Ninja Foodi Smart XL Grill then place the grill grate in the pot. 2. Start by mixing the first seven ingredients in a suitable bowl. 3. Spread this mixture in a 10-inch baking pan and refrigerate for one hour. 4. Flip the pan on a plate and cut the grits mixture into 4 triangles. 5. Select the "Grill" Mode, set the temperature to MED. 6. Use the arrow keys on the display to select the time to 10 minutes 7. Press the START/STOP button to initiate preheating. 8. Place the grits in the Ninja Foodi Smart XL Grill. 9. Cover the hood and allow the grill to cook. 10. Flip the grits once cooked halfway through. 11. Serve warm.

Serving Suggestion: Serve these grits with hot sauce or any other tangy sauce you like.
Variation Tip: Add sautéed ground chicken or pork.
Nutritional Information per Serving: Calories 197 | Fat 15g | Sodium 548mg | Carbs 59g | Fiber 4g | Sugar 1g | Protein 7.9g

Breakfast Potato Casserole

Prep time: 10 minutes | Cook Time: 35 minutes | Serves: 10

Ingredients:

7 eggs

8 ounces cheddar cheese, grated

1 pound sausage, cooked

20 ounces frozen hash browns, diced

½ cup unsweetened almond milk

1 onion, chopped and sautéed

Pepper

Salt

Directions:

1. In a bowl, whisk eggs with milk, pepper, and salt. Add remaining ingredients and mix well. 2. Pour egg mixture into the greased baking dish. 3. Select Bake mode, set the temperature to 350°F/175°C and time to 35 minutes. 4. Press START/STOP to begin preheating. 5. Once preheated, place the baking dish in the Ninja Foodi Smart XL Grill. 6. Close the hood and grill. 7. Serve, when done.

Serving Suggestion: Serve warm.

Variation Tip: You can use any non-dairy milk.

Nutritional Information per Serving: Calories 446 | Fat 30.7g |Sodium 743mg | Carbs 21.6g | Fiber 2.1g | Sugar 1.7g | Protein 20.2g

Kale and Sausage Delight

Prep time: 10 minutes | Cook Time: 10 minutes|Servings: 4

Ingredients

Olive oil as needed

1 cup mushrooms

2 cups kale, fine chopped

4 sausage links

4 medium eggs

1 medium yellow onion, sweet

Directions:

1. Open the lid of your Ninja Foodi Smart XL Grill and arrange the Grill Grate. 2. Pre-heat your Ninja Foodi Smart XL Grill and select the "GRILL" function and set the temperature to "HI" for 5 minutes. 3. Once you hear the beeping sound, arrange sausages over the grill grate. 4. Cook for 2 minutes, flip and cook for 3 minutes more. 5. Take a baking pan and spread out the kale, onion, mushroom, sausage and crack an egg on top. Cook on BAKE mode on 350°F/175°C for about 5 minutes more. 6. Serve and enjoy!

Serving Suggestion: Serve with bread.

Variation Tip: use fresh baked vegetables as side.

Nutritional Information per Serving: Calories 236 | Carbohydrates 17g | Protein 18g | Fat 12g | Sodium 369mg| Fiber 4g

Ninja Foodi Bread and Bacon Cups

Prep time: 12 minutes | Cook Time: 10 minutes | Serves: 4

Ingredients:

4 bread slices

8 tomato slices

4 eggs

¼ teaspoon balsamic vinegar

2 bacon slices, chopped

2 tablespoons shredded mozzarella cheese

¼ teaspoon maple syrup

½ tablespoon fresh parsley, chopped

Salt and black pepper, to taste

Directions:

1. Place the bread slices in lightly greased ramekins and top them with tomato and bacon slices. 2. Top the mixture with cheese, eggs and maple syrup. 3. Drizzle with vinegar and sprinkle salt, pepper and parsley on the top. 4. Meanwhile, arrange the "Crisper Basket" in the cooking pot of Ninja Foodi Smart XL Grill and close the hood. 5. Select the "Air Crisp" button and set the temperature to 320°F/160°C and the time to 10 minutes. 6. Press START/STOP to begin preheating. 7. Place the ramekins in "Crisper Basket" when the Ninja Foodi Smart XL Grill shows "Add Food". 8. Cook for about 10 minutes and take out. 9. Serve and enjoy!

Serving Suggestions: Top with mayonnaise before serving.

Variation Tip: Add chopped bell pepper to enhance taste.

Nutritional Information per Serving: Calories: 185 |Fat: 11.2g|Sat Fat: 4.2g|Carbohydrates: 7g|Fiber: 0.6g|Sugar: 1.8g|Protein: 14g

Stuffed up Bacon and Pepper

Prep time: 10 minutes | Cook Time: 15 minutes | Servings: 4

Ingredients

Chopped parsley, for garnish
Salt and pepper to taste
4 whole large eggs

4 bell pepper, seeded and tops removed
4 slices bacon, cooked and chopped
1 cup cheddar cheese, shredded

Directions:

1. Take the bell pepper and divide the cheese and bacon evenly between them. 2. Crack eggs into each of the bell pepper. 3. Season the bell pepper with salt and pepper. 4. Pre-heat your Ninja Foodi Smart XL Grill in "AIR CRISP" mode with temperature to 390°F/200°C for 15 minutes. 5. Once you hear the beep, transfer the bell pepper to cooking basket. 6. Transfer your prepared pepper to Ninja Foodi Smart XL Grill and cook for 10-15 minutes until the eggs are cooked, and the yolks are just slightly runny.
Serving Suggestion: Serve, Garnish with a bit of parsley.
Variation Tip: use chopped dill for garnish.
Nutritional Information per Serving: Calories: 326| Fat: 23 g| Carbohydrates: 10 g| Fiber: 2 g| Sodium: 781 mg| Protein: 22 g

Cinnamon Oatmeal

Prep time: 10 minutes | Cook Time: 30 minutes | Serves: 8

Ingredients:

2 eggs
3 cups rolled oats
¼ cup butter, melted
½ cup maple syrup
1½ cups unsweetened almond milk

1 teaspoon ground cinnamon
1 teaspoon vanilla
1½ teaspoon baking powder
Pinch of salt

Directions:

1. Place the cooking pot in the Ninja Foodi Smart XL Grill. 2. In a bowl, whisk eggs with milk, cinnamon, vanilla, baking powder, butter, maple syrup and salt. Add oats and stir well. 3. Pour oat mixture into the greased baking pan. 4. Select the "Bake" Mode, set the temperature to 350°F/175°C. 5. Use the right arrow keys on the display to set the cooking time to 30 minutes. 6. Press the START/STOP button to initiate preheating. 7. Once Ninja Foodi Smart XL Grill is preheated, place your own bake pan in the Ninja Foodi Smart XL Grill the cooking pot. 8. Cover the hood and let the appliance cook. 9. Serve
Serving Suggestion: Top with some milk and serve.
Variation Tip: You can use any non-dairy milk.
Nutritional Information per Serving: Calories 245 | Fat 9.5g |Sodium 114mg | Carbs 35.2g | Fiber 3.5g | Sugar 12.2g | Protein 5.7g

Delicious Banana Bread

Prep time: 10 minutes | Cook Time: 40 minutes | Serves: 12

Ingredients:

4 ripe bananas, mashed
¼ cup butter, melted
1 teaspoon baking soda
1 teaspoon baking powder

1¼ cups flour
1 teaspoon vanilla
1 cup sugar
½ teaspoon salt

Directions:

1. Place the cooking pot in the Ninja Foodi Smart XL Grill. 2. In a mixing bowl, mix flour, baking soda, sugar, baking powder and salt. 3. Add mashed bananas and vanilla and mix until well combined. 4. Pour batter into the greased loaf pan. 5. Select the Bake Mode and set the temperature to 350°F/175°C. 6. Use the Arrow keys to set the time to 40 minutes. 7. Press the START/STOP button to initiate preheating. 8. Once preheated, place the baking dish in the Ninja Foodi Smart XL Grill. 9. Cover the hood and let the appliance cook. 10. Serve, when done.
Serving Suggestion: Slice and serve.
Variation Tip: You can also use melted vegan butter.
Nutritional Information per Serving: Calories 181 | Fat 3g |Sodium 4mg | Carbs 35g | Fiber 1g | Sugar 21g | Protein 1g

Banana Oat Muffins

Prep time: 10 minutes | Cook Time: 20 minutes | Serves: 12

Ingredients:

1 egg
1 cup banana, mashed
2¼ cups old-fashioned oats
½ teaspoon cinnamon
1 teaspoon baking powder

1 teaspoon vanilla
¼ cup honey
¾ cup milk
¼ teaspoon salt

Directions:

1. Place the cooking pot in the Ninja Foodi Smart XL Grill. 2. In a bowl, mix oats, cinnamon, baking powder and salt and set aside. 3. In a separate bowl, whisk egg with honey, vanilla, milk and mashed banana. 4. Add oat mixture into the egg mixture and mix until well combined. 5. Pour oat mixture into the greased silicone muffin molds. 6. Select the Bake Mode and set the temperature to 350°F/175°C. 7. Use the Arrow keys to set the time to 20 minutes. 8. Press the START/STOP button to initiate preheating. 9. Once preheated, place the baking dish in the Ninja Foodi Smart XL Grill. 10. Cover the hood and let the appliance cook. 11. Serve, when done.
Serving Suggestion: Allow to cool completely then serve.
Variation Tip: You can also use almond milk instead of milk.
Nutritional Information per Serving: Calories 103 | Fat 1.8g |Sodium 64mg | Carbs 19.9g | Fiber 1.9g | Sugar 8.5g | Protein 3g

Homely Zucchini Muffin

Prep time: 5-10 minutes | Cook Time: 7 minutes|Servings: 4

Ingredients

4 whole eggs
1 zucchini, grated
2 tbsp. almond flour

½ tsp salt
1 tsp butter

Directions:

1. Add zucchini, salt, and almond flour into a mixing bowl. 2. Mix them well. 3. Grease muffin molds with butter. 4. Add zucchini mixture to them. 5. Arrange muffin tins in your Ninja Foodi Smart XL Grill. 6. Then close the lid and cook on "AIR CRISP" mode for 7 minutes at 375°F/190°C.
Serving Suggestion: Serve warm with tea.
Variation Tip: use cheese inside the muffin for fun.
Nutritional Information per Serving: Calories: 94| Fat: 8 g| Carbohydrates: 2 g| Fiber: 0.5 g| Sodium: 209 mg| Protein: 7 g

Ninja Foodi Smart XL Grill Bean

Prep time: 5 minutes | Cook Time: 10 minutes|Servings: 4

Ingredients

Fresh ground black pepper
Flaky sea salt
Pinch of pepper

1 lemon, juiced
2 tablespoons oil
1-pound green bean, trimmed

Directions:

1. Take a medium bowl and add the green bean. 2. Mix and stir well. 3. Select the "GRILL" function, adjust temperature to "MAX" and time to 10 minutes. Press START/STOP to preheat your Ninja Foodi Smart XL Grill. 4. Wait until you hear a beep. Transfer beans to the grill grate, cook for 8-10 minutes. 5. Toss well to ensure that all sides cooked evenly. 6. Squeeze a bit of lemon juice on the top. 7. Season with salt, pepper, and pepper flakes according to your taste. 8. Enjoy!
Serving Suggestion: Serve with bread.
Variation Tip: use chopped dill for garnish.
Nutritional Information per Serving: Calories 100 | Carbohydrates 10g | Protein 2g | Fat 7g | Sodium 30mg| Fiber 4g

Mushroom Pepper

Prep time: 10 minutes | Cook Time: 10 minutes|Servings: 4

Ingredients

4 cremini mushrooms, sliced
4 large eggs
½ cup cheddar cheese, shredded
½ onion, chopped

¼ cup whole milk
Sea salt
½ bell pepper, seeded and diced
Black pepper

Directions:

1. Add eggs and milk into a medium bowl. 2. Whisk them together. 3. Add mushrooms, onion, bell pepper, and cheese. 4. Mix them well. 5. Select the "BAKE" function of Ninja Foodi Smart XL Grill and adjust temperature to 400°F/200°C for 10 minutes. 6. Pour the egg mixture into the baking pan and spread evenly. 7. Let it pre-heat until you hear a beep. 8. Then close the lid. 9. Cook for 10 minutes. 10. Serve and enjoy!

Serving Suggestion: Serve and enjoy.

Variation Tip: Add melted cheese for extra flavor.

Nutritional Information per Serving: Calories 153 | Carbohydrates 5g | Protein 11g | Fat 10g | Sodium 494mg| Fiber 1g

Epic Breakfast Burrito

Prep time: 5-10 minutes | Cook Time: 30 minutes|Servings: 4

Ingredients

12 tortillas
Salt and pepper to taste
2 cups potatoes, diced
3 cups cheddar cheese, shredded

10 whole eggs, beaten
1-pound breakfast sausage
1 tsp. olive oil

Preparation:

1. Pour olive oil into a pan over medium heat. 2. Cook potatoes and sausage for 7 to 10 minutes, stirring frequently. 3. Spread this mixture on the bottom of the Ninja Foodi Smart XL Grill cooking pot. 4. Season with salt and pepper. 5. Pour the eggs and cheese on top. 6. Select the "Bake" setting of Ninja Foodi Smart XL Grill at 325°F/160°C and bake for 20 minutes. 7. Top the tortilla with the cooked mixture and roll. 8. Sprinkle cheese on the top side. Add Crisper basket to Ninja Foodi Smart XL Grill. 9. Select the "AIR CRISP" and crisp the Burritos for 10 minutes at 375°F/190°C. 10. Serve and enjoy!

Serving Suggestion: Serve with your favorite sauce.

Variation Tip: use variation with vegetables.

Nutritional Information per Serving: Calories: 400| Fat: 20 g| Carbohydrates: 36 g| Fiber: 5 g| Sodium: 675 mg| Protein: 22 g

Ninja Foodi Bacon Bombs

Prep time: 5 minutes | Cook Time: 7 minutes | Serves: 2

Ingredients:

2 eggs, lightly beaten
1 tablespoon cream cheese, softened
½ cup whole-wheat pizza dough, freshly prepared

2 bacon slices, crisped and crumbled
½ tablespoon fresh chives, chopped

Directions:

1. In a Ninja Foodi Smart XL Grill, press the "Bake" button and set the time to 6 minutes at 350°F/175°C. 2. Press START/STOP to begin preheating. 3. Meanwhile, add eggs in a non-stick pan and stir-fry for about 1 minute. 4. Add in chives, bacon and cream cheese. Stir well and set aside. 5. Now, cut the pizza dough in two pieces and roll each into circles. 6. Put the bacon mixture in the center of the dough pieces and seal the edges with water. 7. When the Ninja Foodi Smart XL Grill shows "Add Food", place the dough pieces in it and bake for about 6 minutes. 8. Take out, serve and enjoy!

Serving Suggestions: Serve with chopped cilantro on the top.

Variation Tip: Use jalapenos to enhance taste.

Nutritional Information per Serving: Calories: 216 |Fat: 14.2g|Sat Fat: 5.6g|Carbohydrates: 6.8g|Fiber: 1g|Sugar: 1.1g|Protein: 14.5g

Ninja Foodi Pumpkin Bread

Prep time: 15 minutes | Cook Time: 25 minutes | Serves: 8

Ingredients:

½ cup coconut flour

2 teaspoons baking powder

½ teaspoon ground cinnamon

½ cup chopped pumpkin

4 tablespoons unsweetened almond milk

1½ teaspoons pumpkin pie spice

4 eggs

2 teaspoons vanilla extract

Salt, to taste

Directions:

1. Add flour, spices, salt and baking powder in a large bowl. Mix well. 2. Meanwhile, add eggs, pumpkin, vanilla extract and almond milk in another bowl. Mix properly. 3. Now, combine the two mixtures and pour in the baking dish. 4. Arrange the "Crisper Basket" in the pot of Ninja Foodi Smart XL Grill and select "Air Crisp". Set its temperature to 350°F/175°C and time to 25 minutes. 5. Press START/STOP to begin preheating. 6. When it shows "Add Food", place the baking dish in the "Crisper Basket" and cook for 25 minutes at 350°F/175°C. 7. Take out the bread and set aside to cool. 8. Slice and serve.

Serving Suggestions: Serve with maple syrup on the top.

Variation Tip: Coconut flour can be replaced with almond flour.

Nutritional Information per Serving: Calories: 77 |Fat: 3.3g|Sat Fat: 1.3g|Carbohydrates: 8.1g|Fiber: 3.7g|Sugar: 0.9g|Protein: 4.1g

Simple Zucchini Egg Muffins

Prep time: 5-10 minutes | Cook Time: 7 minutes|Servings: 4

Ingredients

4 whole eggs

2 tbsps. almond flour

1 zucchini, grated

1 tsp butter

½ tsp salt

Preparation:

1. Take a small-sized bowl and add almond flour, salt, zucchini. Mix well. 2. Take muffin molds and grease them gently, add the zucchini mix. 3. Arrange your molds in Ninja Foodi Smart XL Grill and cook on "AIR CRISP" mode for 7 minutes at a temperature of 375°F/190°C. 4. Serve and enjoy the meal once complete!

Serving Suggestion: Serve in breakfast.

Variation Tip: Add mushroom for taste.

Nutritional Information per Serving: Calories: 94|Fat: 8 g| Carbohydrates: 2 g| Fiber: 0.5 g| Sodium: 209 mg |Protein: 7 g

Ninja Foodi Eggs with Ham

Prep time: 15 minutes | Cook Time: 13 minutes | Serves: 4

Ingredients:

4 teaspoons unsalted butter, softened

8 eggs, divided

4 tablespoons heavy cream

6 tablespoons grated parmesan cheese

¼ pound ham, thinly sliced

¼ teaspoon smoked paprika

4 teaspoons fresh chives, minced

Salt and black pepper, to taste

Directions:

1. Arrange a "Crisper Basket" in the Ninja Foodi Smart XL Grill cooking pot and press the "Air Crisp" button. Set the temperature to 320°F/160°C and the time to 13 minutes. 2. Press START/STOP to begin preheating. 3. Meanwhile, spread butter in the bottom of a baking pan and place ham slices on it. 4. Now, add two eggs, cream, salt and black pepper in a large bowl. Whisk properly. 5. Pour the mixture on the ham slices and crack remaining eggs on it. 6. Sprinkle with paprika, cheese and chives and place the baking pan in the "Crisper Basket" as soon as the Ninja Foodi Smart XL Grill shows "Add Food". 7. Cook for 13 minutes at 320°F/160°C and take out. 8. Slice and serve.

Serving Suggestions: Top with jalapenos before serving.

Variation Tip: Mozzarella cheese can also be used.

Nutritional Information per Serving: Calories: 393 |Fat: 29.6g|Sat Fat: 15.4g|Carbohydrates: 3.8g|Fiber: 0.5g|Sugar: 0.7g|Protein: 29.7g

The Broccoli and Maple Mix

Prep time: 5-10 minutes | Cook Time: 10 minutes|Servings: 4

Ingredients

2 heads broccoli, cut into florets	4 tablespoons balsamic vinegar
4 tbsps. soy sauce	2 tsp. canola oil
2 tsp. maple syrup	Red pepper flakes and sesame seeds for garnish

Preparation:

1. Take a shallow mixing bowl and add vinegar, soy sauce, oil, maple syrup. 2. Whisk the whole mixture thoroughly. 3. Add broccoli to the mix. 4. Keep it aside. Set your Ninja Foodi Smart XL Grill to "GRILL" mode at the "MAX" heat. 5. Set the timer to 10 minutes. 6. Once you hear the beep, add prepared broccoli over Grill Grate. 7. Cook for 10 minutes. 8. Serve and enjoy!

Serving Suggestion: Serve topped with sesame seeds, pepper flakes.

Variation Tip: use your favorite vegetables.

Nutritional Information per Serving: Calories: 141| Fat: 7 g, Fat: 1 g, Carbohydrates: 14 g, Fiber: 4 g, Sodium: 853 mg, Protein: 4 g

Veggie Packed Egg Muffin

Prep time: 5-10 minutes | Cook Time: 7 minutes|Servings: 4

Ingredients

4 whole eggs	1 zucchini, grated
2 tbsps. almond flour	½ tsp salt
1 tsp butter	

Preparation:

1. Add almond flour, zucchini, and salt into a mixing bowl. 2. Mix them well. 3. Grease muffin molds with butter. 4. Adds zucchini mixture to them. 5. Arrange muffin tins in your Ninja Foodi Smart XL Grill and lock the lid. 6. Select the "AIR CRISP" mode of Ninja Foodi Smart XL Grill for 7 minutes at 375°F/190°C and cook.

Serving Suggestion: Serve warm.

Variation Tip: use chopped dill for taste.

Nutritional Information per Serving: Calories: 94| Fat: 8 g| Carbohydrates: 2 g| Fiber: 0.5 g| Sodium: 209 mg| Protein: 7 g

Greek Egg Muffins

Prep time: 10 minutes | Cook Time: 20 minutes | Serves: 12

Ingredients:

8 eggs	¼ cup milk
1 cup spinach, chopped	½ onion, diced
⅓ cup Feta cheese, crumbled	Pepper
½ cup sun-dried tomatoes, sliced	Salt
1 tablespoon basil leaves, chopped	

Directions:

1. Place the cooking pot in the Ninja Foodi Smart XL Grill. 2. In a bowl, whisk eggs with garlic powder, pepper, and salt. 3. Add onion, tofu and cheese and stir well. 4. Pour egg mixture into the silicone muffin molds. 5. Select the Bake Mode and set the temperature to 390°F/200°C. 6. Use the Arrow keys to set the time to 20 minutes. 7. Press the START/STOP button to initiate preheating. 8. Once preheated, place the muffin molds in the Ninja Foodi Smart XL Grill. 9. Cover the hood and allow the grill to cook. 10. Serve, when done.

Serving Suggestion: Serve warm.

Variation Tip: Add ¼ teaspoon Italian seasoning for more flavor.

Nutritional Information per Serving: Calories 59 | Fat 3.9g |Sodium 104mg | Carbs 1.5g | Fiber 0.3g | Sugar 1g | Protein 4.7g

Butternut Squash with Italian Herbs

Prep time: 5-10 minutes | Cook Time: 16 minutes|Servings: 4

Ingredients

1 medium butternut squash, peeled, seeded, and cut into ½ inch slices	1 and ½ tsp oregano, dried
1 tsp dried thyme	¼ tsp. black pepper
1 tablespoon olive oil	½ tsp. salt

Directions:

1. Add all the Ingredients into a mixing bowl and mix it. 2. Pre-heat your Ninja Foodi Smart XL Grill by selecting the "GRILL" option and setting it to "MED.". 3. Set the timer to 16 minutes. 4. Allow it to pre-heat until you hear a beep. 5. Arrange squash slices over the grill grate. 6. Cook for 8 minutes. 7. Flip them and cook for 8 minutes more. 8. Serve and enjoy!

Serving Suggestion: Serve with your favorite drink.

Variation Tip: use chopped dill for garnish.

Nutritional Information per Serving: Calories 238 | Carbohydrates 36g | Protein 158g | Fat 12g | Sodium 128mg| Fiber 3g

Delicious Berry Oatmeal

Prep time: 10 minutes | Cook Time: 20 minutes | Serves: 4

Ingredients:

1 egg	1 cup blueberries
2 cups old-fashioned oats	½ cup blackberries
½ cup strawberries, sliced	1½ teaspoon baking powder
¼ cup maple syrup	½ teaspoon salt
1½ cups milk	

Directions:

1. Place the cooking pot in the Ninja Foodi Smart XL Grill. 2. In a bowl, mix oats, salt, and baking powder. 3. Add egg, vanilla, maple syrup and milk and stir well. Add berries and stir well. 4. Pour mixture into the greased baking dish. 5. Select the Bake Mode and set the temperature to 375°F/190°C. 6. Use the Arrow keys to set the time to 20 minutes. 7. Press the START/STOP button to initiate preheating. 8. Once preheated, place the baking dish in the Ninja Foodi Smart XL Grill. 9. Cover the hood and allow the grill to cook. 10. Serve, when done.

Serving Suggestion: Allow to cool completely then serve.

Variation Tip: Add almond milk instead of milk.

Nutritional Information per Serving: Calories 461 | Fat 8.4g |Sodium 353mg | Carbs 80.7g | Fiber 10.1g | Sugar 23.4g | Protein 15g

Ninja Foodi Breakfast Sausages

Prep time: 10 minutes | Cook Time: 20 minutes | Serves: 6

Ingredients:

2 teaspoons chili flakes	1 teaspoon paprika
2 teaspoons dried thyme	4 teaspoons brown sugar
1 teaspoon cayenne	2 teaspoons onion powder
4 teaspoons tabasco	6 teaspoons garlic, minced
3 pounds ground sausage	Salt and black pepper, to taste

Directions:

1. In a Ninja Foodi Smart XL Grill, press the "Grill" button, set the temperature to HI heat and time to 20 minutes. 2. Press START/STOP to begin preheating. 3. Meanwhile, add ground sausage, tabasco sauce, herbs and spices in a large bowl. Mix well. 4. Make sausage shaped patties out of the mixture and set aside. 5. When the Ninja Foodi Smart XL Grill shows "Add Food", add in sausages and grill for 20 minutes. 6. Flip halfway through and take out the sausages. 7. Serve and enjoy!

Serving Suggestions: Serve with bread.

Variation Tip: Brown sugar can be replaced with white sugar.

Nutritional Information per Serving: Calories: 787 |Fat: 64.5g|Sat Fat: 20.7g|Carbohydrates: 4.2g|Fiber: 0.5g|Sugar: 2.4g|Protein: 44.5g

Ninja Foodi Swiss-Cheese Sandwiches

Prep time: 10 minutes | Cook Time: 18 minutes | Serves: 4

Ingredients:

6 tablespoons half and half cream

2 eggs

¾ cup Swiss cheese, sliced

1 teaspoon powdered sugar

2 teaspoons butter, melted

4 bread slices

½ teaspoon vanilla extract

¼ pound deli turkey, sliced

¼ pound deli ham, sliced

Directions:

1. In a Ninja Foodi Smart XL Grill, press the "Grill" button and set the time to 18 minutes at MED. 2. Press START/STOP to begin preheating. 3. Meanwhile, add half and half cream and vanilla extract in a bowl. Mix well. 4. Take two bread slices and top them with ham, turkey and Swiss cheese slices. 5. Cover them with remaining bread slices and dip them in egg mixture. 6. Now, place the sandwiches in the Ninja Foodi Smart XL Grill when it shows "Add Food". 7. Grill for about 18 minutes and flip halfway through. 8. Dish out and top with powdered sugar. 9. Serve and enjoy!

Serving Suggestions: Top with raspberry jam before serving.

Variation Tip: Powdered sugar can be omitted.

Nutritional Information per Serving: Calories: 260 |Fat: 15.9g|Sat Fat: 8g|Carbohydrates: 10.8g|Fiber: 0.7g|Sugar: 2.7g|Protein: 18.1g

Ninja Foodi Breakfast Frittata

Prep time: 15 minutes | Cook Time: 10 minutes | Serves: 6

Ingredients:

1 cup grated parmesan cheese, divided

2 bacon slices, chopped

2 tablespoons olive oil

12 cherry tomatoes, halved

6 eggs

12 fresh mushrooms, sliced

Salt and black pepper, to taste

Directions:

1. Press the "Grill" button in a Ninja Foodi Smart XL Grill and set the time to 10 minutes at MED. 2. Press START/STOP to begin preheating. 3. Meanwhile, add tomatoes, bacon, mushrooms, black pepper, and salt in a large bowl. Mix well. 4. Take another bowl and beat eggs and cheese in it. 5. When the Ninja Foodi Smart XL Grill shows "Add Food", place the bacon mixture and top with eggs mixture. 6. Grill for 10 minutes and flip halfway through. 7. Dish out and serve hot.

Serving Suggestions: Top with chopped cilantro before serving.

Variation Tip: You can also use canola oil instead of olive oil.

Nutritional Information per Serving: Calories: 204 |Fat: 13.3g|Sat Fat: 3.6|Carbohydrates: 11.4g|Fiber: 3.3g|Sugar: 7.4g|Protein: 12.7g

Ninja Foodi Cinnamon Buttered Toasts

Prep time: 10 minutes | Cook Time: 5 minutes | Serves: 6

Ingredients:

½ cup sugar

1½ teaspoons vanilla extract

½ cup salted butter, softened

1½ teaspoons ground cinnamon

¼ teaspoon freshly ground black pepper

12 whole-wheat bread slices

Directions:

1. Add vanilla, sugar, black pepper, cinnamon and butter in a large bowl. Mix until a smooth batter is formed. 2. Spread the mixture on the bread-slices and set aside. 3. Meanwhile, arrange the "Crisper Basket" in a Ninja Foodi Smart XL Grill and close the lid. 4. Select "Air Crisp", set the temperature to 400°F/200°C and set the time to 5 minutes. 5. Press START/STOP to begin preheating. 6. When the Ninja Foodi Smart XL Grill shows "Add Food", place the bread slices in the "Crisper Basket" and cook for 5 minutes. 7. Take out and serve.

Serving Suggestions: Cut the slices diagonally before serving.

Variation Tip: You can omit black pepper.

Nutritional Information per Serving: Calories: 353 |Fat: 17.3g|Sat Fat: 10.2g|Carbohydrates: 42.1g|Fiber: 5g|Sugar: 20.3g|Protein: 7.5g

Energetic Bagel Platter

Prep time: 5-10 minutes | Cook Time: 8 minutes|Servings: 4

Ingredients

4 bagels, halved
2 tbsp. coconut flakes
1 cup fine sugar

2 tbsp. black coffee, prepared and cooled down
¼ cup of coconut milk

Directions:

1. Take your Ninja Foodi Smart XL Grill and open the lid. 2. Arrange grill grate and close top. 3. Pre-heat Ninja Foodi Smart XL Grill by selecting the "GRILL" option and setting it to "MED" for 8 minutes 4. Let it pre-heat until you hear a beep. 5. Arrange bagels over grill grate and lock lid. 6. Cook for 2 minutes. 7. Flip sausages and cook for 2 minutes more. 8. Repeat the same procedure to grill remaining Bagels. 9. Take a mixing bowl and mix the remaining Ingredients Pour the sauce over grilled bagels 10. Serve and enjoy!

Serving Suggestion: Serve with sauce.
Variation Tip: add fried egg for taste.
Nutritional Information per Serving: Calories 300 | Carbohydrates 42g | Protein 18g | Fat 23g | Sodium 340mg| Fiber 4g

Morning Frittata

Prep time: 10 minutes | Cook Time: 10 minutes|Servings: 4

Ingredients

4 large eggs
4 cremini mushrooms, sliced
½ bell pepper, seeded and diced
½ cup shredded cheddar cheese

½ onion, chopped
¼ cup whole milk
Salt and pepper to taste

Preparation:

1. Add eggs and milk into a medium-sized bowl. 2. Whisk it and then season with salt and pepper. 3. Then add bell pepper, onion, mushroom, cheese. Mix them well. 4. Preheat Ninja Foodi Smart XL Grill by selecting the "BAKE" option and setting it to 400°F/200°C. 5. Set the timer to 10 minutes. 6. Let it pre-heat until you hear a beep. 7. Pour Egg Mixture in your bake pan, spread well. 8. Transfer to Ninja Foodi Smart XL Grill and lock lid. 9. Bake for 10 minutes until lightly golden. 10. Serve and enjoy!

Serving Suggestion: Serve warm with tea.
Variation Tip: use your favorite vegetables for taste.
Nutritional Information per Serving: Calories: 153| Fat: 10 g| Carbohydrates: 5 g| Fiber: 1 g| Sodium: 177 mg| Protein: 11 g

• Chapter 2 Poultry Recipes •

Grilled Chicken Wings with Jaew

Prep time: 15 minutes | Cook Time: 30 minutes | Serves: 4

Ingredients:

Jaew
½ cup fish sauce
3 tbsp. fresh lime juice
2 tbsp. granulated sugar

Wings
⅓ cup oyster sauce
¼ cup Thai seasoning sauce
2 tbsp. granulated sugar

2 tsp. red Thai chili powder
1½ tsp. toasted sesame seeds

2 tbsp. vegetable oil
1½ tsp. black pepper
30 chicken wing flats

Directions:

1. Place the cooking pot in the Ninja Foodi Smart XL Grill then set a grill grate inside. 2. Mix chili powder, sugar, lime juice, and fish sauce in a bowl. 3. Stir in sesame seeds, and mix well then keep 3 tbsp. marinade aside. 4. Mix the remaining marinade with the chicken in a large bowl. 5. Cover and refrigerate for 30 minutes for marinating. 6. Mix the reserved marinade and remaining ingredients in a bowl. 7. Thread the chicken on the wooden skewers and brush the prepared glaze over them. 8. Select the "Grill" Mode, set the temperature to MED. 9. Press the START/STOP button to initiate preheating. 10. Once preheated, place the chicken in the Ninja Foodi Smart XL Grill. 11. Cover the hood and cook for 10 to 15 minutes per side until golden brown and tender. 12. Serve warm.
Serving Suggestion: Serve the wings with yogurt sauce.
Variation Tip: Coat the chicken with parmesan before cooking.
Nutritional Information per Serving: Calories 344 | Fat 13g |Sodium 216mg | Carbs 7g | Fiber 3g | Sugar 4g | Protein 31g

Balinese Grilled Chicken

Prep time: 15 minutes | Cook Time: 10 minutes | Serves: 6

Ingredients:

3 tbsp. coconut oil
5 garlic cloves, smashed
2 tbsp. fresh makrut lime juice
1 tbsp. peeled fresh turmeric root, chopped
1 tbsp. peeled fresh ginger, chopped

1 tbsp. kosher salt
1 tsp. tamarind paste
1 tsp. ground coriander
3 lbs. chicken pieces

Directions:

1. Place the cooking pot in the Ninja Foodi Smart XL Grill then set a grill grate inside. 2. Blend coconut oil and all other ingredients except chicken in a food processor. 3. Leave this mixture for 20 minutes then add the chicken and mix well. 4. Cover and marinate the chicken for 1 hour in the refrigerator. 5. Plug the thermometer into the appliance. 6. Select the "Grill" Mode, set the temperature to MED then select the PRESET. 7. Use the right arrow keys on the display to select "CHICKEN" and set the doneness to WELL. 8. Press the START/STOP button to initiate preheating. 9. Once preheated, place the chicken in the Ninja Foodi Smart XL Grill. 10. Insert the thermometer probe into the thickest part of the chicken. 11. Cover the hood and allow the grill to cook. 12. Serve warm.
Serving Suggestion: Serve the chicken with mayonnaise dip.
Variation Tip: Add shredded cheese on top.
Nutritional Information per Serving: Calories 380 | Fat 19g |Sodium 318mg | Carbs 9g | Fiber 5g | Sugar 3g | Protein 26g

Kewpie-Marinated Chicken

Prep time: 15 minutes | Cook Time: 25 minutes | Serves: 6

Ingredients:

1 cup Kewpie mayonnaise
2 tsp. lime zest
1½ tbsp. ground cumin
1½ tbsp. hot paprika

Kosher salt
Black pepper
Two 3-lb. whole chickens, cut into pieces
olive oil, for brushing

Directions:

1. Mix mayonnaise with 1 tsp. black pepper, 1 tbsp. salt, paprika, cumin and lime juice and zest. 2. Remove the chicken bones and flatten the meat with a mallet. 3. Cut slits over the chicken and place in a tray. 4. Spread and rub the prepared marinade over the chicken. 5. Cover and refrigerate for 2 hours. 6. Place the cooking pot in the Ninja Foodi Smart XL Grill then set a grill grate inside. 7. Plug the thermometer into the appliance. 8. Select the "Grill" Mode, set the temperature to MED then select the PRESET. 9. Use the right arrow keys on the display to select "CHICKEN" and set the doneness to WELL. 10. Press the START/STOP button to initiate preheating. 11. Once preheated, place the chicken in the Ninja Foodi Smart XL Grill. 12. Insert the thermometer probe into the thickest part of the chicken. 13. Cover the hood and allow the grill to cook. 14. Serve warm.
Serving Suggestion: Serve the chicken with yogurt dip and peas snaps.
Variation Tip: Add grilled zucchini to the recipe as well.
Nutritional Information per Serving: Calories 375 | Fat 16g |Sodium 255mg | Carbs 4.1g | Fiber 1.2g | Sugar 5g | Protein 24.1g

Grilled Duck Breast

Prep time: 15 minutes | Cook Time: 10 minutes | Serves: 4

Ingredients:

4 large duck or small goose breasts, sliced

Salt, to taste

Olive or vegetable oil

Black pepper, to taste

Directions:

1. Season the duck breasts with black pepper, salt and oil. 2. Place the cooking pot in the Ninja Foodi Smart XL Grill then set a grill grate inside. 3. Plug the thermometer into the appliance. 4. Select the "Grill" Mode, set the temperature to MED then select the PRESET. 5. Use the right arrow keys on the display to select "CHICKEN" and set the doneness to WELL. 6. Press the START/STOP button to initiate preheating. 7. Once preheated, place the chicken in the Ninja Foodi Smart XL Grill. 8. Insert the thermometer probe into the thickest part of the duck. 9. Cover the hood and allow the grill to cook. 10. Serve warm.

Serving Suggestion: Serve the duck with keto bread.

Variation Tip: Add a pinch of sugar to season the duck mildly sweet.

Nutritional Information per Serving: Calories 278 | Fat 4g |Sodium 232mg | Carbs 14g | Fiber 1g | Sugar 0g | Protein 21g

Grilled Chicken with Banana Pepper Dip

Prep time: 15 minutes | Cook Time: 28 minutes | Serves: 6

Ingredients:

3 tbsp. olive oil

2 medium banana peppers sliced

4 oz. feta cheese, crumbled

3 tsp. fresh lemon juice

½ tsp. kosher salt

¼ tsp. black pepper

1 oz. pita bread

1 (6-oz.) boneless chicken breast

4 grape tomatoes, halved

1 small Persian cucumber, halved

1 tbsp. red onion, chopped

5 pitted kalamata olives, halved

2 tsp. torn fresh mint

Directions:

1. Sauté banana peppers with 1 tbsp. oil in a skillet for 6 minutes. 2. Allow them to cool then blend with 2 tbsp. lemon juice in a blender until smooth. 3. Stir in black pepper and salt then mix well. 4. Rub the chicken with black pepper, salt and oil. 5. Place the cooking pot in the Ninja Foodi Smart XL Grill then set a grill grate inside. 6. Plug the thermometer into the appliance. 7. Select the "Grill" Mode, set the temperature to MED then select the PRESET. 8. Use the right arrow keys on the display to select "CHICKEN" and set the doneness to WELL. 9. Press the START/STOP button to initiate preheating. 10. Once preheated, place the chicken in the Ninja Foodi Smart XL Grill. 11. Insert the thermometer probe into the thickest part of the chicken. 12. Cover the hood and allow the grill to cook. 13. Transfer the chicken to a plate and cook the pita for 4 minutes per side. 14. Mix tomatoes with other ingredients in a bowl. 15. Slice the chicken and serve with banana pepper dip, pita and tomato mixture. 16. Serve.

Serving Suggestion: Serve the chicken with cucumber salad.

Variation Tip: Add Brussels sprouts to the meal.

Nutritional Information per Serving: Calories 348 | Fat 12g |Sodium 710mg | Carbs 24g | Fiber 5g | Sugar 3g | Protein 34g

Peruvian Chicken Skewers

Prep time: 15 minutes | Cook Time: 10 minutes | Serves: 4

Ingredients:

½ cup ají panca paste

5 tbsp. olive oil

3 tbsp. red wine vinegar

2 tbsp. gochujang

1 tbsp. tamari or soy sauce

1½ tsp. toasted cumin seeds

¼ tsp. dried Mexican oregano

⅛ tsp. black pepper

1 large garlic clove

1½ lbs. boneless chicken thighs, cut into cubes

huacatay Dipping Sauce

Directions:

1. Mix chicken cubes with gochujang and other ingredients in a bowl. 2. Cover and refrigerate for 30 minutes then thread the chicken on the wooden skewers. 3. Place the cooking pot in the Ninja Foodi Smart XL Grill then set a grill grate inside. 4. Select the "Grill" Mode, set the temperature to MED. 5. Press the START/STOP button to initiate preheating. 6. Once preheated, place the chicken in the Ninja Foodi Smart XL Grill. 7. Cover the hood and allow the grill to cook for 10 minutes, flipping halfway through. 8. Serve warm with dipping sauce.

Serving Suggestion: Serve the chicken with roasted cauliflower mash.

Variation Tip: Add some BBQ sauce to the seasoning.

Nutritional Information per Serving: Calories 329 | Fat 5g |Sodium 510mg | Carbs 17g | Fiber 5g | Sugar 4g | Protein 21g

Chicken Thigh Yakitori

Prep time: 15 minutes | Cook Time: 10 minutes | Serves: 4

Ingredients:

⅓ cup mild tare sauce
3 tbsp. tamari
1½ tbsp. wasabi paste
4 skinless, boneless chicken thighs

3 scallions, cut into 1-inch lengths
Olive oil
Salt, to taste

Directions:

1. Mix wasabi with tamari and tare sauce in a bowl. 2. Toss in chicken pieces and mix well to coat. 3. Thread these chicken pieces and scallions over the wooden skewers then drizzle oil and salt. 4. Place the cooking pot in the Ninja Foodi Smart XL Grill then set a grill grate inside. 5. Select the "Grill" Mode, set the temperature to MED. 6. Press the START/STOP button to initiate preheating. 7. Once preheated, place the chicken in the Ninja Foodi Smart XL Grill. 8. Cover the hood and allow the grill to cook for 5 minutes per side. 9. Serve warm.

Serving Suggestion: Serve the grilled chicken with cucumber dip.
Variation Tip: Drizzle dried herbs on top and press before grilling.
Nutritional Information per Serving: Calories 357 | Fat 12g |Sodium 48mg | Carbs 16g | Fiber 2g | Sugar 0g | Protein 24g

Grilled Wild Duck Breast

Prep time: 15 minutes | Cook Time: 10 minutes | Serves: 8

Ingredients:

¼ cup Worcestershire sauce
2 tbsp. olive oil
½ tsp. hot sauce

2 tbsp. garlic, minced
¼ tsp. black pepper
8 boned duck breast halves

Directions:

1. Place duck breasts in a tray. 2. Mix oil and rest of the ingredients together and then pour over the duck. 3. Rub well and cover to refrigerate for 30 minutes. 4. Place the cooking pot in the Ninja Foodi Smart XL Grill then set a grill grate inside. 5. Plug the thermometer into the appliance. 6. Select the "Grill" Mode, set the temperature to MED then select the PRESET. 7. Use the right arrow keys on the display to select "CHICKEN" and set the doneness to WELL. 8. Press the START/STOP button to initiate preheating. 9. Once preheated, place the chicken in the Ninja Foodi Smart XL Grill. 10. Insert the thermometer probe into the thickest part of the duck. 11. Cover the hood and allow the grill to cook. 12. Serve warm.

Serving Suggestion: Serve the duck with a kale salad on the side.
Variation Tip: Add lemon juice for a refreshing taste.
Nutritional Information per Serving: Calories 297 | Fat 25g |Sodium 122mg | Carbs 23g | Fiber 0.4g | Sugar 1g | Protein 43g

Tomato Turkey Burgers

Prep time: 15 minutes | Cook Time: 14 minutes | Serves: 6

Ingredients:

1 large red onion, chopped
6 Ciabatta rolls, sliced in half
1 cup (4 ounces) Feta cheese
⅔ cup sun-dried tomatoes, chopped

¼ teaspoon salt
¼ teaspoon black pepper
2 pounds lean ground turkey

Directions:

1. Take all the ingredients for burgers in a bowl except the Ciabatta rolls. 2. Mix well and make six patties out of this turkey mixture. 3. Place the cooking pot in the Ninja Foodi Smart XL Grill then place the grill grate in the pot. 4. Plug the thermometer into the appliance. 5. Select the "Grill" Mode, set the temperature to MED then select the PRESET. 6. Use the right arrow keys on the display to select "CHICKEN" and set the doneness to WELL. 7. Press the START/STOP button to initiate preheating. 8. Place the 2 patties in the Ninja Foodi Smart XL Grill. 9. Insert the thermometer probe into the thickest part of the patties. 10. Cover the hood and allow the grill to cook for 7 minutes per side. 11. Grill the remaining patties in a similar way. 12. Serve with Ciabatta rolls.

Serving Suggestion: Serve the turkey meatballs with toasted bread slices.
Variation Tip: Add canned corn kernels to the burgers.
Nutritional Information per Serving: Calories 301 | Fat 16g | Sodium 412mg | Carbs 32g | Fiber 0.2g | Sugar 1g | Protein 28.2g

Sriracha Wings

Prep time: 15 minutes | Cook Time: 25 minutes | Serves: 6

Ingredients:

12 chicken wings
1 tablespoon canola oil
2 teaspoons ground coriander
Glaze:
½ cup orange juice
⅓ cup Sriracha chili sauce
¼ cup butter, cubed

½ teaspoon garlic salt
¼ teaspoon black pepper

3 tablespoons honey
2 tablespoons lime juice
¼ cup fresh cilantro, chopped

Directions:

1. Season the wings with all their seasoning in a suitable bowl. 2. Mix well, then cover to refrigerate for 2 hours of marinating. 3. Meanwhile, prepare the sauce by cooking its ingredients in a saucepan for 4 minutes. 4. Place the cooking pot in the Ninja Foodi Smart XL Grill then place the grill grate in the pot. 5. Select the "Grill" Mode, set the temperature to MED. 6. Press the START/STOP button to initiate preheating. 7. Place the chicken wings in the Ninja Foodi Smart XL Grill. 8. Cover the hood and allow the grill to cook for 15 minutes. 9. Flip the grilled wings and continue cooking for another 10 minutes. 10. Drizzle the prepared sauce over the wings in a bowl. 11. Toss well and serve.
Serving Suggestion: Serve the wings with fresh cucumber and couscous salad.
Variation Tip: Toss the wings, the pork rinds and the bacon serving.
Nutritional Information per Serving: Calories 352 | Fat 2.4g | Sodium 216mg | Carbs 16g | Fiber 2.3g | Sugar 1.2g | Protein 27g

Grilled Chicken with Mustard Barbecue Sauce

Prep time: 15 minutes | Cook Time: 20 minutes | Serves: 4

Ingredients:

2 tbsp. olive oil
¼ cup apple cider vinegar
¼ cup light brown sugar
2 tbsp. honey
2 tsp. Worcestershire sauce
1 tsp. garlic powder
1 tsp. paprika

¼ tsp. cayenne pepper
½ cup 2 tbsp. mustard
6 lb. bone-in chicken breasts
Kosher salt
2 large sweet onions, sliced
1 (15-oz.) jar pickled green beans
2 lb. tomatoes, sliced into rounds

Directions:

1. Mix the oil, vinegar, sugar, honey, Worcestershire sauce, garlic powder, paprika, cayenne, and ½ cup mustard in a bowl. 2. Rub the chicken with 2 tbsp. salt. 3. Place the cooking pot in the Ninja Foodi Smart XL Grill then set a grill grate inside. 4. Select the "Grill" Mode, set the temperature to MED. 5. Press the START/STOP button to initiate preheating. 6. Once preheated, place the chicken in the Ninja Foodi Smart XL Grill. 7. Cover the hood and allow the grill to cook for 10 minutes per side. 8. Meanwhile, mix rest of the tomato salad ingredients (mustard, onions, green beans and tomatoes) in a bowl. 9. Serve the grilled chicken with this salad. 10. Enjoy.
Serving Suggestion: Serve the chicken with garlic butter and sautéed broccoli.
Variation Tip: Drizzle paprika on top for more spice.
Nutritional Information per Serving: Calories 401 | Fat 7g |Sodium 269mg | Carbs 25g | Fiber 4g | Sugar 12g | Protein 26g

Spice-Rubbed Duck Breast

Prep time: 15 minutes | Cook Time: 24 minutes | Serves: 4

Ingredients:

2 cups orange juice
1 pint blackberries
1 tbsp. dry mustard
1 tbsp. sweet paprika
1 tsp. ground chili de arbol
½ tsp. ground cinnamon

½ tsp. five-spice powder
½ tsp. ground coriander
4 duck breasts
Kosher salt
Freshly ground black pepper
Olive oil

Directions:

1. Boil orange juice and black berries in a saucepan and cook for 10 minutes stirring it occasionally. 2. Stir in the rest of the spices to this sauce, mix well and allow it to cool. 3. Place duck breasts in a tray then pour the sauce over the duck breasts. 4. Rub well and cover and refrigerate for 30 minutes. 5. Place the cooking pot in the Ninja Foodi Smart XL Grill then set a grill grate inside. 6. Plug the thermometer into the appliance. 7. Select the "Grill" Mode, set the temperature to MED then select the PRESET. 8. Use the right arrow keys on the display to select "CHICKEN" and set the doneness to WELL. 9. Press the START/STOP button to initiate preheating. 10. Once preheated, place the chicken in the Ninja Foodi Smart XL Grill. 11. Insert the thermometer probe into the thickest part of the duck. 12. Cover the hood and allow the grill to cook. 13. Serve warm.
Serving Suggestion: Serve the duck with fresh kale salad.
Variation Tip: Add shredded cheese to the duck.
Nutritional Information per Serving: Calories 440 | Fat 5g |Sodium 244mg | Carbs 16g | Fiber 1g | Sugar 1g | Protein 27g

Huli Huli Chicken Wings

Prep time: 15 minutes | Cook Time: 33 minutes | Serves: 6

Ingredients:

1 cup unsweetened pineapple juice
1 cup chicken stock
½ cup soy sauce
½ cup packed light brown sugar
⅓ cup ketchup
2 tsp. grated peeled fresh ginger

1½ tsp. garlic, chopped
2 lbs. whole chicken wings
½ tsp. kosher salt
1 (3-lb.) fresh pineapple, peeled and cut into ½ -inch slices
Sliced scallions

Directions:

1. Mix pineapple juice, garlic, ginger, ketchup, brown sugar, soy sauce, and stock in a bowl. 2. Keep 1 cup of this marinade aside and mix the remaining with chicken in a ziplock bag. 3. Seal the bag, and refrigerate for 3 hours for marinating. 4. Remove the chicken from the marinade and season with salt. 5. Place the cooking pot in the Ninja Foodi Smart XL Grill then set a grill grate inside. 6. Select the "Grill" Mode, set the temperature to MED. 7. Press the START/STOP button to initiate preheating. 8. Once preheated, place the chicken in the Ninja Foodi Smart XL Grill. 9. Cover the hood and allow the grill to cook for 15 minutes. 10. Flip the chicken pieces and grill for another 10 minutes. 11. Grill the pineapple pieces for 4 minutes per side. 12. Pour the remaining marinade over the chicken and garnish with scallions. 13. Serve warm with grilled pineapple.
Serving Suggestion: Serve the chicken with fried rice.
Variation Tip: You can add dried herbs for seasoning as well.
Nutritional Information per Serving: Calories 373 | Fat 8g |Sodium 146mg | Carbs 28g | Fiber 5g | Sugar 1g | Protein 23g

Chicken and Tomatoes

Prep time: 15 minutes | Cook Time: 10 minutes | Serves: 4

Ingredients:

2 tablespoons olive oil
1 garlic clove, minced
½ teaspoon salt
¼ cup fresh basil leaves

8 plum tomatoes
¾ cup vinegar
4 chicken breast, boneless skinless

Directions:

1. Take the first five ingredients together in a blender jug. 2. Blend them well, then add four tomatoes to blend again. 3. Take chicken in a suitable bowl and pour ⅔ cup of the prepared marinade. 4. Mix well and refrigerate the chicken for one hour. 5. Place the cooking pot in the Ninja Foodi Smart XL Grill then place the grill grate in the pot. 6. Plug the thermometer into the appliance. 7. Select the "Grill" Mode, set the temperature to MED then select the PRESET. 8. Use the right arrow keys on the display to select "CHICKEN" and set the doneness to WELL. 9. Press the START/STOP button to initiate preheating. 10. Place the chicken in the Ninja Foodi Smart XL Grill. 11. Insert the thermometer probe into the thickest part of the chicken. 12. Cover the hood and allow the grill to cook. 13. Flip the grilled chicken and continue grilling until it is al dente. 14. Cook the remaining chicken in a similar way. 15. Serve.
Serving Suggestion: Serve the chicken and tomatoes with a kale salad on the side.
Variation Tip: Add lemon juice for a refreshing taste.
Nutritional Information per Serving: Calories 335 | Fat 25g | Sodium 122mg | Carbs 13g | Fiber 0.4g | Sugar 1g | Protein 33g

Bourbon Drumsticks

Prep time: 15 minutes | Cook Time: 40 minutes | Serves: 6

Ingredients:

1 cup ketchup
2 tablespoons brown sugar
12 chicken drumsticks
2 tablespoons bourbon
4 teaspoons Barbecue seasoning

1 tablespoon Worcestershire sauce
⅔ cup Dr. Pepper spice
2 teaspoons dried minced onion
⅛ teaspoon salt
¼ teaspoon celery salt, optional

Directions:

1. Take the first eight ingredients in a saucepan. 2. Stir cook for ten minutes on a simmer until the sauce thickens. 3. Place the cooking pot in the Ninja Foodi Smart XL Grill then place the grill grate in the pot. 4. Select the "Grill" Mode, set the temperature to MED. 5. Press the START/STOP button to initiate preheating. 6. Place the chicken in the Ninja Foodi Smart XL Grill. 7. Cover the hood and allow the grill to cook for 10 minutes. 8. Flip the grilled chicken and baste it with the remaining sauce. 9. Continue grilling for another 10 minutes until al dente. 10. Cook the remaining drumsticks in a similar way. 11. Garnish with remaining sauce on top. 12. Serve.
Serving Suggestion: Serve the drumsticks with fresh herbs on top and a bowl of steamed rice.
Variation Tip: Use honey or maple syrup for the marinade.
Nutritional Information per Serving: Calories 388 | Fat 8g | Sodium 611mg | Carbs 8g | Fiber 0g | Sugar 4g | Protein 13g

Spinach Turkey Burgers

Prep time: 15 minutes | Cook Time: 19 minutes | Serves: 8

Ingredients:

1 tablespoon avocado oil
2 pounds turkey ground
2 shallots, chopped
2½ cups spinach, chopped
3 garlic cloves, minced

⅔ cup Feta cheese, crumbled
¾ teaspoon Greek seasoning
½ teaspoon salt
¼ teaspoon black pepper
8 hamburger buns, split

Directions:

1. Start by sautéing shallots in a skillet for two minutes, then add garlic and spinach. 2. Cook for 45 seconds, then transfers to a suitable bowl. 3. Add all the seasoning, beef, and Feta cheese to the bowl. 4. Mix well, then make eight patties of ½ inch thickness. 5. Place the cooking pot in the Ninja Foodi Smart XL Grill then place the grill grate in the pot. 6. Plug the thermometer into the appliance. 7. Select the "Grill" Mode, set the temperature to MED then select the PRESET. 8. Use the right arrow keys on the display to select "CHICKEN" and set the doneness to WELL. 9. Press the START/STOP button to initiate preheating. 10. Place the patties in the Ninja Foodi Smart XL Grill. 11. Insert the thermometer probe into the thickest part of the patties. 12. Cover the hood and allow the grill to cook for 8 minutes per side. 13. Serve the patties in between the buns with desired toppings. 14. Enjoy.

Serving Suggestion: Serve the burgers with roasted green beans and mashed potatoes.
Variation Tip: Add chopped kale instead of spinach to make the burgers.
Nutritional Information per Serving: Calories 529 | Fat 17g | Sodium 422mg | Carbs 55g | Fiber 0g | Sugar 1g | Protein 41g

Montreal Chicken Sandwiches

Prep time: 15 minutes | Cook Time: 12 minutes | Serves: 4

Ingredients:

¼ cup mayonnaise
1 tablespoon Dijon mustard
1 tablespoon honey
4 chicken breasts, halves
½ teaspoon Montreal seasoning

4 slices Swiss cheese
4 hamburger buns, split
2 bacon strips, cooked and crumbled
Lettuce leaves and tomato slices, optional

Directions:

1. First, pound the chicken with a mallet into ½ inch thickness. 2. Now season it with steak seasoning and rub it well. 3. Place the cooking pot in the Ninja Foodi Smart XL Grill then place the grill grate in the pot. 4. Select the "Grill" Mode, set the temperature to MED. 5. Press the START/STOP button to initiate preheating. 6. Place the chicken in the Ninja Foodi Smart XL Grill. 7. Cover the hood and allow the grill to cook for 6 minutes per side. 8. Cook the remaining chicken in a similar way. 9. Mix mayonnaise with honey and mustard in a bowl. 10. Place the one chicken piece on top of each half of the bun. 11. Top it with a mayo mixture, one cheese slice, and other toppings. 12. Place the other bun halve on top. 13. Serve.

Serving Suggestion: Serve the sandwiches with roasted veggies.
Variation Tip: Replace chicken with the turkey meat to make these sandwiches.
Nutritional Information per Serving: Calories 284 | Fat 25g | Sodium 460mg | Carbs 36g | Fiber 0.4g | Sugar 2g | Protein 26g

Chicken with Grilled Apples

Prep time: 15 minutes | Cook Time: 12 minutes | Serves: 4

Ingredients:

4 chicken breasts, halved
4 teaspoons chicken seasoning
1 large apple, wedged
1 tablespoon lemon juice

4 slices Provolone cheese
½ cup Alfredo sauce
¼ cup Blue cheese, crumbled

Directions:

1. Take chicken in a bowl and season it with chicken seasoning. 2. Toss apple with lemon juice in another small bowl. 3. Place the cooking pot in the Ninja Foodi Smart XL Grill then place the grill grate in the pot. 4. Select the "Grill" Mode, set the temperature to MED. 5. Press the START/STOP button to initiate preheating. 6. Place the chicken in the Ninja Foodi Smart XL Grill. 7. Cover the hood and allow the grill to cook for 16 minutes, flipping halfway through. 8. Now grill the apple in the same grill for 2 minutes per side. 9. Serve the chicken with apple, blue cheese and alfredo sauce. 10. Enjoy.

Serving Suggestion: Serve the chicken with apples with white rice or vegetable chow mein.
Variation Tip: Wrap the chicken with bacon before grilling for more taste.
Nutritional Information per Serving: Calories 231 | Fat 20.1g | Sodium 364mg | Carbs 30g | Fiber 1g | Sugar 1.4g | Protein 15g

Grilled Red Curry Chicken

Prep time: 15 minutes | Cook Time: 30 minutes | Serves: 6

Ingredients:

1 (3-pounds) chicken wings, tips removed

¼ cup unsweetened coconut milk

2 tablespoons red curry paste

1 teaspoon dark brown sugar

Salt and freshly ground pepper, to taste

Directions:

1. Mix coconut milk with red curry paste, brown sugar, black pepper, salt in a bowl. 2. Toss in chicken wings and mix well. 3. Cover and marinate the wings for one hour in the refrigerator. 4. Place the cooking pot in the Ninja Foodi Smart XL Grill then place the grill grate in the pot. 5. Select the "Grill" Mode, set the temperature to MED. 6. Press the START/STOP button to initiate preheating. 7. Place the wings in the Ninja Foodi Smart XL Grill. 8. Cover the hood and allow the grill to cook for 10 minutes. 9. Flip the wings and grill for 20 minutes. 10. Serve warm.

Serving Suggestion: Serve the curry chicken with a warmed tortilla.

Variation Tip: Add dried herbs to the seasoning.

Nutritional Information per Serving: Calories 405 | Fat 20g | Sodium 941mg | Carbs 26.1g | Fiber 0.9g | Sugar 0.9g | Protein 45.2g

Grilled Chicken Breasts with Grapefruit Glaze

Prep time: 15 minutes | Cook Time: 16 minutes | Serves: 4

Ingredients:

2 garlic cloves, minced

1 teaspoon grapefruit zest

½ cup grapefruit juice

1 tablespoon cooking oil

2 tablespoons honey

½ teaspoon salt

¼ teaspoon black pepper

4 bone-in chicken breasts

Directions:

1. Mix garlic, black pepper, salt, honey, oil, grapefruit juice and zest in a small saucepan. 2. Cook the grapefruit mixture for 5 to 7 minutes until it thickens. 3. Pour this glaze over the chicken breasts. 4. Place the cooking pot in the Ninja Foodi Smart XL Grill then place the grill grate in the pot. 5. Plug the thermometer into the appliance. 6. Select the "Grill" Mode, set the temperature to MED then select the PRESET. 7. Use the right arrow keys on the display to select "CHICKEN" and set the doneness to WELL. 8. Press the START/STOP button to initiate preheating. 9. Place the chicken in the Ninja Foodi Smart XL Grill. 10. Insert the thermometer probe into the thickest part of the chicken. 11. Cover the hood and allow the grill to cook for 8 minutes per side. 12. Slice and serve warm.

Serving Suggestion: Serve the chicken breasts with warmed pita bread.

Variation Tip: Add maple syrup instead of honey.

Nutritional Information per Serving: Calories 380 | Fat 8g | Sodium 339mg | Carbs 33g | Fiber 1g | Sugar 2g | Protein 21g

Chicken Breasts with Pineapple Relish

Prep time: 15 minutes | Cook Time: 15 minutes | Serves: 4

Ingredients:

Marinade

1 ripe pineapple, peeled but left whole

1 jalapeño chili

½ red onion

½ cup vinegar

Grilled Pineapple Relish

½ peeled pineapple, chopped

Oil, for coating

Honey, for coating

Salt, for seasoning

1 tbsp. roasted garlic

1 tbsp. salt

4 boneless chicken breasts

1 jalapeño chili

½ red onion, peeled and halved

¼ cup vinegar

½ cup cilantro leaves, chopped

Directions:

1. Blend all the marinade ingredients in a blender and pour over the chicken in a bowl. 2. Mix well, cover and refrigerate for 1 hour. 3. Meanwhile, mix the remaining relish ingredients in a bowl and keep it aside. 4. Place the cooking pot in the Ninja Foodi Smart XL Grill then set a grill grate inside. 5. Plug the thermometer into the appliance. 6. Select the "Grill" Mode, set the temperature to MED then select the PRESET. 7. Use the right arrow keys on the display to select "CHICKEN" and set the doneness to WELL. 8. Press the START/STOP button to initiate preheating. 9. Once preheated, place the chicken in the Ninja Foodi Smart XL Grill. 10. Insert the thermometer probe into the thickest part of the chicken. 11. Cover the hood and allow the grill to cook. 12. Serve the chicken with the relish.

Serving Suggestion: Serve the chicken with parsley on top.

Variation Tip: Coat the chicken with lemon juice for some zest.

Nutritional Information per Serving: Calories 418 | Fat 22g |Sodium 350mg | Carbs 22g | Fiber 0.7g | Sugar 1g | Protein 24.3g

Chicken Kebabs with Currants

Prep time: 15 minutes | Cook Time: 16 minutes | Serves: 6

Ingredients:

2 medium red bell peppers, cubed
1 cup dried currants
1 (14-ounce) jar sweet pickled red peppers, cubed
½ cup of the juices from pickles

2 tablespoons olive oil
Kosher salt, to taste
3 pounds boneless chicken thighs, cut into 1-inch-wide strips
3 pounds boneless chicken breasts, cut into strips

Directions:

1. Toss chicken with olive oil, peppers, pickle juices, salt and currants. 2. Cover and refrigerate the chicken for 30 minutes for marinating. 3. Thread the marinated chicken on the wooden skewers. 4. Place the cooking pot in the Ninja Foodi Smart XL Grill then place the grill grate in the pot. 5. Select the "Grill" Mode, set the temperature to MED. 6. Press the START/STOP button to initiate preheating. 7. Place the chicken in the Ninja Foodi Smart XL Grill. 8. Cover the hood and allow the grill to cook for 8 minutes per side. 9. Serve warm.

Serving Suggestion: Serve the chicken kebabs with steaming white rice.
Variation Tip: Add one tablespoon lemon juice to the seasoning and marinate.
Nutritional Information per Serving: Calories 361 | Fat 16g | Sodium 189mg | Carbs 19.3g | Fiber 0.3g | Sugar 18.2g | Protein 33.3g

Turkey Meatballs

Prep time: 10 minutes | Cook Time: 20 minutes | Serves: 4

Ingredients:

1 egg, lightly beaten
1 pound ground turkey
¼ cup basil, chopped
1 tablespoon lemongrass, chopped
1½ tablespoon fish sauce

1 teaspoon garlic, minced
½ cup almond flour
Pepper
Salt

Directions:

1. Place the cooking pot in the Ninja Foodi Smart XL Grill, then place the Crisper Basket in the pot. 2. Add all ingredients into a bowl and mix until well combined. 3. Make balls from the meat mixture. 4. Select the "Air Crisp" Mode, set the temperature to 380°F/195°C. 5. Press the START/STOP button to initiate preheating. 6. Once preheated, place the meatballs in the Ninja Foodi Smart XL Grill. 7. Cover the hood and allow the grill to cook for 20 minutes. 8. Serve, when done.

Serving Suggestion: Allow to cool completely then serve.
Variation Tip: Add some chili flakes for more flavor.
Nutritional Information per Serving: Calories 327 | Fat 20.6g |Sodium 697mg | Carbs 5.1g | Fiber 1.7g | Sugar 1.6g | Protein 36g

Barbecued Turkey

Prep time: 15 minutes | Cook Time: 30 minutes | Serves: 6

Ingredients:

1 cup Greek yogurt
½ cup lemon juice
⅓ cup canola oil
½ cup fresh parsley, minced
1 (3 pounds) turkey breast half, bone-in
½ cup green onions, chopped

4 garlic cloves, minced
4 tablespoons dill, fresh minced
1 teaspoon dried rosemary, crushed
1 teaspoon salt
½ teaspoon black pepper

Directions:

1. Take the first ten ingredients in a bowl and mix well. 2. Mix turkey with this marinade in a suitable bowl for seasoning. 3. Cover it to marinate for eight hours of marinating. 4. Place the cooking pot in the Ninja Foodi Smart XL Grill then place the grill grate in the pot. 5. Plug the thermometer into the appliance. 6. Select the "Grill" Mode, set the temperature to MAX then select the PRESET. 7. Use the right arrow keys on the display to select "CHICKEN" and set the doneness to WELL. 8. Press the START/STOP button to initiate preheating. 9. Place the turkey in the Ninja Foodi Smart XL Grill. 10. Insert the thermometer probe into the thickest part of the turkey. 11. Cover the hood and allow the grill to cook for 15 minutes. 12. Flip the turkey and continue grilling for another 15 minutes until al dente. 13. Grill until the internal temperature reaches 165°F/75°C. 14. Slice and serve.

Serving Suggestion: Serve the turkey with avocado guacamole.
Variation Tip: Add sweet paprika for a tangy taste.
Nutritional Information per Serving: Calories 440 | Fat 14g | Sodium 220mg | Carbs 22g | Fiber 0.2g | Sugar 1g | Protein 37g

Grilled Chicken with Grapes

Prep time: 15 minutes | Cook Time: 55 minutes | Serves: 6

Ingredients:

1 cup whole buttermilk
1 cup water
½ cup yellow onion, sliced
2 tablespoons light brown sugar
1½ tablespoons hot sauce
1 tablespoon salt

1 teaspoon black pepper
3 garlic cloves, smashed
3 boneless, skin-on chicken breasts
6 boneless, skin-on chicken thighs
1 pound Bronx grapes, separated into small clusters

Directions:

1. Mix chicken with the rest of the ingredients except the grapes. 2. Cover and marinate the chicken for 30 minutes in the refrigerator. 3. Place the cooking pot in the Ninja Foodi Smart XL Grill then place the grill grate in the pot. 4. Select the "Grill" Mode, set the temperature to MED. 5. Press the START/STOP button to initiate preheating. 6. Place the chicken in the Ninja Foodi Smart XL Grill. 7. Cover the hood and allow the grill to cook for 25 minutes, flipping halfway through. 8. Grill the grapes for 5 minutes per side until slightly charred. 9. Serve chicken with grilled grapes. 10. Enjoy.
Serving Suggestion: Serve the chicken with tomato sauce and toasted bread slices.
Variation Tip: Add butter sauce on top of the chicken before cooking.
Nutritional Information per Serving: Calories 419 | Fat 13g | Sodium 432mg | Carbs 9.1g | Fiber 3g | Sugar 1g | Protein 33g

Piri Piri Chicken

Prep time: 15 minutes | Cook Time: 8 minutes | Serves: 2

Ingredients:

1 small red bell pepper, chopped
½ cup cilantro leaves
1 small shallot, chopped
2 tablespoons red wine vinegar
2 tablespoons olive oil
1 tablespoon paprika
2 garlic cloves, crushed

2 Piri Piri chilies stemmed
1½ teaspoons dried oregano
1 tablespoon Kosher salt
1¼ pounds chicken pieces
Canola oil for brushing
1 pound Shishito peppers

Directions:

1. Mix chicken piece with rest of the ingredients in a bowl. 2. Cover and refrigerate the chicken for 30 minutes for marinating. 3. Place the cooking pot in the Ninja Foodi Smart XL Grill then place the grill grate in the pot. 4. Select the "Grill" Mode, set the temperature to MED. 5. Press the START/STOP button to initiate preheating. 6. Place the chicken in the Ninja Foodi Smart XL Grill. 7. Cover the hood and allow the grill to cook for 4 minutes per side. 8. Serve warm.
Serving Suggestion: Serve the chicken with roasted veggies on the side.
Variation Tip: Add sweet paprika for more taste.
Nutritional Information per Serving: Calories 334 | Fat 16g | Sodium 462mg | Carbs 31g | Fiber 0.4g | Sugar 3g | Protein 35.3g

Juicy Greek Turkey Meatballs

Prep time: 10 minutes | Cook Time: 25 minutes | Serves: 6

Ingredients:

2 eggs
2 pounds of ground turkey
1 teaspoon fresh mint, chopped
½ cup parsley, chopped
½ cup onion, minced
½ cup breadcrumbs

1 teaspoon cumin
1 teaspoon oregano
1 tablespoon garlic, minced
½ teaspoon pepper
Pepper
Salt

Directions:

1. Place the cooking pot in the Ninja Foodi Smart XL Grill. 2. Add all ingredients into the bowl and mix until well combined. 3. Make small balls from the meat mixture and place into the baking dish. 4. Select the "Bake" Mode, set the temperature to 375°F/190°C. 5. Press the START/STOP button to initiate preheating. 6. Once preheated, place the meatball in the Ninja Foodi Smart XL Grill. 7. Cover the hood and allow the grill to cook for 25 minutes. 8. Serve, when done.
Serving Suggestion: Serve warm.
Variation Tip: Add one tablespoon of fresh chopped basil.
Nutritional Information per Serving: Calories 362 | Fat 18.7g |Sodium 280mg | Carbs 8.7g | Fiber 1.1g | Sugar 1.2g | Protein 44.9g

Garlic Butter Chicken Wings

Prep time: 10 minutes | Cook Time: 20 minutes | Serves: 2

Ingredients:

1 pound chicken wings
2 tablespoons butter, melted
1½ tablespoon ranch seasoning

1 tablespoon garlic, minced
Pepper
Salt

Directions:

1. Place the cooking pot in the Ninja Foodi Smart XL Grill then place the Crisper Basket in the pot. 2. In a bowl, toss chicken wings with butter, garlic, ranch seasoning, pepper and salt. Cover and place in the refrigerator for one hour. 3. Select the "Air Crisp" Mode, set the temperature to 360°F/180°C. 4. Press the START/STOP button to initiate preheating. 5. Once preheated, place the chicken in the Ninja Foodi Smart XL Grill. 6. Cover the hood and allow the grill to cook for 20 minutes. 7. Serve, when done.
Serving Suggestion: Allow to cool completely then serve.
Variation Tip: Once cooked then sprinkle some grated Parmesan cheese.
Nutritional Information per Serving: Calories 539 | Fat 28.4g |Sodium 355mg | Carbs 1.4g | Fiber 0.1g | Sugar 0.1g | Protein 66g

Tasty Chicken Drumsticks

Prep time: 10 minutes | Cook Time: 25 minutes | Serves: 6

Ingredients:

6 chicken drumsticks
½ teaspoon ground cumin
½ teaspoon garlic powder
2 tablespoons olive oil

¾ teaspoon paprika
Pepper
Salt

Directions:

1. Place the cooking pot in the Ninja Foodi Smart XL Grill then place the Crisper Basket in the pot. 2. In a bowl, toss chicken drumsticks with oil, paprika, garlic powder, cumin, pepper and salt. 3. Select the "Air Crisp" Mode, set the temperature to 400°F/200°C. 4. Press the START/STOP button to initiate preheating. 5. Once preheated, place the chicken in the Ninja Foodi Smart XL Grill. 6. Cover the hood and allow the grill to cook for 25 minutes. 7. Serve, when done.
Serving Suggestion: Serve warm.
Variation Tip: Add your choice of seasonings.
Nutritional Information per Serving: Calories 120 | Fat 7.4g |Sodium 64mg | Carbs 0.4g | Fiber 0.2g | Sugar 0.1g | Protein 12.8g

Grilled Chicken Thighs with Pickled Peaches

Prep time: 15 minutes | Cook Time: 57 minutes | Serves: 4

Ingredients:

Peaches
6 medium peaches
1½ cups distilled white vinegar
1 cup sugar
1 stalk of lemongrass, sliced
1 (1-inch piece) ginger, peeled and sliced
Chicken
1 tablespoon Sorghum syrup
Kosher salt, to taste
Black pepper, to taste
8 bone-in chicken thighs
½ cup, 1 tablespoon olive oil

½ teaspoon whole black peppercorns
5 allspice berries
2 whole cloves
1 (3-inch) cinnamon stick

1 tablespoon red wine vinegar
2 garlic cloves, chopped
¼ cup parsley, basil and tarragon, chopped
4 cups arugula, thick stems discarded

Directions:

1. Mix 8 cups water with 2 tablespoons of salt and Sorghum syrup in a bowl. 2. Add chicken to the Sorghum water and cover to refrigerate overnight. 3. Remove the chicken to a bowl, then add garlic, herbs, one teaspoon pepper, vinegar and ½ cup olive oil. 4. Place the cooking pot in the Ninja Foodi Smart XL Grill then place the grill grate in the pot. 5. Plug the thermometer into the appliance. 6. Select the "Grill" Mode, set the temperature to MED then select the PRESET. 7. Use the right arrow keys on the display to select "CHICKEN" and set the doneness to WELL. 8. Press the START/STOP button to initiate preheating. 9. Place the chicken in the Ninja Foodi Smart XL Grill. 10. Insert the thermometer probe into the thickest part of the chicken. 11. Cover the hood and allow the grill to cook for 6 minutes per side. 12. Transfer the grilled chicken to a plate. 13. Add water to a saucepan and boil it. 14. Carve an X on top of the peaches and boil them in the water, then cook for 2 minutes. 15. Transfer the peaches to an ice bath, then peel the peaches. 16. Cut the peaches in half and remove the pit from the center. 17. Mix the rest of the ingredients for peaches and one ½ cups water in a saucepan. 18. Allow the glaze to cool, and toss in peaches. 19. Cover and refrigerate the peaches overnight. 20. Grill the peaches in the Ninja Foodi Smart XL Grill for 10 minutes per side. 21. Serve the chicken and peaches with arugula. 22. Enjoy.
Serving Suggestion: Serve the peach chicken with a fresh crouton salad.
Variation Tip: Add a drizzle of cheese on top of the chicken after grilling.
Nutritional Information per Serving: Calories 545 | Fat 7.9g | Sodium 581mg | Carbs 41g | Fiber 2.6g | Sugar 0.1g | Protein 42.5g

Juicy Chicken Tenders

Prep time: 10 minutes | Cook Time: 20 minutes | Serves: 4

Ingredients:

1 pound chicken tenders
2 tablespoons fresh tarragon, chopped
½ cup whole grain mustard
1 teaspoon garlic, minced

½ ounces of fresh lemon juice
½ teaspoon paprika
Pepper
Salt

Directions:

1. Place the cooking pot in the Ninja Foodi Smart XL Grill. 2. Add all ingredients except chicken to the bowl and mix well. 3. Add chicken tenders to the bowl and mix until well coated. 4. Transfer chicken to a baking dish. 5. Select the "Bake" Mode, set the temperature to 400°F/200°C. 6. Press the START/STOP button to initiate preheating. 7. Once preheated, place the chicken in the Ninja Foodi Smart XL Grill. 8. Cover the hood and allow the grill to cook for 20 minutes. 9. Serve, when done.

Serving Suggestion: Serve warm.
Variation Tip: Add your choice of seasonings.
Nutritional Information per Serving: Calories 241 | Fat 9.5g |Sodium 273mg | Carbs 2.9g | Fiber 0.2g | Sugar 0.1g | Protein 33.1g

Thai Grill Chicken

Prep time: 10 minutes | Cook Time: 10 minutes | Serves: 4

Ingredients:

4 chicken breasts, boneless & skinless
For Marinade:
1½ tablespoon Thai red curry
½ cup coconut milk

1 teaspoon brown sugar
1½ tablespoon fish sauce

Directions:

1. Place the cooking pot in the Ninja Foodi Smart XL Grill then place the grill grate in the pot. 2. Add chicken and marinade ingredients into the zip-lock bag. Seal bag and place in the refrigerator for four hours. 3. Plug the thermometer into the appliance. 4. Select the "Grill" Mode, set the temperature to HI then select the PRESET. 5. Use the right arrow keys on the display to select "CHICKEN" and set the doneness to WELL. 6. Press the START/STOP button to initiate preheating. 7. Once preheated, place the chicken in the Ninja Foodi Smart XL Grill. 8. Insert the thermometer probe into the thickest part of the chicken. 9. Cover the hood and allow the grill to cook. 10. Serve, when done.

Serving Suggestion: Serve warm and enjoy.
Variation Tip: None
Nutritional Information per Serving: Calories 352 | Fat 18g |Sodium 651mg | Carbs 2.7g | Fiber 0.7g | Sugar 2g | Protein 43.3g

Grilled BBQ Turkey

Prep time: 5-10 min | Cook Time: 30 min.|Servings: 5-6

Ingredients

½ cup minced parsley
½ cup chopped green onions
4 garlic cloves, minced
1 cup Greek yogurt
½ cup lemon juice
1 tsp dried rosemary, crushed

⅓ cup canola oil
4 tbsp. minced dill
1 tsp salt
½ tsp pepper
1-3 pounds turkey breast half, bone in

Directions:

1. In a mixing bowl, combine all the Ingredients except the turkey. Add and coat the turkey evenly. Refrigerate for 8 hours to marinate. 2. Take Ninja Foodi Smart XL Grill, arrange it over your kitchen platform, and open the top lid. 3. Arrange the Grill Grate and close the top lid. 4. Select the "GRILL" function and select the "HI" setting. Adjust the timer to 30 minutes and then press "START/STOP." Ninja Foodi Smart XL Grill will start pre-heating. 5. Ninja Foodi Smart XL Grill is preheated and ready to cook when it starts to beep. After you hear a beep, open the top lid. 6. Arrange the turkey over the grill grate. 7. Close the top lid and cook for 15 minutes. Now open the top lid, flip the turkey. 8. Close the top lid and cook for 15 more minutes. Cook until the food thermometer reaches 165°F/75°C. 9. Slice and serve.

Serving Suggestion: Serve with grill veggies.
Variation Tip: add red pepper flakes for spiciness.
Nutritional Information per Serving: Calories: 426|Fat: 8.5g| Carbohydrates: 22g| Fiber: 3g| Sodium: 594mg| Protein: 38g

Chicken Cheese Patties

Prep time: 10 minutes | Cook Time: 25 minutes | Serves: 4

Ingredients:

1 egg
1 pound ground chicken
⅛ teaspoon red pepper flakes
2 garlic cloves, minced
½ cup onion, minced
¾ cup breadcrumbs

1 cup Cheddar cheese, shredded
1 cup carrot, grated
1 cup cauliflower, grated
Pepper
Salt

Directions:

1. Place the cooking pot in the Ninja Foodi Smart XL Grill. 2. Add all ingredients into the bowl and mix until well combined. 3. Make patties from the meat mixture and place in the baking dish. 4. Select the "Bake" Mode, set the temperature to 400°F/200°C. 5. Press the START/STOP button to initiate preheating. 6. Once preheated, place the chicken in the Ninja Foodi Smart XL Grill. 7. Cover the hood and allow the grill to cook for 25 minutes. 8. Serve, when done.

Serving Suggestion: Serve warm.
Variation Tip: Add your choice of seasonings.
Nutritional Information per Serving: Calories 451 | Fat 20g |Sodium 503mg | Carbs 20.9g | Fiber 2.6g | Sugar 4.1g | Protein 44.9g

Mexican Chicken

Prep time: 10 minutes | Cook Time: 30 minutes | Serves: 6

Ingredients:

4 chicken breasts, skinless & boneless
1 ¾ cups Cheddar cheese, shredded
1 teaspoon taco seasoning
12 ounces of salsa

¼ teaspoon ground cumin
¼ teaspoon garlic powder
Pepper
Salt

Directions:

1. Place the cooking pot in the Ninja Foodi Smart XL Grill then set a grill grate inside. 2. Place chicken into the baking dish and sprinkle with cumin, garlic powder, pepper and salt. 3. Pour salsa over chicken. Sprinkle cheese on top of chicken. 4. Plug the thermometer into the appliance. 5. Select the "Bake" Mode, set the temperature to 375°F/190°C then select the PRESET. 6. Use the right arrow keys on the display to select "CHICKEN" and set the doneness to WELL. 7. Press the START/STOP button to initiate preheating. 8. Once preheated, place the chicken in the Ninja Foodi Smart XL Grill. 9. Insert the thermometer probe into the thickest part of the chicken. 10. Cover the hood and allow the grill to cook. 11. Serve, when done.

Serving Suggestion: Serve warm.
Variation Tip: None
Nutritional Information per Serving: Calories 334 | Fat 18.2g |Sodium 656mg | Carbs 4.1g | Fiber 0.9g | Sugar 1.9g | Protein 37.3g

Crispy Cajun Chicken

Prep time: 10 minutes | Cook Time: 25 minutes | Serves: 2

Ingredients:

2 chicken breasts
1 teaspoon Cajun seasoning
2 tablespoons mayonnaise
¾ cup breadcrumbs

1 teaspoon garlic powder
1 teaspoon paprika
Pepper
Salt

Directions:

1. Place the cooking pot in the Ninja Foodi Smart XL Grill then place the baking dish in the pot. 2. In a shallow dish, mix breadcrumbs, paprika, garlic powder, Cajun seasoning, pepper and salt. 3. Brush chicken with mayo and coat with breadcrumb mixture. 4. Plug the thermometer into the appliance. 5. Select the "Bake" Mode, set the temperature to 400°F/200°C then select the PRESET. 6. Use the right arrow keys on the display to select "CHICKEN" and set the doneness to WELL. 7. Press the START/STOP button to initiate preheating. 8. Once preheated, place the chicken in the Ninja Foodi Smart XL Grill. 9. Insert the thermometer probe into the thickest part of the chicken. 10. Cover the hood and allow the grill to cook. 11. Serve, when done.

Serving Suggestion: Serve warm.
Variation Tip: None

Nutritional Information per Serving: Calories 503 | Fat 18g |Sodium 630mg | Carbs 34.3g | Fiber 2.4g | Sugar 3.9g | Protein 48.2g

Grill Pesto Chicken Breast

Prep time: 10 minutes | Cook Time: 30 minutes | Serves: 4

Ingredients:

4 chicken breasts, boneless & skinless
8 ounces of Mozzarella cheese, sliced
1 tablespoon garlic, minced
2 tomatoes, sliced

½ cup pesto
2 tablespoons fresh basil
Pepper
Salt

Directions:

1. Place the cooking pot in the Ninja Foodi Smart XL Grill then set a baking dish inside. 2. Place chicken into the baking dish and sprinkle with garlic and basil. 3. Pour pesto over chicken. Arrange tomato slices and cheese on top of the chicken. 4. Plug the thermometer into the appliance. 5. Select the "Bake" Mode, set the temperature to 400°F/200°C then select the PRESET. 6. Use the right arrow keys on the display to select "CHICKEN" and set the doneness to WELL. 7. Press the START/STOP button to initiate preheating. 8. Once preheated, place the chicken in the Ninja Foodi Smart XL Grill. 9. Insert the thermometer probe into the thickest part of the chicken. 10. Cover the hood and allow the grill to cook. 11. Serve, when done.
Serving Suggestion: Serve warm with plain rice.
Variation Tip: Add chili flakes for more flavor.
Nutritional Information per Serving: Calories 587 | Fat 34g |Sodium 698mg | Carbs 7.1g | Fiber 1.3g | Sugar 3.6g | Protein 62g

Creamy Chicken Breasts

Prep time: 10 minutes | Cook Time: 55 minutes | Serves: 4

Ingredients:

4 chicken breasts
¾ cup Parmesan cheese, grated
1 cup sour cream
1 cup Mozzarella cheese, shredded
1 teaspoon garlic powder

1 teaspoon dried basil
1 teaspoon dried oregano
Pepper
Salt

Directions:

1. Place the cooking pot in the Ninja Foodi Smart XL Grill. 2. Season chicken with pepper and salt and place into the baking dish. 3. Mix together sour cream, Parmesan cheese, Mozzarella cheese, oregano, basil, garlic powder and salt and pour over chicken. 4. Plug the thermometer into the appliance. 5. Select the "Bake" Mode, set the temperature to 375°F/190°C then select the PRESET. 6. Use the right arrow keys on the display to select "CHICKEN" and set the doneness to WELL. 7. Press the START/STOP button to initiate preheating. 8. Once preheated, place the chicken in the Ninja Foodi Smart XL Grill. 9. Insert the thermometer probe into the thickest part of the chicken. 10. Cover the hood and allow the grill to cook. 11. Serve, when done.
Serving Suggestion: Serve warm.
Variation Tip: Add ¼ teaspoon of Italian seasonings.
Nutritional Information per Serving: Calories 574 | Fat 33.2g |Sodium 838mg | Carbs 3.5g | Fiber 0.2g | Sugar 0.3g | Protein 58.3g

Balsamic Chicken

Prep time: 10 minutes | Cook Time: 25 minutes | Serves: 4

Ingredients:

4 chicken breasts, boneless & skinless
½ cup Balsamic vinegar
2 tablespoons soy sauce
¼ cup olive oil

2 teaspoons dried oregano
1 teaspoon garlic, minced
Pepper
Salt

Directions:

1. Place the cooking pot in the Ninja Foodi Smart XL Grill then set a grill grate inside. 2. Place chicken into the baking dish. 3. Mix together remaining ingredients and pour over chicken. 4. Plug the thermometer into the appliance. 5. Select the "Bake" Mode, set the temperature to 400°F/200°C then select the PRESET. 6. Use the right arrow keys on the display to select "CHICKEN" and set the doneness to WELL. 7. Press the START/STOP button to initiate preheating. 8. Once preheated, place the chicken in the Ninja Foodi Smart XL Grill. 9. Insert the thermometer probe into the thickest part of the chicken. 10. Cover the hood and allow the grill to cook. 11. Serve, when done.
Serving Suggestion: Serve warm.

Nutritional Information per Serving: Calories 399 | Fat 23.5g |Sodium 617mg | Carbs 1.6g | Fiber 0.4g | Sugar 0.3g | Protein 42.9g

Marinated Grill Chicken Breast

Prep time: 10 minutes | Cook Time: 10 minutes | Serves: 4

Ingredients:

4 chicken breasts, boneless & skinless

For marinade:

½ cup orange juice

1 tsp garlic, minced

3 tablespoons olive oil

½ teaspoon allspice

¾ teaspoon ground nutmeg

Directions:

1. Place the cooking pot in the Ninja Foodi Smart XL Grill then set a grill grate inside. 2. Add chicken and marinade ingredients into the zip-lock bag. Seal bag and place in the refrigerator for two hours. 3. Plug the thermometer into the appliance. 4. Select the "Grill" Mode, set the temperature to HI then select the PRESET. 5. Use the right arrow keys on the display to select "CHICKEN" and set the doneness to WELL. 6. Press the START/STOP button to initiate preheating. 7. Once preheated, place the chicken in the Ninja Foodi Smart XL Grill. 8. Insert the thermometer probe into the thickest part of the chicken. 9. Cover the hood and allow the grill to cook. 10. Serve, when done.

Serving Suggestion: Serve warm.

Variation Tip: Add fresh chopped parsley once cooked.

Nutritional Information per Serving: Calories 385 | Fat 21.6g |Sodium 126mg | Carbs 3.8g | Fiber 0.2g | Sugar 2.7g | Protein 42.5g

Ninja Foodi Barbeque Chicken Breasts

Prep time: 5 minutes | Cook Time: 22 minutes | Serves: 2

Ingredients:

2 chicken breasts, skinless and boneless

½ cup barbeque sauce

1 tablespoon olive oil

Salt and black pepper, to taste

Directions:

1. Rub chicken breasts with salt, pepper and half tablespoon olive oil. Set aside. 2. Meanwhile, arrange "Grill Grate" in a Ninja Foodi Smart XL Grill and press the "Grill" button. 3. Set the time to 22 minutes and temperature to MED heat. 4. Press START/STOP to begin preheating. 5. When it shows "Add Food", place chicken breasts in it and cook for 10 minutes. 6. Flip the breasts and pour barbeque sauce and remaining olive oil on them. 7. Cook for 12 minutes and take out. 8. Serve and enjoy!

Serving Suggestions: Serve with lime wedges.

Variation Tip: Olive oil can be replaced with corn oil.

Nutritional Information per Serving: Calories: 420 |Fat: 17.6g|Sat Fat: 3.9g|Carbohydrates: 22.7g|Fiber: 0.4g|Sugar: 16.3g|Protein: 40.5g

Delicious Maple Glazed Chicken

Prep time: 10 minutes | Cook Time: 15 minutes|Servings: 4

Ingredients

2 pounds chicken wings, bone-in

1 tsp black pepper, ground

¼ cup teriyaki sauce

1 cup maple syrup

⅓ cup soy sauce

3 garlic cloves, minced

2 tsp garlic powder

2 tsp onion powder

Directions:

1. Take a mixing bowl, add garlic, soy sauce, black pepper, maple syrup, garlic powder, onion powder, and teriyaki sauce, combine well. 2. Add the chicken wings and combine well to coat. 3. Arrange the Grill Grate in the Ninja Foodi Smart XL Grill and close the lid. 4. Pre-heat Ninja Foodi Smart XL Grill by selecting the "GRILL" function and setting it to "MED" and timer to 10 minutes. 5. Let it pre-heat until you hear a beep. 6. Arrange the chicken wings over the grill grate lock lid and cook for 5 minutes. 7. Flip the chicken and close the lid, cook for 5 minutes more. 8. Cook until its internal temperature reaches 165°F/75°C. 9. Serve warm and enjoy!

Serving Suggestion: Serve with chilled wine.
Variation Tip: add pepper flakes for more spice.
Nutritional Information per Serving: Calories: 543| Fat: 26 g| Carbohydrates: 46 g| Fiber: 4 g| Sodium: 648 mg | Protein: 42 g

Sweet and Sour Chicken BBQ

Prep time: 10 minutes | Cook Time: 40 minutes|Servings: 4

Ingredients

6 chicken drumsticks
¾ cup of sugar
1 cup of soy sauce
1 cup of water
¼ cup garlic, minced

¼ cup tomato paste
¾ cup onion, minced
1 cup white vinegar
Salt and pepper, to taste

Directions:

1. Take a Ziploc bag and add all Ingredients into it. 2. Marinate for at least 2 hours in your refrigerator. 3. Insert the Crisper Basket, and close the hood. 4. Pre-heat Ninja Foodi Smart XL Grill by selecting the "AIR CRISP" mode at 390°F/200°C for 40 minutes. 5. Place the grill pan accessory in the Grill. 6. Flip the chicken after every 10 minutes. 7. Take a saucepan and pour the marinade into it and heat over medium flame until sauce thickens. 8. Brush with the glaze.
Serving Suggestion: Serve warm and enjoy.
Variation Tip: use salt and pepper instead of BBQ sauce for variation.
Nutritional Information per Serving: Calories: 460| Fat: 20 g| Carbohydrates: 26 g| Fiber: 3 g| Sodium: 126 mg| Protein: 28 g

Alfredo Chicken Apples

Prep time: 5-10 minutes | Cook Time: 20 minutes|Servings: 4

Ingredients

1 large apple, wedged
1 tablespoon lemon juice
4 chicken breasts, halved
4 tsp chicken seasoning

4 slices provolone cheese
¼ cup blue cheese, crumbled
½ cup Alfredo sauce

Directions:

1. Take a bowl and add chicken, season it well. 2. Take another bowl and add in apple, lemon juice. 3. Pre-heat Ninja Foodi Smart XL Grill by selecting the "GRILL" mode and setting it to "MED" and timer to 20 minutes. 4. Let it pre-heat until you hear a beep. 5. Arrange chicken over Grill Grate, lock lid and cook for 8 minutes, flip and cook for 8 minutes more. 6. Grill apple in the same manner for 2 minutes per side. 7.
Serving Suggestion: Serve chicken with pepper, apple, blue cheese, and Alfredo sauce and Enjoy!
Variation Tip: use pears for variations.
Nutritional Information per Serving: Calories: 247|Fat: 19 g| Carbohydrates: 29 g| Fiber: 6 g |Sodium: 853 mg| Protein: 14 g

The Tarragon Chicken Meal

Prep time: 10 minutes | Cook Time: 5 minutes|Servings: 4

Ingredients

For Chicken
1 and ½ pounds chicken tenders
Salt as needed
3 tbsps. tarragon leaves, chopped
1 tsp lemon zest, grated
2 tbsps. fresh lemon juice
2 tbsps. extra virgin olive oil

For Sauce
2 tbsps. fresh lemon juice
2 tbsps. butter, salted
½ cup heavy whip cream

Directions:

1. Prepare your chicken by taking a baking dish and arranging the chicken over the dish in a single layer. 2. Season generously with salt and pepper. 3. Sprinkle chopped tarragon and lemon zest all around the tenders. 4. Drizzle lemon juice and olive oil on top. 5. Let them sit for 10 minutes. 6. Drain them well. 7. Insert Grill Grate in your Ninja Foodi Smart XL Grill and select the "GRILL" mode and set to "HI" temperature. 8. Set timer to 4 minutes. 9. Once you hear the beep, place chicken tenders in your grill grate. 10. Let it cook for 3-4 minutes until cooked completely. 11. Do in batches if needed. 12. Transfer the cooked chicken tenders to a platter. 13. For the sauce, take a small-sized saucepan. 14. Add cream, butter and lemon juice and bring to a boil. 15. Once thickened enough, pour the mix over chicken. 16. Serve and enjoy!

Serving Suggestion: Serve with pita bread.
Variation Tip: use chopped dill for garnish.
Nutritional Information per Serving: Calories: 263|Fat: 18 g| Carbohydrates: 7 g| Fiber: 1 g| Sodium: 363 mg| Protein: 19 g

Greek Chicken

Prep time: 10 minutes | Cook Time: 20 minutes | Serves: 4

Ingredients:

4 chicken breast, boneless and halves
3 tablespoons olive oil
3 tablespoons capers, rinsed and drained
10 olives, pitted and halved

2 cups cherry tomatoes
Pepper
Salt

Directions:

1. Place the cooking pot in the Ninja Foodi Smart XL Grill then set a grill grate inside. 2. In a bowl, mix tomatoes, capers, olives and oil. Set aside. 3. Season chicken with pepper and salt. 4. Place chicken in the baking dish. Top with tomato mixture. 5. Plug the thermometer into the appliance. 6. Select the "Bake" Mode, set the temperature to 400°F/200°C then select the PRESET. 7. Use the right arrow keys on the display to select "CHICKEN" and set the doneness to WELL. 8. Press the START/STOP button to initiate preheating. 9. Once preheated, place the chicken in the Ninja Foodi Smart XL Grill. 10. Insert the thermometer probe into the thickest part of the chicken. 11. Cover the hood and allow the grill to cook. 12. Serve, when done.
Serving Suggestion: Serve warm.
Variation Tip: Add ¼ teaspoon of Italian seasonings.
Nutritional Information per Serving: Calories 156 | Fat 12.6g |Sodium 345mg | Carbs 4.5g | Fiber 1.7g | Sugar 2.4g | Protein 7.9g

Chapter 3 Beef and Lamb Recipes

Grilled Stuffed Flank Steak

Prep time: 15 minutes | Cook Time: 10 minutes | Serves: 2

Ingredients:

¼ cup vegetable oil

2 cups thinly sliced scallions

3 tbsp. minced fresh ginger

1 (2½ lbs.) whole flank steak

Kosher salt and black pepper, to taste

1 cup teriyaki sauce

Directions:

1. Sauté ginger and scallions with oil in a skillet for 30 seconds then allow them to cool. 2. Cut the steak in ½ inch thick slices and cut each slice into 2-3 smaller rectangles. 3. Season the steaks with black pepper and salt then top each piece with the scallion mixture. 4. Roll the steak pieces and secure them a toothpick. 5. Place the cooking pot in the Ninja Foodi Smart XL Grill then set a grill grate inside. 6. Plug the thermometer into the appliance. 7. Select the "Grill" Mode, set the temperature to HI then select the PRESET. 8. Use the right arrow keys on the display to select "BEEF" and set the doneness to MED WELL. 9. Press the START/STOP button to initiate preheating. 10. Once preheated, place the steak in the Ninja Foodi Smart XL Grill. 11. Insert the thermometer probe into the thickest part of the steak. 12. Cover the hood and allow the grill to cook. 13. Serve warm.

Serving Suggestion: Serve the steaks with scallions on top.

Variation Tip: Add 1 tbsp. lime juice to the seasoning.

Nutritional Information per Serving: Calories 431 | Fat 20.1g | Sodium 364mg | Carbs 13g | Fiber 1g | Sugar 1.4g | Protein 25g

Teriyaki Beef Kebabs

Prep time: 15 minutes | Cook Time: 16 minutes | Serves: 4

Ingredients:

1 tbsp. olive oil

1 tbsp. grated ginger

1 tbsp. minced garlic

1 tsp. red pepper flakes

¾ cup teriyaki sauce

¾ cup pineapple juice

2 tbsp. soy sauce

1 tbsp. dark brown sugar

1 tsp. sesame oil

1½ lbs. beef sirloin tips, cubed

½ pineapple, peeled, cored, cubed

1 large sweet onion, cubed

2 red bell peppers, cubed

Directions:

1. Sauté red pepper, garlic and ginger with oil in a saucepan for 1 minute. 2. Stir in brown sugar, soy sauce, ¼ cup pineapple juice and teriyaki sauce then cook for 5 minutes on a simmer. 3. Remove from the heat and allow the sauce to cool. 4. Mix half of this marinade with ½ pineapple juice in a bowl. 5. Pour this mixture into a ziplock and add beef cubes. 6. Seal the bag, shake well and refrigerate for 5 hours. 7. Thread the beef, bell peppers, onion and pineapple on the wooden skewers, alternately. 8. Place the cooking pot in the Ninja Foodi Smart XL Grill then set a grill grate inside. 9. Select the "Grill" Mode, set the temperature to MED. 10. Press the START/STOP button to initiate preheating. 11. Once preheated, place the skewers in the Ninja Foodi Smart XL Grill. 12. Cover the hood and allow the grill to cook for 10 minutes, flipping halfway through. 13. Serve warm.

Serving Suggestion: Serve the kebabs with a kale cucumber salad.

Variation Tip: Add crumbled bacon on top before serving.

Nutritional Information per Serving: Calories 325 | Fat 16g | Sodium 431mg | Carbs 12g | Fiber 1.2g | Sugar 4g | Protein 23g

Cumin Lamb Skewers

Prep time: 15 minutes | Cook Time: 10 minutes | Serves: 4

Ingredients:

1 tbsp. red chili flakes

1 tbsp. whole cumin seed

2 tsp. whole fennel seed

1 tsp. kosher salt

2 tsp. granulated garlic

2 lbs. boneless lamb shoulder, cubed

1 tbsp. vegetable or canola oil

2 tsp. Shaoxing wine

Directions:

1. Grind all the spices, garlic, and salt, in a mortar. 2. Mix the spice-mixture with wine, and oil in a large bowl. 3. Toss in the lamb cubes, mix well to coat and cover then refrigerate for 30 minutes. 4. Thread the lamb cubes on the wooden skewers. 5. Place the cooking pot in the Ninja Foodi Smart XL Grill then set a grill grate inside. 6. Select the "Grill" Mode, set the temperature to MED. 7. Press the START/STOP button to initiate preheating. 8. Once preheated, place the skewers in the Ninja Foodi Smart XL Grill. 9. Cover the hood and allow the grill to cook for 10 minutes, flipping halfway through. 10. Serve warm.

Serving Suggestion: Serve the skewers with grilled zucchini salad.

Variation Tip: Add crushed red pepper on top before serving.

Nutritional Information per Serving: Calories 380 | Fat 20g | Sodium 686mg | Carbs 13g | Fiber 1g | Sugar 1.2g | Protein 21g

Steakhouse Kebabs

Prep time: 10 minutes | Cook Time: 10 minutes | Serves: 4

Ingredients:

¼ cup olive oil
¼ cup Worcestershire sauce
3 tbsp. soy sauce
1 tbsp. lemon juice
1 tbsp. Dijon mustard
1 tbsp. minced garlic

2 tsp. dark brown sugar
2 tsp. black pepper
1½ lbs. beef sirloin tips, cubed
8 oz. cremini mushrooms, halved
1 large red onion, cubed

Directions:

1. Mix black pepper, brown sugar, garlic, mustard, lemon juice, soy sauce, oil and Worcestershire sauce in a bowl. 2. Add this mixture to a ziplock bag and Once preheated, place the beef and mushrooms in the bag. 3. Seal the bag, shake well and refrigerate for 1 hour. 4. Thread mushrooms and beef on the skewer alternately. 5. Place the cooking pot in the Ninja Foodi Smart XL Grill then set a grill grate inside. 6. Select the "Grill" Mode, set the temperature to MED. 7. Press the START/STOP button to initiate preheating. 8. Once preheated, place the skewers in the Ninja Foodi Smart XL Grill. 9. Cover the hood and allow the grill to cook for 10 minutes, flipping halfway through. 10. Serve warm.
Serving Suggestion: Serve the kebabs with mashed cauliflower.
Variation Tip: Dust the beef with almond flour before grilling for more texture.
Nutritional Information per Serving: Calories 391 | Fat 5g |Sodium 88mg | Carbs 3g | Fiber 0g | Sugar 0g | Protein 27g

Ninja Foodi Beef Satay

Prep time: 10 minutes | Cook Time: 15 minutes | Serves: 4

Ingredients:

4 tablespoons olive oil
2 tablespoons fish sauce
2 tablespoons sugar
½ cup peanuts, roasted and chopped
2 tablespoons garlic, minced
1 cup chopped cilantro

2 pounds beef steak, cubed
2 tablespoons minced ginger
2 teaspoons ground coriander
2 tablespoons soy sauce
2 teaspoons Sriracha sauce
Salt, to taste

Directions:

1. Press "Grill" button in a Ninja Foodi Smart XL Grill and set the time to 15 minutes. Adjust the temperature to MED heat. 2. Press START/STOP to begin preheating. 3. Add all the ingredients except beef steak and olive oil in a bowl. Mix well. 4. When the Ninja Foodi Smart XL Grill shows "Add food", dip beef steaks in the mixture and place it in "Crisper Basket". 5. Drizzle with olive oil and grill for 15 minutes. 6. Flip halfway through and dish out. 7. Serve and enjoy!
Serving Suggestions: Serve with rice.
Variation Tip: Add red chili powder to enhance taste.
Nutritional Information per Serving: Calories: 691 |Fat: 37.3g|Sat Fat: 8.6g|Carbohydrates: 13.4g|Fiber: 2.2g|Sugar: 7.4g|Protein: 75.1g

Grilled Beef Skewers

Prep time: 10 minutes | Cook Time: 10 minutes | Serves: 4

Ingredients:

4 tbsp. minced fresh lemongrass
3 fresh bay leaves, chopped
2 tsp. fresh thyme leaves
1 tsp. lemon zest
1 tsp. lime zest
2 tsp. fresh peeled ginger, diced
8 medium garlic cloves, crushed
1½ tsp. turmeric powder

1½ tsp. fresh juice from 1 lemon
1 tsp. kosher salt
1 tbsp. sugar
1 tsp. cinnamon
1 lb. beef sirloin steak, sliced
2 tsp. Asian fish sauce
1 tbsp. vegetable oil

Directions:

1. Grind ginger, garlic, lime zest, lemon zest, thyme bay leaves and lemon grass in a mortar with a pestle. 2. Stir in cinnamon, sugar, salt, lemon juice and turmeric to form a paste. 3. Add this paste, oil, fish sauce and beef to a mixing bowl. 4. Mix well, and thread the beef on the wooden skewers. 5. Place the cooking pot in the Ninja Foodi Smart XL Grill then set a grill grate inside. 6. Select the "Grill" Mode, set the temperature to MED. 7. Press the START/STOP button to initiate preheating. 8. Once preheated, place the skewers in the Ninja Foodi Smart XL Grill. 9. Cover the hood and allow the grill to cook for 10 minutes, flipping halfway through. 10. Serve warm.
Serving Suggestion: Serve the skewers with mashed cauliflower.
Variation Tip: Use BBQ sauce for the change of taste.
Nutritional Information per Serving: Calories 305 | Fat 25g |Sodium 532mg | Carbs 13g | Fiber 0.4g | Sugar 2g | Protein 28.3g

Beef with Pesto

Prep time: 15 minutes | Cook Time: 14 minutes | Serves: 2

Ingredients:

2 cups Penne pasta, uncooked

2 (6 ounces) beef tenderloin steaks

¼ teaspoon salt

¼ teaspoon black pepper

5 ounces fresh baby spinach, chopped

2 cups grape tomatoes, halved

⅓ cup pesto

¼ cup walnuts, chopped

¼ cup Feta cheese, crumbled

Directions:

1. At first, prepared the pasta as per the given instructions on the pack. 2. Drain and rinse, then keep this pasta aside. 3. Now season the tenderloin steaks with salt and black pepper. 4. Place the cooking pot in the Ninja Foodi Smart XL Grill then place the grill grate in the pot. 5. Plug the thermometer into the appliance. 6. Select the "Grill" Mode, set the temperature to MAX then select the PRESET. 7. Use the right arrow keys on the display to select "BEEF" and set the doneness to MED WELL. 8. Press the START/STOP button to initiate preheating. 9. Place the beef in the Ninja Foodi Smart XL Grill. 10. Insert the thermometer probe into the thickest part of the beef. 11. Cover the hood and allow the grill to cook for 7 minutes per side. 12. Toss the pasta with spinach, tomatoes, walnuts and pesto in a bowl. 13. Slice the grilled steak and top the salad with the steak. 14. Garnish with cheese. 15. Enjoy.

Serving Suggestion: Serve the beef with toasted bread slices.

Variation Tip: Add crumbled bacon to the mixture.

Nutritional Information per Serving: Calories 325 | Fat 16g | Sodium 431mg | Carbs 22g | Fiber 1.2g | Sugar 4g | Protein 23g

Garlic Rosemary Lamb Chops

Prep time: 10 minutes | Cook Time: 10 minutes | Serves: 6

Ingredients:

2 pounds of lamb chops

1 tablespoon rosemary, chopped

¼ cup olive oil

1 tablespoon garlic, minced

1 lemon zest

Pepper

Salt

Directions:

1. Place the cooking pot in the Ninja Foodi Smart XL Grill then place the grill grate in the pot. 2. Add lamb chops and remaining ingredients into the zip-lock bag. Seal bag and place in the refrigerator overnight. 3. Select the "Grill" Mode, set the temperature to HI. 4. Press the START/STOP button to initiate preheating. 5. Once preheated, place the lamb in the Ninja Foodi Smart XL Grill. 6. Cover the hood and allow the grill to cook for 10 minutes. 7. Serve, when done.

Serving Suggestion: Serve warm.

Variation Tip: None

Nutritional Information per Serving: Calories 357 | Fat 19.6g |Sodium 143mg | Carbs 0.8g | Fiber 0.3g | Sugar 0g | Protein 42.6g

Beef Chimichurri Skewers

Prep time: 15 minutes | Cook Time: 10 minutes | Serves: 4

Ingredients:

⅓ cup fresh basil

⅓ cup fresh cilantro

⅓ cup fresh parsley

1 tablespoon red wine vinegar

Juice of ½ lemon

1 Garlic clove, minced

1 shallot, minced

½ teaspoon crushed red pepper flakes

½ cup olive oil, divided

Salt to taste

Black pepper to taste

1 red onion, cubed

1 red pepper, cubed

1 orange pepper, cubed

1 yellow pepper, cubed

1½ pound sirloin steak, fat trimmed and diced

Directions:

1. First take basil, parsley, vinegar, lemon juice, red pepper, shallots, garlic and cilantro in a blender jug. 2. Blend well, then add ¼ cup olive oil, salt and pepper and mix again. 3. Now thread the steak, peppers and onion on the skewers. 4. Drizzle salt, black pepper and remaining oil over the skewers. 5. Place the cooking pot in the Ninja Foodi Smart XL Grill then place the grill grate in the pot. 6. Select the Grill Mode, set the temperature to MED. 7. Press the Start/Stop button to Initiate preheating. 8. Place skewers in the Ninja Foodi Smart XL Grill. 9. Cover the Ninja Foodi Smart XL Grill's Hood and let the appliance cook. 10. Place four skewers in the Ninja Foodi Smart XL Grill. 11. Close the hood and grill for 5 to 6 minutes per side. 12. Grill the skewers in a batch until all are cooked. 13. Serve warm with green sauce.

Serving Suggestion: Serve the skewers with fresh green and mashed potatoes.

Variation Tip: Add a drizzle of herbs on top of the skewers.

Nutritional Information per Serving: Calories 301 | Fat 5g | Sodium 340mg | Carbs 24.7g | Fiber 1.2g | Sugar 1.3g | Protein 15.3g

Steak Bread Salad

Prep time: 15 minutes | Cook Time: 8 minutes | Serves: 2

Ingredients:

2 teaspoons chili powder
2 teaspoons brown sugar
½ teaspoon salt
½ teaspoon black pepper
1 beef top Sirloin steak, diced
2 cups bread, cubed
2 tablespoons olive oil

1 cup ranch salad dressing
2 tablespoons horseradish, grated
1 tablespoon prepared mustard
3 large tomatoes, diced
1 medium cucumber, chopped
1 small red onion, thinly sliced

Directions:

1. First, mix the chili powder with salt, pepper and brown sugar in a bowl 2. Sauté the bread cubes with oil in a skillet for 10 minutes until golden. 3. Take a small bowl and mix horseradish with mustard and salad dressing. 4. Season the steak with black pepper, salt and olive oil. 5. Place the cooking pot in the Ninja Foodi Smart XL Grill then place the grill grate in the pot. 6. Plug the thermometer into the appliance. 7. Select the "Grill" Mode, set the temperature to MAX then select the PRESET. 8. Use the right arrow keys on the display to select "BEEF" and set the doneness to MED WELL. 9. Press the START/STOP button to initiate preheating. 10. Place the steak in the Ninja Foodi Smart XL Grill. 11. Insert the thermometer probe into the thickest part of the steak. 12. Cover the hood and allow the grill to cook for 4 minutes per side. 13. Toss the sautéed bread cubes with the rest of the ingredients and dressing mix in a salad bowl. 14. Slice the grilled steak and serve on top of the salad. 15. Enjoy.

Serving Suggestion: Serve the steak bread salad with crispy bacon on top.
Variation Tip: Grill bread cubes in the Ninja Foodi Smart XL Grill for more texture.
Nutritional Information per Serving: Calories 380 | Fat 20g | Sodium 686mg | Carbs 33g | Fiber 1g | Sugar 1.2g | Protein 21g

Sweet Chipotle Ribs

Prep time: 15 minutes | Cook Time: 20 minutes | Serves: 8

Ingredients:

6 pounds baby back ribs
Sauce:
3 cups ketchup
2 (11.2 ounces) beer bottles
2 cups barbecue sauce
⅔ cup honey
1 small onion, chopped
¼ cup Worcestershire sauce

2 tablespoons Dijon mustard
2 tablespoons chipotle in Adobo sauce, chopped
4 teaspoons ground chipotle pepper
1 teaspoon salt
1 teaspoon garlic powder
½ teaspoon black pepper

Directions:

1. First, wrap the ribs in a large foil and keep it aside. 2. Insert the thermometer probe into the thickest part of the meat and connect it to the appliance. 3. Place the cooking pot in the Ninja Foodi Smart XL Grill then place the grill grate in the pot. 4. Plug the thermometer into the appliance. 5. Select the "Grill" Mode, set the temperature to MAX then select the PRESET. 6. Use the right arrow keys on the display to select "BEEF" and set the doneness to MED WELL. 7. Press the START/STOP button to initiate preheating. 8. Place the ribs in the Ninja Foodi Smart XL Grill. 9. Insert the thermometer probe into the thickest part of the ribs. 10. Cover the hood and allow the grill to cook. 11. Take the rest of the ingredients in a saucepan and cook for 45 minutes on a simmer. 12. Brush the grilled ribs with the prepared sauce generously. 13. Place the ribs back into the grill and continue grilling for 10 minutes per side. 14. Serve.

Serving Suggestion: Serve these ribs with rice, pasta or spaghetti.
Variation Tip: Add maple syrup instead of honey.
Nutritional Information per Serving: Calories 425 | Fat 14g | Sodium 411mg | Carbs 44g | Fiber 0.3g | Sugar 1g | Protein 8.3g

Ninja Foodi Herbed Lamb Chops

Prep time: 5 minutes | Cook Time: 12 minutes | Serves: 2

Ingredients:

1 pound lamb chops
1 tablespoon herb and garlic seasoning
1 teaspoon olive oil

2 tablespoons herbed butter
Salt and black pepper, to taste

Directions:

1. Press "Air Crisp" in a Ninja Foodi Smart XL Grill. Set the temperature to 350°F/175°C and adjust the time to 12 minutes. 2. Press START/STOP to begin preheating. 3. Meanwhile, add lamb chops, herbed butter, olive oil, herb and garlic seasoning in a bowl. Mix well. 4. When the Ninja Foodi Smart XL Grill shows "Add Food", place lamb chops in it and cook for 12 minutes. 5. Dish out and serve warm.

Serving Suggestions: Serve with chopped mint leaves on the top.
Variation Tip: You can add some herbs to enhance taste.
Nutritional Information per Serving: Calories: 797 |Fat: 45g|Sat Fat: 17.3g|Carbohydrates: 4g|Fiber: 0g|Sugar: 1g|Protein: 86.7g

Steak with Salsa Verde

Prep time: 15 minutes | Cook Time: 18 minutes | Serves: 2

Ingredients:

¼ teaspoon salt
¼ teaspoon black pepper
1 cup Salsa Verde
½ cup fresh cilantro leaves

1 ripe avocado, diced
1 beef flank steak, diced
1 medium tomato, seeded and diced

Directions:

1. First, rub the steak with salt and pepper to season well. 2. Place the cooking pot in the Ninja Foodi Smart XL Grill then place the grill grate in the pot. 3. Plug the thermometer into the appliance. 4. Select the "Grill" Mode, set the temperature to MAX then select the PRESET. 5. Use the right arrow keys on the display to select "BEEF" and set the doneness to MED WELL. 6. Press the START/STOP button to initiate preheating. 7. Place the beef in the Ninja Foodi Smart XL Grill. 8. Insert the thermometer probe into the thickest part of the beef. 9. Cover the hood and allow the grill to cook for 9 minutes per side until al dente. 10. During this time, blend salsa with cilantro in a blender jug. 11. Slice the steak and serve it with salsa, tomato and avocado.

Serving Suggestion: Serve the steak with sweet potato casserole.

Variation Tip: Add cheese on top of the steak and then bake after grilling.

Nutritional Information per Serving: Calories 425 | Fat 15g | Sodium 345mg | Carbs 12.3g | Fiber 1.4g | Sugar 3g | Protein 23.3g

Beef Cheese Burgers

Prep time: 15 minutes | Cook Time: 20 minutes | Serves: 4

Ingredients:

½ cup shredded Cheddar cheese
6 tablespoons chili sauce, divided

1 tablespoon chili powder
1 pound ground beef

To serve:

4 hamburger buns, split

Lettuce leaves, tomato slices and mayonnaise

Directions:

1. First, take all the ingredients for patties in a bowl. 2. Thoroughly mix them together, then make 4 of the ½ inch patties out of it. 3. Place the cooking pot in the Ninja Foodi Smart XL Grill then place the grill grate in the pot. 4. Select the "Grill" Mode, set the temperature to MAX. 5. Press the START/STOP button to initiate preheating. 6. Place the patties in the Ninja Foodi Smart XL Grill. 7. Cover the hood and allow the grill to cook for 5 minutes per side. 8. Serve with buns, lettuce, tomato, and mayonnaise.

Serving Suggestion: Serve the beef cheeseburgers with mayo dip.

Variation Tip: Add butter to the patties before cooking.

Nutritional Information per Serving: Calories 405 | Fat 22.7g | Sodium 227mg | Carbs 26.1g | Fiber 1.4g | Sugar 0.9g | Protein 45.2g

Grilled Beef Burgers

Prep time: 5-10 minutes | Cook Time: 10 minutes|Servings: 4

Ingredients

4 pounces cream cheese
4 slices bacon, cooked and crumbled
2 seeded jalapeño peppers, stemmed, and minced
½ cup shredded Cheddar cheese
½ tsp. chili powder
¼ tsp. paprika

¼ tsp. ground black pepper
2 pounds ground beef
4 hamburger buns
4 slices pepper Jack cheese
Optional - Lettuce, sliced tomato, and sliced red onion

Directions:

1. In a mixing bowl, combine the peppers, Cheddar cheese, cream cheese, and bacon until well combined. 2. Prepare the ground beef into 8 patties. Add the cheese mixture onto four of the patties; arrange a second patty on top of each to prepare four burgers. press gently. 3. In another bowl, combine the chili powder, paprika, and pepper. Sprinkle the mixture onto the sides of the burgers. 4. Take Ninja Foodi Smart XL Grill, organize it over your kitchen stage, and open the top cover. 5. Organize the flame broil mesh and close the top cover. 6. Select ROAST mode at 350°F/175°C and set the time to 5 minutes. Press SATRT/STOP to begin preheating. 7. Ninja Foodi Smart XL Grill is preheated and prepared to cook when it begins to blare. After you hear a blare, open the top. Arrange the burgers over the Grill Grate. 8. Close the top lid and allow it to cook until the timer reads zero. Cook for 3-4 more minutes, if needed. 9. Cook until the food thermometer reaches 145°F/60°C. Serve warm.

Serving Suggestion: Serve warm with buns.

Variation Tip: Add your choice of toppings: pepper Jack cheese, lettuce, tomato, and red onion.

Nutritional Information per Serving: Calories: 783| Fat: 38g| Carbohydrates: 25g| Fiber: 3g| Sodium: 1259mg| Protein: 57.5g

Crusted Beef Burger

Prep time: 15 minutes | Cook Time: 10 minutes | Serves: 4

Ingredients:

½ cup seasoned bread crumbs
1 large egg, lightly beaten
½ teaspoon salt
½ teaspoon black pepper

1 pound ground beef
1 tablespoon olive oil
4 sesame seed hamburger buns, split

Directions:

1. Take all the ingredients for a burger in a suitable bowl except the oil and the buns. 2. Mix them thoroughly together and make four of the ½ inch patties. 3. Brush these patties with olive oil. 4. Place the cooking pot in the Ninja Foodi Smart XL Grill then place the grill grate in the pot. 5. Select the Grill Mode, set the temperature to LOW and press PRESET. 6. Press the START/STOP button to Initiate preheating. 7. Place 2 patties in the Ninja Foodi Smart XL Grill and insert the probe into any patty. 8. Cover the Ninja Foodi Smart XL Grill's Hood and cook for 5 minutes per side. 9. Grill the remaining 2 patties in the same way. 10. Serve with buns.
Serving Suggestion: Serve the burgers with sautéed green beans and mashed potatoes.
Variation Tip: Insert a cheese cube at the center of each patty.
Nutritional Information per Serving: Calories 395 | Fat 9.5g | Sodium 655mg | Carbs 13.4g | Fiber 0.4g | Sugar 0.4g | Protein 28.3g

Lamb Skewers

Prep time: 15 minutes | Cook Time: 8 minutes | Serves: 4

Ingredients:

1 (10 ounces) pack couscous
1½ cup yogurt
1 tablespoon, 1 teaspoon cumin
2 garlic cloves, minced
Juice of 2 lemons
Salt to taste
Black pepper to taste
1½ pound leg of lamb, boneless, diced

2 tomatoes, seeded and diced
½ English cucumber, seeded and diced
½ small red onion, chopped
¼ cup fresh parsley, chopped
¼ cup fresh mint, chopped
3 tablespoons olive oil
Lemon wedges, for serving

Directions:

1. First, cook the couscous as per the given instructions on the package, then fluff with a fork. 2. Whisk yogurt with garlic, cumin, lemon juice, salt and black pepper in a large bowl. 3. Add lamb and mix well to coat the meat. 4. Separately toss red onion with cucumber, tomatoes, parsley, mint, lemon juice, olive oil, salt and couscous in a salad bowl. 5. Place the cooking pot in the Ninja Foodi Smart XL Grill then place the grill grate in the pot. 6. Thread the seasoned lamb on eight skewers and drizzle salt and black pepper over them. 7. Select the Grill Mode, set the temperature to MED. 8. Press the Start/Stop button to Initiate preheating. 9. Place skewers in the Ninja Foodi Smart XL Grill. 10. Cover the Ninja Foodi Smart XL Grill's Hood and grill for 7 to 8 minutes. 11. Cook the remaining skewers in a similar way. 12. Serve warm with prepared couscous.
Serving Suggestion: Serve the Lamb Skewers with quinoa salad.
Variation Tip: Add BBQ sauce to the lamb cube skewers.
Nutritional Information per Serving: Calories 448 | Fat 23g | Sodium 350mg | Carbs 18g | Fiber 6.3g | Sugar 1g | Protein 40.3g

Korean Beef Steak

Prep time: 15 minutes | Cook Time: 12 minutes | Serves: 2

Ingredients:

½ cup 1 tablespoon soy sauce
¼ cup 2 tablespoons vegetable oil
½ cup rice wine vinegar
4 garlic cloves, minced
2 tablespoons ginger, minced
2 tablespoon honey
3 tablespoons sesame oil

3 tablespoons Sriracha
1½ pound flank steak
1 teaspoon sugar
1 teaspoon crushed red pepper flakes
2 cucumbers, cut lengthwise, seeded and sliced
Salt to taste

Directions:

1. Mix ½ cup soy sauce, half of the rice wine, honey, ginger, garlic, 2 tablespoons Sriracha sauce, 2 tablespoons sesame oil and vegetable oil in a large bowl. 2. Pour half of this sauce over the steak and rub it well. 3. Cover the steak and marinate for 10 minutes. 4. For the salad, mix remaining rice wine vinegar, sesame oil, sugar, red pepper flakes, Sriracha sauce, soy sauce and salt in a salad bowl. 5. Place the cooking pot in the Ninja Foodi Smart XL Grill then place the grill grate in the pot. 6. Select the Grill Mode, set the temperature to MED. 7. Press the Start/Stop button to Initiate preheating. 8. Place steak in the Ninja Foodi Smart XL Grill. 9. Cover the Ninja Foodi Smart XL Grill's Hood and cook for 6 minutes per side. 10. Slice and serve with cucumber salad.
Serving Suggestion: Serve the flank steak with sautéed vegetables and toasted bread slices.
Variation Tip: Use maple syrup instead of honey for a unique sweet taste.
Nutritional Information per Serving: Calories 309 | Fat 25g | Sodium 463mg | Carbs 9.9g | Fiber 0.3g | Sugar 0.3g | Protein 18g

Delicious Pot Roast

Prep time: 10 minutes | Cook Time: 6 hours | Serves: 6

Ingredients

Seasoning Blend
2 tsp thyme leaves dried
2 tsp sea salt
1 tsp black pepper
Pot Roast Ingredients
1-2 tbsp. avocado oil
3-4(1 lbs.) Chuck Roast
1 onion
4 cups beef stock divided

1 tsp garlic powder
1 tsp onion powder
½ tsp red pepper flakes

¼ cup flour
6 carrots
6 small potatoes

Directions:

1. Add the oil to the inner pan of the Ninja Foodi Smart XL Grill and preheat on "GRILL" function and set the temperature to "HI" for 10 minutes. 2. Combine the seasoning in a bowl and rub onto both sides of the chuck roast. When the grill has preheated, place the roast on the bottom of the inner pan. Close the lid and grill on high for 5 minutes. 3. Flip and grill another 5 minutes. 4. Cut your onion into chunks and add to the pan. Pour in 2 cups of beef stock and select the "ROAST" function on 250°F/120°C and set the time for 3 hours. 5. After the 3 hours, remove the meat and make the gravy by combining the remaining beef stock and flour with some of the liquid in the pan into a large glass Mason jar with a lid and shake until well combined. 6. Pour into the pan. Put the roast in along with the vegetables and set the grill to the ROAST setting on 250°F/120°C for another 3 hours. 7. The total cook time will depend on your roast, so start checking it after the 1st hour and give it a flip.
Serving Suggestion: Serve with the vegetables.
Variation Tip: For keto version uses ½ cup of coconut flour for gravy.
Nutritional Information per Serving: Calories 658 | Carbohydrates 44g | Protein 52g | Fat 31g | Sodium 156mg| Fiber 6g

Lemon Garlic Lamb Chops

Prep time: 10 minutes | Cook Time: 10 minutes | Serves: 4

Ingredients:

1½ pound lamb chops
2 teaspoons oregano
1 lemon zest
¼ cup olive oil

4 garlic cloves, minced
1 lemon juice
Pepper
Salt

Directions:

1. Place the cooking pot in the Ninja Foodi Smart XL Grill then place the grill grate in the pot. 2. Add lamb chops and remaining ingredients into the zip-lock bag. Seal bag and place in the refrigerator for overnight. 3. Insert the thermometer probe into the thickest part of the meat and connect it to the appliance. 4. Plug the thermometer into the appliance. 5. Select the "Grill" Mode, set the temperature to HI then select the PRESET. 6. Use the right arrow keys on the display to select "LAMB" and set the doneness to MED WELL. 7. Press the START/STOP button to initiate preheating. 8. Once preheated, place the lamb in the Ninja Foodi Smart XL Grill. 9. Insert the thermometer probe into the thickest part of the lamb. 10. Cover the hood and allow the grill to cook. 11. Serve, when done.
Serving Suggestion: Serve warm.
Variation Tip: Add chili powder for a spicy flavor.
Nutritional Information per Serving: Calories 431 | Fat 25.2g |Sodium 169mg | Carbs 1.5g | Fiber 0.4g | Sugar 0.1g | Protein 48g

Ninja Foodi Herbed Beef Steak

Prep time: 15 minutes | Cook Time: 8 minutes | Serves: 8

Ingredients:

4 tablespoons melted butter
4 (¾ pounds) strip steaks

4 tablespoons herb and garlic seasoning
Salt and black pepper, to taste

Directions:

1. Rub beef steak with salt, pepper, melted butter, herb and garlic seasoning. Set aside. 2. Meanwhile, arrange "Grill Grate" in a Ninja Foodi Smart XL Grill and press the "Grill" button. 3. Adjust the time to 8 minutes and temperature to HI heat. 4. Press START/STOP to begin preheating. 5. When it shows "Add Food", place marinated beef steak in it and cook for about 8 minutes. 6. Flip halfway through and dish out. 7. Serve and enjoy!
Serving Suggestions: Top with yogurt before serving.
Variation Tip: You can add green chili sauce to enhance taste.
Nutritional Information per Serving: Calories: 372 |Fat: 16.4g|Sat Fat: 7.7g|Carbohydrates: 1g|Fiber: 0g|Sugar: 0g|Protein: 51.7g

Fajita Skewers

Prep time: 15 minutes | Cook Time: 7 minutes | Serves: 4

Ingredients:

1 pound sirloin steak, cubed
1 bunch scallions, cut into large pieces
1 pack flour tortillas, torn
4 large Bell peppers, cubed

8 skewers
Olive oil, for drizzling
Salt to taste
Black pepper to taste

Directions:

1. Thread the steak, tortillas, peppers and scallions on the skewers. 2. Drizzle salt, black pepper and olive oil over the skewers. 3. Place the cooking pot in the Ninja Foodi Smart XL Grill then place the grill grate in the pot. 4. Select the Grill Mode, set the temperature to MED. 5. Press the Start/Stop button to Initiate preheating. 6. Place skewers in the Ninja Foodi Smart XL Grill. 7. Cover the Ninja Foodi Smart XL Grill's Hood and let the appliance cook for 14 minutes, continue rotating the skewers every 4 minutes. 8. Cook the skewers in batches until all are grilled. 9. Serve warm.

Serving Suggestion: Serve the Fajita Skewers with mashed potatoes.
Variation Tip: Add more veggies of your choice to the skewers.
Nutritional Information per Serving: Calories 537 | Fat 20g | Sodium 719mg | Carbs 25.1g | Fiber 0.9g | Sugar 1.4g | Protein 37.8g

Moink Balls

Prep time: 15 minutes | Cook Time: 10 minutes | Serves: 4

Ingredients:

1½ lb. ground beef chuck
¾ cup fresh breadcrumbs
2 large eggs, beaten
2 tsp. minced garlic

½ lb. bacon, halved
¼ cup rub
1 cup of barbecue sauce

Directions:

1. Mix beef with garlic, eggs, and breadcrumbs in a bowl. 2. Make 1 inch round balls out of this mixture. 3. Stick a toothpick in each ball and coat each with the rub. 4. Place the cooking pot in the Ninja Foodi Smart XL Grill then set a grill grate inside. 5. Select the "Grill" Mode, set the temperature to MED. 6. Press the START/STOP button to initiate preheating. 7. Once preheated, place the moink balls in the Ninja Foodi Smart XL Grill. 8. Cover the hood and cook for 5 minutes per side. 9. Serve warm.

Serving Suggestion: Serve the moink balls with cream cheese dip.
Variation Tip: Serve the balls on top of a lettuce bed.
Nutritional Information per Serving: Calories 376 | Fat 21g |Sodium 476mg | Carbs 12g | Fiber 3g | Sugar 4g | Protein 20g

Spinach Salad with Steak & Blueberries

Prep time: 30 minutes | Cook Time: 30 minutes|Servings: 4

Ingredients

1 cup fresh blueberries, divided
½ cup chopped walnuts, toasted
1 tsp sugar
½ tsp salt, divided
3 tbsps. fruity vinegar, such as raspberry vinegar
1 tablespoon minced shallot

3 tbsps. walnut oil or canola oil
8 cups baby spinach
1 pound sirloin steak
½ tsp freshly ground pepper
¼ cup crumbled feta cheese

Directions:

1. Select the "GRILL" function and adjust temperature to "HI" and preheat the Ninja Foodi Smart XL Grill for 8 minutes. 2. Pulse quarter cup blueberries, quarter cup walnuts, vinegar, shallots, ¼ tsp salt, and sugar in a food processor to form a paste. With the running motor, add oil until incorporated. Then transfer the dressing to a big bowl. 3. Sprinkle the steak with pepper and the left quarter with tsp salt. 4. Insert grill grate in the unit and close the hood. Cook the steak for 15 minutes, flipping every 5 minutes for even cooking. 5. Add the spinach to a bowl with the dressing and toss to coat. Divide the spinach among four plates. Slice the steak thinly, crosswise.

Serving Suggestion: Serve top spinach with the feta, steak, and remaining blueberries and walnuts.
Variation Tip: use fresh berries of your choice.
Nutritional Information per Serving: Calories 412 | Carbohydrates 64.3g | Protein 16.1g | Fat 10.1g | Sodium 895mg| Fiber 2g

Delicious Beef Meatballs

Prep time: 10 minutes | Cook Time: 10 minutes | Serves: 4

Ingredients:

1 egg, lightly beaten
1 pound ground beef
1 tablespoon garlic, minced
½ cup Cheddar cheese, shredded
¼ cup fresh parsley, chopped

¼ cup onion, chopped
2 tablespoons taco seasoning
Pepper
Salt

Directions:

1. Place the cooking pot in the Ninja Foodi Smart XL Grill then place the Crisper Basket in the pot. 2. Add meat and remaining ingredients into the bowl and mix until well combined. 3. Make small balls from the meat mixture. 4. Plug the thermometer into the appliance. 5. Select the "Air Crisp" Mode, set the temperature to 400°F/200°C then select the PRESET. 6. Use the right arrow keys on the display to select "BEEF" and set the doneness to MED WELL. 7. Press the START/STOP button to initiate preheating. 8. Once preheated, place the meatballs in the Ninja Foodi Smart XL Grill. 9. Insert the thermometer probe into the thickest part of the meatballs. 10. Cover the hood and allow the grill to cook. 11. Serve, when done.

Serving Suggestion: Serve warm.

Variation Tip: Add your choice of seasonings.

Nutritional Information per Serving: Calories 291 | Fat 12.9g |Sodium 219mg | Carbs 1.9g | Fiber 0.3g | Sugar 0.5g | Protein 39.6g

Flavorful Lamb Chops

Prep time: 10 minutes | Cook Time: 30 minutes | Serves: 4

Ingredients:

4 lamb chops
1 teaspoon ginger
1 teaspoon cinnamon
1½ teaspoon tarragon

¼ cup brown sugar
1 teaspoon garlic powder
Pepper
Salt

Directions:

1. Place the cooking pot in the Ninja Foodi Smart XL Grill and set a baking dish inside. 2. Add lamb chops and remaining ingredients into the zip-lock bag. Seal bag and place in the refrigerator for overnight. 3. Plug the thermometer into the appliance. 4. Select the "Bake" Mode, set the temperature to 375°F/190°C then select the PRESET. 5. Use the right arrow keys on the display to select "LAMB" and set the doneness to MED WELL. 6. Press the START/STOP button to initiate preheating. 7. Once preheated, place the lamb in the Ninja Foodi Smart XL Grill. 8. Insert the thermometer probe into the thickest part of the lamb. 9. Cover the hood and allow the grill to cook for 30 minutes, turn lamb chops after 20 minutes. 10. Serve, when done.

Serving Suggestion: Serve warm.

Variation Tip: Once cooked sprinkle with chopped parsley.

Nutritional Information per Serving: Calories 649 | Fat 24g |Sodium 290mg | Carbs 10.3g | Fiber 0.5g | Sugar 9g | Protein 92.1g

Ninja Foodi Korean BBQ Beef

Prep time: 10 minutes | Cook Time: 15 minutes | Serves: 4

Ingredients:

2 pounds steak
½ cup cornstarch
1 cup soy sauce
2 tablespoons barbeque sauce
2 teaspoons water
2 teaspoons ground ginger

1 cup brown sugar
4 tablespoons white wine vinegar
1 teaspoon sesame seeds
2 garlic cloves, crushed
Salt and pepper, to taste

Directions:

1. Add in cornstarch and water and cook until the sauce thickens. Take out and set aside. 2. Add all the rest ingredients except steak in a pan. Cook well. 3. Meanwhile, press the "Grill" button in a Ninja Foodi Smart XL Grill and set the time to 10 minutes. Adjust the temperature to MED heat. 4. Cover steak with cornstarch and place it in the Ninja Foodi Smart XL Grill when it shows "Add Food". 5. Cook for 10 minutes at medium pressure and take out. 6. Top with barbeque sauce and serve.

Serving Suggestions: Top with fresh cilantro before serving.

Variation Tip: You can use chopped green bell pepper to enhance taste.

Nutritional Information per Serving: Calories: 708 |Fat: 11.8g|Sat Fat: 4g|Carbohydrates: 59.3g|Fiber: 0.9g|Sugar: 38.4g|Protein: 86.3g

Cheese Beef Meatballs

Prep time: 10 minutes | Cook Time: 10 minutes | Serves: 4

Ingredients:

1 egg
1 pound ground beef
¼ cup onions, chopped
½ cup Cheddar cheese, shredded

2 tablespoons taco seasoning
Pepper
Salt

Directions:

1. Place the cooking pot in the Ninja Foodi Smart XL Grill then set a Crisper Basket inside. 2. Add all ingredients into the bowl and mix until well combined. 3. Make small balls from the meat mixture. 4. Select the "Air Crisp" Mode, set the temperature to 400°F/200°C then select the PRESET. 5. Press the START/STOP button to initiate preheating. 6. Once preheated, place the meatballs in the Ninja Foodi Smart XL Grill. 7. Cover the hood and allow the grill to cook. 8. Serve, when done.
Serving Suggestion: Garnish with parsley and serve.
Variation Tip: Add your choice of seasonings.
Nutritional Information per Serving: Calories 286 | Fat 12.9g |Sodium 217mg | Carbs 1g | Fiber 0.2g | Sugar 0.5g | Protein 39.4g

Grill Lamb Chops

Prep time: 10 minutes | Cook Time: 10 minutes | Serves: 4

Ingredients:

2 pounds of lamb chops
¼ cup fresh lime juice
¼ cup olive oil
¼ teaspoon red pepper flakes, crushed

2 teaspoons garlic, minced
2 teaspoons dried oregano
½ teaspoon pepper
1 teaspoon salt

Directions:

1. Place the cooking pot in the Ninja Foodi Smart XL Grill then set a Crisper Basket inside. 2. Add lamb chops and remaining ingredients into the zip-lock bag. Seal bag and place in the refrigerator overnight. 3. Plug the thermometer into the appliance. 4. Select the "Air Crisp" Mode, set the temperature to 400°F/200°C then select the PRESET. 5. Use the right arrow keys on the display to select "LAMB" and set the doneness to MED WELL. 6. Press the START/STOP button to initiate preheating. 7. Once preheated, place the lamb in the Ninja Foodi Smart XL Grill. 8. Insert the thermometer probe into the thickest part of the lamb. 9. Cover the hood and allow the grill to cook. 10. Serve, when done.
Serving Suggestion: Serve warm.
Variation Tip: Add your choice of seasonings.
Nutritional Information per Serving: Calories 535 | Fat 29.3g |Sodium 754mg | Carbs 1.1g | Fiber 0.4g | Sugar 0g | Protein 63.9g

Steak Pineapple Mania

Prep time: 5-10 minutes | Cook Time: 8 minutes|Servings: 4-5

Ingredients

½ medium pineapple, cored and diced
1 jalapeño pepper, seeded, stemmed, and diced
1 medium red onion, diced
4 (6-8-ounce) filet mignon steaks
1 tablespoon canola oil

Sea salt and ground black pepper to taste
1 tablespoon lime juice
¼ cup chopped cilantro leaves
Chili powder and ground coriander to taste

Directions:

1. Rub the fillets with the oil evenly, and then season with the salt and black pepper. 2. Take Ninja Foodi Smart XL Grill, arrange it over your kitchen platform, and open the top lid. 3. Arrange the Grill Grate and close the top lid. 4. Select "GRILL" function and select the "HI" temperature setting. Adjust the timer to 8 minutes and then select "START/STOP." Ninja Foodi Smart XL Grill will start preheating. 5. Ninja Foodi Smart XL Grill is preheated and ready to cook when it starts to beep. After you hear a beep, open the top lid. 6. Arrange the fillets over the Grill Grate. Close the top lid and cook for 4 minutes. Now open the top lid, flip the fillets. 7. Close the top lid and cook for 4 more minutes. Cook until the food thermometer reaches 130°F/55°C. 8. In a mixing bowl, add the pineapple, onion, and jalapeño. Combine well. Add the lime juice, cilantro, chili powder, and coriander. Combine again.
Serving Suggestion: Serve the fillets warm with the pineapple mixture on top.
Variation Tip: Add chilies for spicy taste.
Nutritional Information per Serving: Calories: 536| Fat: 22.5g|Carbohydrates: 21g| Fiber: 4g|Sodium: 286mg|Protein: 58g

Lamb Burger Patties

Prep time: 10 minutes | Cook Time: 20 minutes | Serves: 4

Ingredients:

1½ pound ground lamb
1 tablespoon ginger garlic paste
¼ teaspoon paprika
½ teaspoon chili powder

¼ cup green onions, sliced
Pepper
Salt

Directions:

1. Place the cooking pot in the Ninja Foodi Smart XL Grill then set a baking dish inside. 2. Add all ingredients into the bowl and mix until well combined. 3. Make patties from the meat mixture and place into the baking dish. 4. Select the "Bake" Mode, set the temperature to 375°F/190°C. 5. Press the START/STOP button to initiate preheating. 6. Once preheated, place the patties in the Ninja Foodi Smart XL Grill. 7. Cover the hood and allow the grill to cook for 20 minutes. 8. Serve, when done.
Serving Suggestion: Allow to cool completely then serve.
Variation Tip: You can also add your choice of seasoning.
Nutritional Information per Serving: Calories 320 | Fat 12.6g |Sodium 172mg | Carbs 0.7g | Fiber 0.3g | Sugar 0.2g | Protein 47.9g

Greek Lamb Meatballs

Prep time: 10 minutes | Cook Time: 15 minutes | Serves: 4

Ingredients:

1 egg
1 pound ground lamb
1 teaspoon Italian seasoning
¼ teaspoon coriander
½ teaspoon ground cumin
2 teaspoons dried oregano
1 tablespoon mint, chopped

¼ cup parsley, chopped
½ cup breadcrumbs
2½ teaspoons garlic, minced
¼ cup onion, grated
Pepper
Salt

Directions:

1. Place the cooking pot in the Ninja Foodi Smart XL Grill then set a baking dish inside. 2. Add all ingredients into the bowl and mix until well combined. 3. Make small balls from the meat mixture. 4. Select the "Bake" Mode, set the temperature to 400°F/200°C. 5. Press the START/STOP button to initiate preheating. 6. Once preheated, place the meatballs in the Ninja Foodi Smart XL Grill. 7. Cover the hood and allow the grill to cook for 15 minutes. 8. Serve, when done.
Serving Suggestion: Garnish with chopped coriander and serve.
Variation Tip: Add ¼ teaspoon of crushed red pepper flakes.
Nutritional Information per Serving: Calories 294 | Fat 10.7g |Sodium 243mg | Carbs 12.2g | Fiber 1.4g | Sugar 1.4g | Protein 35.5g

Ninja Foodi Asparagus Steak Tips

Prep time: 10 minutes | Cook Time: 15 minutes | Serves: 4

Ingredients:

2 pounds steak cubes
¼ teaspoon cayenne pepper
1 teaspoon dried onion powder
2 pounds asparagus, tough ends trimmed

3 teaspoons olive oil
1 teaspoon dried garlic powder
Salt and black pepper, to taste

Directions:

1. Press "Grill" button in a Ninja Foodi Smart XL Grill and set the time to 15 minutes. Set the temperature to MED heat. 2. Meanwhile, combine steak cubes with cayenne pepper, garlic powder, salt, black pepper and onion powder in a Ziploc bag. Shake properly. 3. Now, add asparagus, salt and olive oil in a bowl. Mix well. 4. Press START/STOP to begin preheating. 5. When the Ninja Foodi Smart XL Grill shows "Add Food", place steak cubes in it and cook for 10 minutes. 6. Add in seasoned asparagus after 10 minutes and cook for 5 minutes. 7. Take out and serve hot.
Serving Suggestions: You can serve with vinegar on the top.
Variation Tip: You can also add chili sauce for spicy taste.
Nutritional Information per Serving: Calories: 404 |Fat: 17.3g|Sat Fat: 6g|Carbohydrates: 9.9g|Fiber: 4.9g|Sugar: 4.7g|Protein: 53.8g

Avocado Salsa Steak

Prep time: 5-10 minutes | Cook Time: 18 minutes|Servings: 4

Ingredients

1 cup cilantro leaves

2 ripe avocados, diced

2 cups salsa Verde

2 beef flank steak, diced

½ tsp. salt

½ tsp. pepper

2 medium tomatoes, seeded and diced

Directions:

1. Rub the beef steak with salt and black pepper to season well. 2. Take Ninja Foodi Smart XL Grill, orchestrate it over your kitchen stage, and open the top cover. 3. Place the Grill Grate and close the lid. Select "GRILL" and select the "MED" temperature setting. Alter the clock to 18 minutes and afterward select "START/STOP." Ninja Foodi Smart XL Grill will begin preheating. 4. Ninja Foodi Smart XL Grill is preheated and prepared to cook when it begins to signal. After you hear a blare, open the top. Arrange the diced steak over the grill grate. 5. Close the top lid and cook for 9 minutes. Now open the top lid, flip the diced steak. 6. Close the top lid and cook for 9 more minutes. 7. In a blender, blend the salsa and cilantro.

Serving Suggestion: Serve the grilled steak with the blended salsa, tomato, and avocado.

Variation Tip: for spicier steak use cayenne pepper.

Nutritional Information per Serving: Calories: 523| Fat: 31.5g|Carbohydrates: 38.5g| Fiber: 2g| Sodium: 301mg| Protein: 41.5g

Lettuce Cheese Steak

Prep time: 5-10 minutes | Cook Time: 16 minutes|Servings: 5-6

Ingredients

4 (8-ounce) skirt steaks

6 cups romaine lettuce, chopped

¾ cup cherry tomatoes halved

¼ cup blue cheese, crumbled

Ocean salt and Ground Black Pepper

2 avocados, peeled and sliced

1 cup croutons

1 cup blue cheese dressing

Directions:

1. Coat steaks with black pepper and salt. 2. Take Ninja Foodi Smart XL Grill, place it over your kitchen stage, and open the top. Organize the Grill Grate and close the top. 3. Click "GRILL" function and choose the "HI" function. Change the clock to 8 minutes and afterward select "START/STOP." Ninja Foodi Smart XL Grill will begin pre-warming. 4. Ninja Foodi Smart XL Grill is preheated and prepared to cook when it begins to blare. After you hear a blare, open the top cover. 5. Fix finely the 2 steaks on the Grill Grate. 6. Close the top cover and cook for 4 minutes. Presently open the top cover, flip the steaks. 7. Close the top cover and cook for 4 additional minutes. Cook until the food thermometer comes to 150°F/65°C. Cook for 3-4 more minutes if needed. Grill the remaining steaks. 8. In a mixing bowl, add the lettuce, tomatoes, blue cheese, and croutons. Combine the Ingredients to mix well with each other.

Serving Suggestion: Serve the steaks warm with the salad mixture, blue cheese dressing, and avocado slices on top.

Variation Tip: use your favorite steak

Nutritional Information per Serving: Calories: 576|, Fat: 21g| Carbohydrates: 23g| Fiber: 6.5g|Sodium: 957mg|Protein: 53.5g

Grilled Steak Salad with Tomatoes & Eggplant

Prep time: 40 minutes | Cook Time: 40 minutes|Servings: 4

Ingredients

1 tablespoon dried oregano

1pound flank steak, trimmed

1 small eggplant cut lengthwise into ½-inch-thick slices

4 tbsps. extra-virgin olive oil, divided

1 tsp salt, divided

¾ tsp freshly ground pepper, divided

2 sweet Italian peppers, cut into 2-inch-wide strips

2 large tomatoes, cut into wedges

1 small red onion, thinly sliced

1 small clove garlic, minced

3 tbsps. red-wine vinegar

Directions:

1. Cook the oregano in a small skillet on medium heat and keep stirring until it is toasted, which will be about two minutes. Transfer it to a bowl. 2. Cut the steak in half, lengthwise; season it with half tsp each salt and pepper. Brush the peppers and eggplant with one tablespoon oil. 3. Insert Grill Grate in the unit and close the hood. Select the "GRILL", set the temperature to "LO", and set time to 30 minutes. 4. Select the option START/STOP to begin preheating. Grill the steak for 30 minutes, flipping halfway for even cooking. 5. Add the tomatoes, garlic, and onion to a bowl with the oregano. Drizzle them with vinegar and the remaining 3 tsp oil. Season them with the remaining half tsp salt and quarter tsp pepper; toss to combine. Chop the eggplant and peppers and cut the steak across the grain into thin slices; add to the bowl and toss to combine.

Serving Suggestion: Serve warm.

Variation Tip: add your favorite veggies for the salad.

Nutritional Information per Serving: Calories 177.6 | Carbohydrates 25.5g | Protein 5 g | Fat 8.9g | Sodium 286.5mg| Fiber 2.5g

Ninja Foodi Lamb Leg Roast

Prep time: 5 minutes | Cook Time: 1 hour 15 minutes | Serves: 2

Ingredients:

2 pounds lamb leg
2 tablespoons olive oil
1 tablespoon fresh rosemary

½ tablespoon black pepper
1½ tablespoons fresh thyme
Salt, to taste

Directions:

1. Press "Roast" button in Ninja Foodi Smart XL Grill and set the temperature to 300°F/150°C. 2. Arrange the "Crisper Basket" in it and adjust the time to 15 minutes. 3. Press START/STOP to begin preheating. 4. Meanwhile, add rosemary, olive oil, black pepper and thyme in a small bowl. Mix well. 5. Rub lamb leg with thyme mixture and set aside. 6. Now, place lamb leg in "Crisper Basket" and cook for 75 minutes. 7. Take out and cover with the foil. 8. Serve and enjoy!
Serving Suggestions: Serve with lime wedges on the top.
Variation Tip: Olive oil can be replaced with vegetable oil.
Nutritional Information per Serving: Calories: 739 |Fat: 36.7g|Sat Fat: 10.1g|Carbohydrates: 6.9g|Fiber: 3.9g|Sugar: 0.1g|Protein: 93.1g

Ninja Foodi Herbed Lamb Leg

Prep time: 10 minutes | Cook Time: 1 hour | Serves: 3

Ingredients:

2 pounds lamb leg
1 fresh thyme sprig
1 tablespoon olive oil

1 fresh rosemary sprig
Salt and black pepper, to taste

Directions:

1. Add thyme, rosemary, salt, black pepper and olive oil in a bowl. Mix well. 2. Coat lamb leg with thyme mixture and set aside. 3. Now, arrange "Crisper Basket" in a Ninja Foodi Smart XL Grill and press the "Air Crisp" button. Set the temperature to 300°F/150°C and adjust time to 60 minutes. 4. Press START/STOP to begin preheating. 5. When it shows "Add Food", place lamb leg in it and cook for 60 minutes at 300°F/150°C. 6. Take out and serve hot.
Serving Suggestions: Serve with rice.
Variation Tip: Black pepper can be replaced with cayenne pepper.
Nutritional Information per Serving: Calories: 587 |Fat: 24.9g|Sat Fat: 7.9g|Carbohydrates: 0.5g|Fiber: 0.3g|Sugar: 0g|Protein: 85.2g

Ninja Foodi Garlic Lamb Chops

Prep time: 10 minutes | Cook Time: 15 minutes | Serves: 2

Ingredients:

2 garlic cloves
½ teaspoon olive oil
½ tablespoon lemon juice

4 lamb chops
½ tablespoon garlic powder
Salt and black pepper, to taste

Directions:

1. Add everything in a large bowl, mix well and set aside. 2. Now, arrange "Crisper Basket" in a Ninja Foodi Smart XL Grill and press the "Air Crisp" button. 3. Set the temperature to 400°F/200°C and adjust the time to 15 minutes. 4. Press START/STOP to begin preheating. 5. When it shows "Add Food", place lamb chops in it and cook for 15 minutes at 400°F/200°C. 6. Flip halfway through and dish out. 7. Serve and enjoy!
Serving Suggestions: Serve with mint leaves on the top.
Variation Tip: You can add more garlic cloves for strong garlicky taste.
Nutritional Information per Serving: Calories: 1079 |Fat: 59.2g|Sat Fat: 33.5g|Carbohydrates: 22.3g|Fiber: 3.1g|Sugar: 2.4g|Protein: 109.5g

Ninja Foodi Buttered Beef Steak

Prep time: 5 minutes | Cook Time: 8 minutes | Serves: 2

Ingredients:

1 tablespoon melted butter
1 pound beef steak

Salt and black pepper, to taste

Directions:

1. Season beef steak with salt, pepper and melted butter. Set aside. 2. Meanwhile, arrange "Grill Grate" in a Ninja Foodi Smart XL Grill and select "Grill" button. 3. Set the time to 8 minutes and temperature to HI heat. 4. Press START/STOP to begin preheating. 5. When it shows "Add Food", place beef steak in it and cook for about 8 minutes. 6. Flip halfway through and take out. 7. Serve and enjoy!
Serving Suggestions: Top with chopped mint leaves serving.
Variation Tip: You can add more butter if you want.
Nutritional Information per Serving: Calories: 472 |Fat: 19.9g|Sat Fat: 9g|Carbohydrates: 0g|Fiber: 0g|Sugar: 0g|Protein: 68.9g

Chapter 4 Pork Recipes

Grilled Pork Chops with Plums

Prep time: 15 minutes | Cook Time: 12 minutes | Serves: 4

Ingredients:

4 tbsp. olive oil
1 tsp. honey
4 bone-in pork rib chops (1" thick), patted dry
Kosher salt and ground pepper, to taste
4 ripe medium plums, halved

1 lemon, halved, seeds removed
8 oz. Halloumi cheese, sliced
2 tbsp. torn oregano leaves
Aleppo-style pepper flakes, for serving

Directions:

1. Season the pork chops with black peppers, salt, 2 tbsp. oil and honey. 2. Toss plums with lemon, halloumi, salt, black pepper and 2 tbsp. oil in a bowl. 3. Place the cooking pot in the Ninja Foodi Smart XL Grill then set a grill grate inside. 4. Select the "Grill" Mode, set the temperature to MED. 5. Press the START/STOP button to initiate preheating. 6. Once preheated, place the pork in the Ninja Foodi Smart XL Grill. 7. Cover the hood and allow the grill to cook for 8 minutes, flipping halfway through. 8. Grill the lemon, plums and halloumi for 2 minutes per side. 9. Slice the pork chops and serve with grilled halloumi, plums and lemon. 10. Garnish with oregano, and peppers. 11. Enjoy.
Serving Suggestion: Serve the pork chops with steaming rice.
Variation Tip: Add 1 tbsp. lemon juice to the seasoning.
Nutritional Information per Serving: Calories 361 | Fat 16g |Sodium 189mg | Carbs 13g | Fiber 0.3g | Sugar 18.2g | Protein 33.3g

Pork Tenderloin with Peach-Mustard Sauce

Prep time: 11 minutes | Cook Time: 12 minutes | Serves: 4

Ingredients:

Peach-Mustard Sauce:
2 large ripe peaches, peeled, diced
¼ cup ketchup
3 tbsp. Dijon mustard
Pork:
2 pork tenderloins
4 tsp. kosher salt
1 tsp. black pepper

1 tsp. light brown sugar
½ tsp. black pepper
½ tsp. kosher salt

Vegetable oil, for grill
½ cup peach preserves

Directions:

1. Blend peaches with ½ tsp. salt, black pepper, brown sugar, mustard and ketchup in a blender. 2. Rub the pork with black pepper and salt then leave for 1 hour. 3. Place the cooking pot in the Ninja Foodi Smart XL Grill then set a grill grate inside. 4. Plug the thermometer into the appliance. 5. Select the "Grill" Mode, set the temperature to MED then select the PRESET. 6. Use the right arrow keys on the display to select "PORK" and set the doneness to MED WELL. 7. Press the START/STOP button to initiate preheating. 8. Once preheated, place the pork in the Ninja Foodi Smart XL Grill. 9. Insert the thermometer probe into the thickest part of the pork. 10. Cover the hood and allow the grill to cook. 11. Slice the pork and serve with peach sauce.
Serving Suggestion: Serve the pork with a fresh spinach salad.
Variation Tip: Add a drizzle of cheese on top of the pork.
Nutritional Information per Serving: Calories 445 | Fat 7.9g |Sodium 581mg | Carbs 14g | Fiber 2.6g | Sugar 0.1g | Protein 42.5g

Beer Bratwurst

Prep time: 15 minutes | Cook Time: 8 minutes | Serves: 4

Ingredients:

2 lbs. boneless pork shoulder, cut into cubes
⅔ lb. boneless veal shoulder, cut into cubes
½ cup pale ale
1 tbsp. fine sea salt
1 tsp. sugar
1 tsp. caraway seeds

½ tsp. dry mustard powder
1 tsp. fresh thyme leaves
½ tsp. ground ginger
¼ tsp. freshly grated nutmeg
Hog casings, rinsed

Directions:

1. Mix nutmeg, ginger, thyme, mustard powder, caraway seeds, sugar and salt in a small bowl. 2. Grind the pork meat in a food processor then add semi frozen ale. 3. Stir in spice mixture, mix well and take 2 tbsp. of the beef mixture to make a sausage. 4. Make more sausages and keep them aside. 5. Place the cooking pot in the Ninja Foodi Smart XL Grill then set a grill grate inside. 6. Select the "Grill" Mode, set the temperature to MED. 7. Press the START/STOP button to initiate preheating. 8. Once preheated, place the pork in the Ninja Foodi Smart XL Grill. 9. Cover the hood and allow the grill to cook for 8 minutes, flipping halfway through. 10. Serve warm.
Serving Suggestion: Serve the bratwurst with roasted veggies.
Variation Tip: Use toasted buns for serving.
Nutritional Information per Serving: Calories 384 | Fat 25g |Sodium 460mg | Carbs 16g | Fiber 0.4g | Sugar 2g | Protein 26g

Grilled Pork Chops with Pineapple Glaze

Prep time: 10 minutes | Cook Time: 14 minutes | Serves: 4

Ingredients:

½ cup pineapple juice
¼ cup honey
¼ cup unseasoned rice vinegar
3 tbsp. Dijon mustard
1 tsp. crushed red pepper flakes

½ tsp. toasted sesame oil
½ tsp. ground turmeric
4 (1"-thick) bone-in pork chops
Kosher salt, to taste

Directions:

1. Mix pineapple juice, honey, rice vinegar, mustard, red pepper flakes, sesame oil and turmeric in a bowl. 2. Mix the pork chops with the marinade in a shallow tray, cover and refrigerate for 30 minutes. 3. Place the cooking pot in the Ninja Foodi Smart XL Grill then set a grill grate inside. 4. Plug the thermometer into the appliance. 5. Select the "Grill" Mode, set the temperature to MED then select the PRESET. 6. Use the right arrow keys on the display to select "PORK" and set the doneness to MED WELL. 7. Press the START/STOP button to initiate preheating. 8. Once preheated, place the pork in the Ninja Foodi Smart XL Grill. 9. Insert the thermometer probe into the thickest part of the pork. 10. Cover the hood and allow the grill to cook. 11. Serve warm.
Serving Suggestion: Serve the pork chops with steamed rice.
Variation Tip: Add butter sauce on top of the pork.
Nutritional Information per Serving: Calories 419 | Fat 13g |Sodium 432mg | Carbs 19g | Fiber 3g | Sugar 1g | Protein 33g

Pork Cutlets with Cantaloupe Salad

Prep time: 15 minutes | Cook Time: 8 minutes | Serves: 4

Ingredients:

4 (½-inch–thick) pork cutlets
Kosher salt, to taste
1 cup grated cantaloupe
4 tbsp. fresh lime juice
2 tbsp. olive oil

4 scallions, sliced
1 red chili, sliced
¼ cup cilantro, chopped
2 tbsp. fish sauce
Crushed salted, roasted peanuts

Directions:

1. Prick the pork with a fork and season with 2 tbsp. lime juice, and cantaloupe in a bowl. 2. Cover and refrigerate for 1 hour. 3. Place the cooking pot in the Ninja Foodi Smart XL Grill then set a grill grate inside. 4. Plug the thermometer into the appliance. 5. Select the "Grill" Mode, set the temperature to MED then select the PRESET. 6. Use the right arrow keys on the display to select "PORK" and set the doneness to MED WELL. 7. Press the START/STOP button to initiate preheating. 8. Once preheated, place the pork in the Ninja Foodi Smart XL Grill. 9. Insert the thermometer probe into the thickest part of the pork. 10. Cover the hood and allow the grill to cook. 11. Mix scallions and other ingredients in a bowl. 12. Serve the pork with the scallions mixture.
Serving Suggestion: Serve the pork with fresh herbs on top and a bowl of rice.
Variation Tip: You can serve the pork with cabbage slaw as well.
Nutritional Information per Serving: Calories 388 | Fat 8g |Sodium 611mg | Carbs 18g | Fiber 0g | Sugar 4g | Protein 13g

Curried Pork Skewers

Prep time: 10 minutes | Cook Time: 23 minutes | Serves: 4

Ingredients:

1 (13½ -oz.) can unsweetened coconut milk
2 tbsp. fish sauce
2 tbsp. Thai thin soy sauce
1 tbsp. sugar
1 tsp. kosher salt
¾ tsp. white pepper

½ tsp. curry powder
½ tsp. ground turmeric
¾ cup sweetened condensed milk
1 (½ lb.) boneless pork shoulder, cut into 4x ½ " strips
4 oz. fatback, cut into ½ " pieces

Directions:

1. Mix coconut milk, turmeric, curry powder, black pepper, salt, sugar, soy sauce and fish sauce in a pan. 2. Cook to a boil then reduce its heat and cook for 15 minutes on a simmer. 3. Allow this mixture to cool, then add black pepper, salt and pork. 4. Mix well, cover and refrigerate for 1 hour. 5. Place the cooking pot in the Ninja Foodi Smart XL Grill then set a grill grate inside. 6. Select the "Grill" Mode, set the temperature to MED. 7. Press the START/STOP button to initiate preheating. 8. Once preheated, place the pork in the Ninja Foodi Smart XL Grill. 9. Cover the hood and allow the grill to cook for 8 minutes, flipping halfway through. 10. Serve warm.
Serving Suggestion: Serve the skewers with roasted green beans and mashed cauliflower.
Variation Tip: Add chopped sautéed kale on top before serving.
Nutritional Information per Serving: Calories 429 | Fat 17g |Sodium 422mg | Carbs 15g | Fiber 0g | Sugar 1g | Protein 41g

Mojo-Marinated Pork Kebabs

Prep time: 15 minutes | Cook Time: 10 minutes | Serves: 4

Ingredients:

Mojo Marinade
2 tbsp. garlic, minced
½ tsp. kosher salt
½ cup fresh sour orange juice
¼ cup olive oil
Brined Pork:
2 quarts' ice-cold water
⅓ cup kosher salt
Skewers:
2 whole mangos, peeled, cored, and cut into 1½ -inch squares

½ tsp. dried oregano
½ tsp. cumin
Black pepper, to taste

¼ cup sugar
2 lbs. center-cut pork chops

Directions:

1. Mix salt, sugar and water in a large pan and soak the pork for 1 hour. 2. Mash garlic, with ½ tsp. salt, cumin, oregano, oil, and orange juice in a mortar. 3. Remove the pork from the brine and cut into cubes. 4. Mix the pork with the marinade in a bowl, cover and refrigerate for 1 hour. 5. Thread the pork and mango cubes on the wooden skewers. 6. Place the cooking pot in the Ninja Foodi Smart XL Grill then set a grill grate inside. 7. Select the "Grill" Mode, set the temperature to MED. 8. Press the START/STOP button to initiate preheating. 9. Once preheated, place the pork in the Ninja Foodi Smart XL Grill. 10. Cover the hood and allow the grill to cook for 10 minutes, flipping halfway through. 11. Serve warm.
Serving Suggestion: Serve the kebabs with cauliflower cheese casserole.
Variation Tip: Add cheese on top of the pork and then bake after grilling.
Nutritional Information per Serving: Calories 425 | Fat 15g |Sodium 345mg | Carbs 23g | Fiber 1.4g | Sugar 3g | Protein 33.3g

Grilled Pork Belly Kebabs

Prep time: 10 minutes | Cook Time: 10 minutes | Serves: 4

Ingredients:

2 tbsp. gochujang
2 tbsp. honey
2 tsp. sake
2 tsp. soy sauce
1 tsp. vegetable oil

1¼ lb. boneless pork belly, cut into cubes
1 small zucchini, cut 1-inch-thick half-moons
½ pint cherry tomatoes
1 red bell pepper, seeded, and cut into 1-inch pieces

Directions:

1. Mix oil, soy sauce, sake, honey and gochujang in a bowl and keep 2 tbsp. of this marinade aside. 2. Add pork to the bowl, mix well, cover and refrigerate for 1 hour. 3. Thread the pork, bell pepper, tomatoes and zucchini on the wooden skewers alternately. 4. Place the cooking pot in the Ninja Foodi Smart XL Grill then set a grill grate inside. 5. Select the "Grill" Mode, set the temperature to MED. 6. Press the START/STOP button to initiate preheating. 7. Once preheated, place the pork in the Ninja Foodi Smart XL Grill. 8. Cover the hood and allow the grill to cook for 10 minutes, flipping halfway through. 9. Pour the reserved marinade on top of the skewers and serve warm.
Serving Suggestion: Serve the kebabs with boiled cauliflower rice or grilled zucchini.
Variation Tip: Add crushed or sliced almonds to the serving.
Nutritional Information per Serving: Calories 361 | Fat 16g |Sodium 515mg | Carbs 13g | Fiber 0.1g | Sugar 18.2g | Protein 33.3g

Bratwurst Potatoes

Prep time: 15 minutes | Cook Time: 50 minutes | Serves: 6

Ingredients:

3 pounds Bratwurst links, uncooked
3 pounds small red potatoes, wedged
1 pound baby carrots
1 large red onion, sliced and rings
2 jars (4-½ ounces) whole mushrooms, drained

¼ cup butter, cubed
1 pack onion soup mix
2 tablespoons soy sauce
½ teaspoon black pepper

Directions:

1. Place two foil packets on the working surface. 2. Divide the potatoes, carrots, onion, brats and mushrooms with the foil. 3. Top them with butter, soup mix, pepper and soy sauce. 4. Seal the foil packets by pinching their ends together. 5. Place one foil packet in the Ninja Foodi Smart XL Grill. 6. Cover the Ninja Foodi Smart XL Grill's Hood, and select the Grill Mode. 7. Select MED cooking temperature and cooking time to 20 minutes. 8. Close the hood and grill for 10 minutes per side. 9. Cook the other half of the brat's mixture in a similar way. 10. Open the packets carefully and be careful of the steam. 11. Serve.
Serving Suggestion: Serve the Bratwurst Potatoes with boiled peas, carrots and potatoes on the side.
Variation Tip: Add butter to the potatoes for more taste.
Nutritional Information per Serving: Calories 345 | Fat 36g | Sodium 272mg | Carbs 41g | Fiber 0.2g | Sugar 0.1g | Protein 22.5g

Chili-Spiced Ribs

Prep time: 15 minutes | Cook Time: 50 minutes | Serves: 6

Ingredients:

Glaze:

1 cup of soy sauce
1 cup packed brown sugar
⅔ cup ketchup

⅓ cup lemon juice
1½ teaspoon fresh ginger root, minced

Ribs:

6 pounds pork baby back ribs
3 tablespoons packed brown sugar
2 tablespoons paprika
2 tablespoons chili powder

3 teaspoons ground cumin
2 teaspoons garlic powder
1 teaspoon salt

Directions:

1. Take the first six ingredients in a suitable bowl and mix well. 2. Place the cooking pot in the Ninja Foodi Smart XL Grill then place the grill grate in the pot. 3. Plug the thermometer into the appliance. 4. Select the "Grill" Mode, set the temperature to MAX then select the PRESET. 5. Use the right arrow keys on the display to select "BEEF" and set the doneness to MED WELL. 6. Press the START/STOP button to initiate preheating. 7. Place the ribs in the Ninja Foodi Smart XL Grill. 8. Insert the thermometer probe into the thickest part of the ribs. 9. Cover the hood and allow the grill to cook. 10. Meanwhile, prepare the sauce by cooking its ingredients for eight minutes in a saucepan. 11. Pour this sauce over the grilled ribs in the Ninja Foodi Smart XL Grill. 12. Grill for another 5 minutes per side. 13. Serve.

Serving Suggestion: Serve the ribs with mashed potatoes.
Variation Tip: Use BBQ sauce for the change of taste.
Nutritional Information per Serving: Calories 305 | Fat 25g | Sodium 532mg | Carbs 2.3g | Fiber 0.4g | Sugar 2g | Protein 18.3g

Crispy Pork Chops

Prep time: 10 minutes | Cook Time: 30 minutes | Serves: 3

Ingredients:

1 egg, lightly beaten
3 pork chops, boneless
½ cup crackers, crushed
4 tablespoons of Parmesan cheese, grated

2 tablespoons milk
Pepper
Salt

Directions:

1. Place the cooking pot in the Ninja Foodi Smart XL Grill. 2. In a small bowl, whisk egg with milk. 3. In a shallow dish, mix cheese, crackers, pepper and salt. 4. Dip pork chops in egg then coat with cheese mixture and place into the baking dish. 5. Plug the thermometer into the appliance. 6. Select the "Bake" Mode, set the temperature to 350°F/175°C then select the PRESET. 7. Use the right arrow keys on the display to select "PORK" and use the left arrows to set the doneness to MED WELL. 8. Press the START/STOP button to initiate preheating. 9. Once preheated, place the pork in the Ninja Foodi Smart XL Grill. 10. Insert the thermometer probe into the thickest part of the pork. 11. Cover the hood and allow the grill to cook. 12. Serve, when done.

Serving Suggestion: Garnish with fresh coriander and serve.
Variation Tip: None
Nutritional Information per Serving: Calories 334 | Fat 24.2g |Sodium 219mg | Carbs 6.9g | Fiber 0.2g | Sugar 0.8g | Protein 20.9g

Chipotle-Raspberry Pork Chops

Prep time: 10 minutes | Cook Time: 10 minutes|Servings: 4

Ingredients

½ cup seedless raspberry
4 bone-in pork loin chops (7 ounces each)

1 chipotle pepper in adobo sauce, finely chopped
½ tsp salt

Directions:

1. Preheat the grill for 5 minutes. 2. In a saucepan, cook and stir and chipotle pepper over medium heat until heated through. Reserve ¼ cup for serving. Sprinkle pork with salt; brush with remaining raspberry sauce. 3. Lightly grease a grill or broiler pan rack. Select the GRILL mode, set the temperature to MAX and time to 10 minutes, Select the option START/STOP to begin cooking, flipping occasionally for even cooking. 4. Serve.

Serving Suggestion: Serve with raspberry sauce.
Variation Tip: for spice add pepper to your taste.
Nutritional Information per Serving: Calories 412 | Carbohydrates 64.3g | Protein 16.1g | Fat 10.1g | Sodium 895mg| Fiber 2g

Ham Pineapple Skewers

Prep time: 15 minutes | Cook Time: 7 minutes | Serves: 4

Ingredients:

1 can (20 ounces) pineapple chunks
½ cup orange marmalade
1 tablespoon mustard
¼ teaspoon ground cloves

1 pound ham, diced
½ pound Swiss cheese, diced
1 medium green pepper, cubed

Directions:

1. Take two tablespoons of pineapple from pineapples in a bowl. 2. Add mustard, marmalade, cloves and mix well and keep it aside. 3. Thread the pineapple, green pepper, cheese and ham over the skewers alternatively. 4. Place the cooking pot in the Ninja Foodi Smart XL Grill then place the grill grate in the pot. 5. Select the "Grill" Mode, set the temperature to MED. 6. Press the START/STOP button to initiate preheating. 7. Place the skewer in the Ninja Foodi Smart XL Grill. 8. Cover the hood and allow the grill to cook for 10 minutes. 9. Continue rotating the skewers every 2 minutes. 10. Pour the sauce on top and serve.

Serving Suggestion: Serve the skewers with cream cheese dip.
Variation Tip: Serve the pineapple skewers on top of the fruit salad.
Nutritional Information per Serving: Calories 276 | Fat 21g | Sodium 476mg | Carbs 12g | Fiber 3g | Sugar 4g | Protein 10g

Raspberry Pork Chops

Prep time: 15 minutes | Cook Time: 10 minutes | Serves: 4

Ingredients:

½ cup seedless raspberry preserves
1 chipotle in Adobo sauce, chopped

½ teaspoon salt
4 bone-in pork loin chops

Directions:

1. Take a small pan and mix preserves with chipotle pepper sauce on medium heat. 2. Keep ¼ cup of this sauce aside and rub the remaining over the pork. 3. Sprinkle salt over the pork and mix well. 4. Place the cooking pot in the Ninja Foodi Smart XL Grill then place the grill grate in the pot. 5. Plug the thermometer into the appliance. 6. Select the "Grill" Mode, set the temperature to MAX then select the PRESET. 7. Use the right arrow keys on the display to select "PORK" and set the doneness to MED WELL. 8. Press the START/STOP button to initiate preheating. 9. Place the pork in the Ninja Foodi Smart XL grill. 10. Insert the thermometer probe into the thickest part of the pork. 11. Cover the hood and allow the grill to cook for 5 to 7 minutes per side. 12. Grill the remaining chops in the same method. 13. Serve with the reserved sauce. 14. Enjoy.

Serving Suggestion: Serve the pork chops with boiled rice or spaghetti.
Variation Tip: Use apple sauce or maple syrup for seasoning.
Nutritional Information per Serving: Calories 361 | Fat 16g |Sodium 515mg | Carbs 19.3g | Fiber 0.1g | Sugar 18.2g | Protein 33.3g

Pork with Salsa

Prep time: 15 minutes | Cook Time: 12 minutes | Serves: 4

Ingredients:

¼ cup lime juice
2 tablespoons olive oil
2 garlic cloves, minced
1½ teaspoon ground cumin
Salsa
1 jalapeno pepper, seeded and chopped
⅓ cup red onion, chopped
2 tablespoons fresh mint, chopped
2 tablespoons lime juice

1½ teaspoons dried oregano
½ teaspoon black pepper
2 pounds pork tenderloin, ¾ inch slices

4 cups pears, peeled and chopped
1 tablespoon lime zest, grated
1 teaspoon sugar
½ teaspoon black pepper

Directions:

1. Season the pork with lime juice, cumin, oregano, oil, garlic and pepper in a suitable bowl. 2. Cover to refrigerate for overnight margination. 3. Place the cooking pot in the Ninja Foodi Smart XL Grill then place the grill grate in the pot. 4. Select the "Grill" Mode, set the temperature to MAX. 5. Press the START/STOP button to initiate preheating. 6. Place the pork in the Ninja Foodi Smart XL Grill. 7. Cover the hood and allow the grill to cook for 6 minutes per side until al dente. 8. Mix the pear salsa ingredients into a separate bowl. 9. Serve the sliced pork with pear salsa.

Serving Suggestion: Serve the pork with mashed potatoes.
Variation Tip: Dust the pork chops with flour before grilling for more texture.
Nutritional Information per Serving: Calories 91 | Fat 5g | Sodium 88mg | Carbs 3g | Fiber 0g | Sugar 0g | Protein 7g

Parmesan Pork Chops

Prep time: 10 minutes | Cook Time: 10 minutes | Serves: 2

Ingredients:

2 pork chops, boneless
3 tablespoons of Parmesan cheese, grated
1 tablespoon olive oil
⅓ cup almond flour
1 teaspoon Cajun seasoning

1 teaspoon dried mix herbs
1 teaspoon paprika
Pepper
Salt

Directions:

1. Place the cooking pot in the Ninja Foodi Smart XL Grill then place the Crisper Basket in the pot. 2. In a bowl, mix Parmesan cheese, paprika, mixed herbs, almond flour and Cajun seasoning. 3. Brush pork chops with oil and coat with cheese mixture. 4. Plug the thermometer into the appliance. 5. Select the "Air Crisp" Mode, set the temperature to 350°F/175°C then select the PRESET. 6. Use the right arrow keys on the display to select "PORK" and set the doneness to MED WELL. 7. Press the START/STOP button to initiate preheating. 8. Once preheated, place the pork in the Ninja Foodi Smart XL Grill. 9. Insert the thermometer probe into the thickest part of the pork. 10. Cover the hood and allow the grill to cook. 11. Serve, when done.
Serving Suggestion: Allow to cool completely then serve.
Variation Tip: You can also add Italian seasoning instead of dried herbs.
Nutritional Information per Serving: Calories 319 | Fat 27g |Sodium 159mg | Carbs 0.6g | Fiber 0.4g | Sugar 0.1g | Protein 18.2g

Grilled Pork Tenderloin Marinated in Spicy Soy Sauce

Prep time: 20 minutes | Cook Time: 140 minutes|Servings: 6

Ingredients

¼ cup reduced-sodium soy sauce
1 tablespoon finely grated fresh ginger
2 tbsps. sugar
1 large garlic clove, minced

1 fresh red Thai chili, minced
1 tablespoon toasted sesame oil
1½ pounds pork tenderloin, trimmed of fat and cut into 1-inch-thick medallions

Directions:

1. Select the "GRILL" function and adjust temperature to "MED" and preheat the Ninja Foodi Smart XL Grill for 8 minutes. 2. Whisk the soy sauce and sugar in a medium bowl until the sugar is dissolved. Stir in ginger, garlic, chili, and oil. 3. Place the pork in a plastic bag. Add the marinade and then seal the bag, squeezing out the air. Turn the bag for coating the medallions. Refrigerate for two hours, turning bag once to redistribute the marinade. 4. Insert Grill Grate in the unit and close the hood. Remove the pork from the marinade. Select the option START/STOP to begin cooking. Cook pork until desire tenderness or until meat reaches to 160°F/70°C internal temperature.
Serving Suggestion: Serve hot with cold wine.
Variation Tip: use cayenne Chile pepper for spice.
Nutritional Information per Serving: Calories 155.5 | Carbohydrates 24.8g | Protein 3g | Fat 5.4g | Sodium 193.7mg| Fiber 1 g

Honey Garlic Pork Chops

Prep time: 10 minutes | Cook Time: 12 minutes | Serves: 4

Ingredients:

4 pork chops
2 tablespoons grainy mustard
2 tablespoons Dijon mustard
¼ cup honey
3 garlic cloves, chopped

1 tablespoon soy sauce
2 tablespoons vinegar
Pepper
Salt

Directions:

1. Place the cooking pot in the Ninja Foodi Smart XL Grill then place the grill grate in the pot. 2. Add pork chops and remaining ingredients into the zip-lock bag. Seal bag and place in the refrigerator for 30 minutes. 3. Plug the thermometer into the appliance. 4. Select the "Grill" Mode, set the temperature to HI then select the PRESET. 5. Use the right arrow keys on the display to select "PORK" and set the doneness to MED WELL. 6. Press the START/STOP button to initiate preheating. 7. Once preheated, place the pork in the Ninja Foodi Smart XL Grill. 8. Insert the thermometer probe into the thickest part of the pork. 9. Cover the hood and allow the grill to cook. 10. Turn pork chops halfway through. 11. Serve, when done.
Serving Suggestion: Serve warm.
Variation Tip: None
Nutritional Information per Serving: Calories 338 | Fat 20.5g |Sodium 444mg | Carbs 19.5g | Fiber 0.4g | Sugar 17.6g | Protein 18.8g

Lemon Basil Pork Chops

Prep time: 10 minutes | Cook Time: 12 minutes | Serves: 4

Ingredients:

4 pork chops
1 cup fresh basil
2 garlic cloves
2 tablespoons olive oil

2 tablespoons fresh lemon juice
Pepper
Salt

Directions:

1. Place the cooking pot in the Ninja Foodi Smart XL Grill then place the grill grate in the pot. 2. Add basil, lemon juice, oil, garlic, pepper and salt into the blender and blend until smooth. 3. Add pork chops and basil mixture into the zip-lock bag. Seal bag and place in the refrigerator for 30 minutes. 4. Plug the thermometer into the appliance. 5. Select the "Grill" Mode, set the temperature to HI then select the PRESET. 6. Use the right arrow keys on the display to select "PORK" and set the doneness to MED WELL. 7. Press the START/STOP button to initiate preheating. 8. Once preheated, place the pork in the Ninja Foodi Smart XL Grill. 9. Insert the thermometer probe into the thickest part of the pork. 10. Cover the hood and allow the grill to cook. 11. Serve, when done.
Serving Suggestion: Serve warm.
Variation Tip: You can also add your choice of seasoning.
Nutritional Information per Serving: Calories 322 | Fat 27g |Sodium 97mg | Carbs 0.8g | Fiber 0.2g | Sugar 0.2g | Protein 18.3g

Flavorful Pork Chops

Prep time: 10 minutes | Cook Time: 14 minutes | Serves: 4

Ingredients:

4 pork loin chops
For Rub:
1 teaspoon paprika
2 tablespoons brown sugar
½ teaspoon Cayenne

½ teaspoon ground mustard
Pepper
Salt

Directions:

1. Place the cooking pot in the Ninja Foodi Smart XL Grill then place the grill grate in the pot. 2. In a small bowl, mix all rub ingredients and rub all over pork chops. 3. Plug the thermometer into the appliance. 4. Select the "Grill" Mode, set the temperature to HI then select the PRESET. 5. Use the right arrow keys on the display to select "PORK" and set the doneness to MED WELL. 6. Press the START/STOP button to initiate preheating. 7. Once preheated, place the pork in the Ninja Foodi Smart XL Grill. 8. Insert the thermometer probe into the thickest part of the pork. 9. Cover the hood and allow the grill to cook. 10. Serve and enjoy.
Serving Suggestion: Garnish with parsley and serve.
Variation Tip: Add your choice of seasonings.
Nutritional Information per Serving: Calories 277 | Fat 20.1g |Sodium 96mg | Carbs 5g | Fiber 0.3g | Sugar 4.5g | Protein 18.2g

Sausage and Pepper Grinders

Prep time: 15 minutes | Cook Time: 26 minutes|Servings: 6

Ingredients

2 bell peppers, cut in quarters, seeds and ribs removed
Kosher salt, as desired
Ground black pepper, as desired
1 white onion, peeled, sliced in 1-inch rings

2 tbsps. canola oil, divided
6 raw sausages (4 ounces each)
6 hot dog buns
Condiments, as desired

Directions:

1. Select the "GRILL" function and adjust temperature to "LO" and preheat the Ninja Foodi Smart XL Grill for 8 minutes before use. 2. Insert Grill Grate in the unit and close the hood. 3. When the unit starts beeping to signal that it has preheated, place steaks on the grill grate. Close hood and cook for 12 minutes. 4. After 12 minutes, transfer the peppers and onions to a medium mixing bowl. Place the sausages on the grill grate; close the hood and cook for 6 minutes. 5. After 6 minutes, flip the sausages. Close the hood and cook for 6 extra minutes. 6. Meanwhile, gently tear up the grilled onions into individual rings and mix them well with the peppers. 7. After 6 minutes, remove the sausages from the Grill Grate. Place the buns, cut-side them down, over the Grill Grate. Close the hood and cook for 2 remaining minutes. 8. When cooking is done, spread any desired condiments on the buns, then place the sausages in buns.
Serving Suggestion: Serve topped each with onions peppers.
Variation Tip: use your preferred condiments.
Nutritional Information per Serving: Calories 155.5 | Carbohydrates 24.8g | Protein 3g | Fat 5.4g | Sodium 193.7mg| Fiber 1g

Juicy Pork Chops

Prep time: 10 minutes | Cook Time: 10 minutes | Serves: 4

Ingredients:

4 pork chops, boneless
1 teaspoon Italian seasoning
1 teaspoon olive oil

¼ teaspoon garlic powder
Pepper
Salt

Directions:

1. Place the cooking pot in the Ninja Foodi Smart XL Grill then set a Crisper Basket inside. 2. In a small bowl, mix oil, Italian seasoning, garlic powder, pepper and salt. 3. Brush pork chops with oil mixture. 4. Plug the thermometer into the appliance. 5. Select the "Air Crisp" Mode, set the temperature to 400°F/200°C then select the PRESET. 6. Use the right arrow keys on the display to select "PORK" and set the doneness to MED WELL. 7. Press the START/STOP button to initiate preheating. 8. Once preheated, place the pork in the Ninja Foodi Smart XL Grill. 9. Insert the thermometer probe into the thickest part of the pork. 10. Cover the hood and allow the grill to cook. 11. Serve, when done.
Serving Suggestion: Garnish with chopped coriander and serve.
Variation Tip: None
Nutritional Information per Serving: Calories 270 | Fat 21.4g |Sodium 95mg | Carbs 0.3g | Fiber 0g | Sugar 0.1g | Protein 18g

Turmeric Pork Chops with Green Onion Rice

Prep time: 15 minutes | Cook Time: 15 minutes|Servings: 4

Ingredients

4 (6-oz.) bone-in pork chops
½ tsp kosher salt, divided
½ tsp black pepper, divided
3 tbsp olive oil, divided
1 large garlic clove, halved
½ tsp ground turmeric
1 tablespoon fish sauce

2 tsp oyster sauce
1 tsp tomato paste
1 bunch green onions
2 (8.8-oz.) packages precooked brown rice
¼ cup fresh cilantro leaves
1 lime, cut into 4 wedges

Directions:

1. Select the "GRILL" function to "HI" temperature setting. Preheat the Ninja Foodi Smart XL Grill for 8 minutes before use. Rub pork with cut sides of garlic; discard garlic. Sprinkle pork with turmeric, ¼ tsp salt, and ¼ tsp pepper. Combine 2 tsp oil, fish sauce, oyster sauce, and tomato paste. 2. Brush both sides of pork with half of the oil mixture. Grill pork for 4 minutes on each side or until the desired of doneness or until internal temperature reaches to 160°F/70°C. Transfer to a plate; brush both sides of pork with the remaining oil mixture. Keep warm. 3. Add onions to grill. Over "MED" setting; grill for 2 minutes. Coarsely chop onions. 4. Heat rice according to package Preparation. Combine green onions, rice, remaining one tablespoon oil, ¼ tsp salt, and ¼ tsp pepper.
Serving Suggestion: Serve rice with pork. Sprinkle with cilantro; serve with lime wedges.
Variation Tip: can be eat without rice and taste will be marvelous.
Nutritional Information per Serving: Calories 412 | Carbohydrates 64.3g | Protein 16.1g | Fat 10.1g | Sodium 895mg| Fiber 2g

Bourbon Pork Chops

Prep time: 5-10 minutes | Cook Time: 20 minutes|Servings: 4

Ingredients

4 boneless pork chops
Ocean salt and ground dark pepper to taste
¼ cup apple cider vinegar
¼ cup soy sauce
3 tbsps. Worcestershire sauce

2 cups ketchup
¾ cup bourbon
1 cup packed brown sugar
½ tablespoon dry mustard powder

Directions:

1. Take Ninja Foodi Smart XL Grill, orchestrate it over your kitchen stage, and open the top cover. Orchestrate the flame broil mesh and close the top cover. 2. Select the "GRILL" function and choose the "MED" setting. Press START/STOP to begin preheating. 3. Ninja Foodi Smart XL Grill is preheated and prepared to cook when it begins to signal. After you hear a signal, open the top. 4. Arrange the pork chops over the Grill Grate. 5. Close the top lid and cook for 8 minutes. Now open the top lid, flip the pork chops. 6. Close the top lid and cook for 8 more minutes. Check the pork chops for doneness, cook for 2 more minutes if required. 7. In a saucepan, heat the soy sauce, sugar, ketchup, bourbon, vinegar, Worcestershire sauce, and mustard powder; stir-cook until boils. 8. Reduce heat and simmer for 20 minutes to thicken the sauce. 9. Coat the pork chops with salt and ground black pepper.
Serving Suggestion: Serve warm with the prepared sauce.
Variation Tip: use beef for variation.
Nutritional Information per Serving: Calories: 346| Fat: 13.5g| Carbohydrates: 27g| Fiber: 0.5g|Sodium: 1324mg|Protein: 27g

Balinese Pork Satay

Prep time: 15 minutes | Cook Time: 15 minutes | Serves: 4

Ingredients:

Spice Paste:

1 (1-inch) knob fresh turmeric, peeled

2 stalks lemongrass, sliced

8 garlic cloves, sliced

2 small shallots, sliced

3 wholes dried Pasilla chili with seeds removed, chopped

Glaze

1 cup Kecap manis

¼ cup sugar

Dipping Sauce

10 oz. roasted peanuts

¼ cup vegetable or canola oil

1 oz. tamarind pulp

2 tbsp. palm sugar

2 tsp. whole coriander seed

1 tbsp. whole white peppercorns

Kosher salt, to taste

2 lbs. boneless pork shoulder, cut into cubes

One (2-inch) knob ginger, chopped

4 medium garlic cloves, chopped

1 tbsp. Kecap manis or fish sauce

Water, as necessary

Sugar, to taste

Directions:

1. Blend all the spice paste ingredients in a mini-food processor. 2. Mix pork with the ¾ of the spice paste in a bowl. 3. Cover and refrigerate the pork for 45 minutes. Thread the pork on the wooden skewers. 4. Place the cooking pot in the Ninja Foodi Smart XL Grill then set a grill grate inside. 5. Select the "Grill" Mode, set the temperature to MED. 6. Press the START/STOP button to initiate preheating. 7. Once preheated, place the pork in the Ninja Foodi Smart XL Grill. 8. Cover the hood and allow the grill to cook for 10 minutes, flipping halfway through. 9. Meanwhile, mix the glaze ingredients and ⅓ spice paste in a saucepan and cook for 5 minutes on a simmer. Pour this glaze over the skewers. Serve warm.

Serving Suggestion: Serve the pork with cauliflower rice.

Variation Tip: Add some BBQ sauce as well for seasoning.

Nutritional Information per Serving: Calories 425 | Fat 14g |Sodium 411mg | Carbs 24g | Fiber 0.3g | Sugar 1g | Protein 28.3g

Korean Chili Pork

Prep time: 5-10 minutes | Cook Time: 8 minutes|Servings: 4

Ingredients

2 pounds pork, cut into ⅛-inch slices

5 minced garlic cloves

3 tbsps. minced green onion

1 yellow onion, sliced

½ cup soy sauce

½ cup brown sugar

3 tbsps. regular chili paste

2 tbsps. sesame seeds

3 tsp black pepper

Red pepper flakes to taste

Directions:

1. Take a zip-lock bag, add all the Ingredients. Shake well and refrigerate for 6-8 hours to marinate. 2. Take Ninja Foodi Smart XL Grill, orchestrate it over your kitchen stage, and open the top. 3. Place the Grill Grate and close the top cover. 4. Click "GRILL" function and choose the "MED" temperature setting. Modify the clock to 8 minutes and afterward select "START/STOP." Ninja Foodi Smart XL Grill will begin to preheat. 5. Ninja Foodi Smart XL Grill is preheated and prepared to cook when it begins to signal. After you hear a signal, open the top. 6. Fix finely sliced pork on the Grill Grate. 7. Cover and cook for 4 minutes. Then open the cover, switch the side of the pork. 8. Cover it and cook for another 4 minutes.

Serving Suggestion: Serve warm with chopped lettuce.

Variation Tip: for spiciness use Korean red chili paste.

Nutritional Information per Serving: Calories: 621| Fat: 31g|Carbohydrates: 29g|Fiber: 3g| Sodium: 1428mg| Protein: 53g

• Chapter 5 Seafood Recipes •

Lemon-Garlic Salmon

Prep time: 15 minutes | Cook Time: 9 minutes | Serves: 4

Ingredients:

2 garlic cloves, minced
2 teaspoons lemon zest, grated
½ teaspoon salt

½ teaspoon fresh rosemary, minced
½ teaspoon black pepper
4 (6 ounces) salmon fillets

Directions:

1. Place the cooking pot in the Ninja Foodi Smart XL Grill then place the grill grate in the pot. 2. Take the first five ingredients in a bowl and mix well. 3. Leave the mixture for 15 minutes, then rub the salmon with this mixture. 4. Place the cooking pot in the Ninja Foodi Smart XL Grill then place the grill grate in the pot. 5. Select the "Grill" Mode, set the temperature to MED. 6. Press the START/STOP button to initiate preheating. 7. Once preheated, place the fish in the Ninja Foodi Smart XL grill. 8. Cover the hood and cook for 6 minutes per side, then serve warm.

Serving Suggestion: Serve the lemon garlic salmon with butter sauce on top.
Variation Tip: Grill the veggies on the side to serve with the salmon.
Nutritional Information per Serving: Calories 392 | Fat 16g | Sodium 466mg | Carbs 3.9g | Fiber 0.9g | Sugar 0.6g | Protein 48g

Shrimp Stuffed Sole

Prep time: 15 minutes | Cook Time: 14 minutes | Serves: 4

Ingredients:

¼ cup soft bread crumbs
¼ cup butter, melted
2 tablespoons whipped cream cheese
2 teaspoons chives, minced
1 garlic clove, minced
1 teaspoon lemon zest, grated
1 can (6 ounces) crabmeat, drained
1 teaspoon parsley, minced

4 sole fillets (6 ounces), cut from a side and insides removed
½ cup shrimp, cooked, peeled and chopped
1½ cups cherry tomatoes
2 tablespoons chicken broth
2 tablespoons lemon juice
½ teaspoon salt
½ teaspoon black pepper

Directions:

1. Place the cooking pot in the Ninja Foodi Smart XL Grill then place the grill grate in the pot. 2. Thoroughly mix crab with shrimp, cream cheese, chives, lemon zest, garlic, parsley, two tablespoons butter and breadcrumbs in a small bowl. 3. Stuff ¼ of this filling into each fillet and secure the ends by inserting the toothpicks. 4. Mix tomatoes with salt, pepper, wine and lemon juice in a separate bowl. 5. Place each stuffed fillet in a foil sheet and top with tomato mixture. 6. Insert the thermometer probe into the thickest part of the meat and connect it to the appliance. 7. Cover and seal the fillets in the foil while leaving a little space for the probe on the side. 8. Place the cooking pot in the Ninja Foodi Smart XL Grill then place the grill grate in the pot. 9. Select the "Grill" Mode, set the temperature to MED then select the PRESET. 10. Use the right arrow keys on the display to select "FISH" and set the doneness to MED. 11. Press the START/STOP button to initiate preheating. 12. Once preheated, place the fish in the Ninja Foodi Smart XL Grill. 13. Place 2 sealed fillets in the Ninja Foodi Smart XL Grill and insert the thermometer into the fish. 14. Cover the hood and grill for 7 minutes per side. Cook the remaining fillets in a similar way. 15. Serve warm.

Serving Suggestion: Serve the Shrimp Stuffed Sole with fried rice.
Variation Tip: Serve the sole fish with breadcrumbs and butter sauce on top.
Nutritional Information per Serving: Calories 321 | Fat 7.4g | Sodium 356mg | Carbs 9.3g | Fiber 2.4g | Sugar 5g | Protein 37.2g

Salmon Lime Burgers

Prep time: 15 minutes | Cook Time: 20 minutes | Serves: 4

Ingredients:

1 pound salmon fillets, cubed
2 tablespoons grated lime zest
1 tablespoon Dijon mustard
3 tablespoons shallot, chopped
2 tablespoons fresh cilantro, minced
1 tablespoon soy sauce

1 tablespoon honey
3 garlic cloves, minced
½ teaspoon salt
¼ teaspoon black pepper
4 hamburger buns, split

Directions:

1. Place the cooking pot in the Ninja Foodi Smart XL Grill then place the grill grate in the pot. 2. Thoroughly mix all the ingredients for burgers in a bowl except the buns. 3. Make four of the ½ patties out of this mixture. 4. Select the "Grill" Mode, set the temperature to MED. 5. Press the START/STOP button to initiate preheating. 6. Once preheated, place the fish patties in the Ninja Foodi Smart XL grill. 7. Cover the hood and allow the grill to cook for 5 minutes per side. 8. Serve warm with buns.

Serving Suggestion: Serve the Salmon Lime Burgers with vegetable rice.
Variation Tip: Add canned corn to the burgers.
Nutritional Information per Serving: Calories 258 | Fat 9g | Sodium 994mg | Carbs 1g | Fiber 0.4g | Sugar 3g | Protein 16g

Salmon Packets

Prep time: 15 minutes | Cook Time: 10 minutes | Serves: 4

Ingredients:

4 (6 ounces) salmon steaks
1 teaspoon lemon-pepper seasoning
1 cup shredded carrots
½ cup julienned sweet yellow pepper
½ cup julienned green pepper

4 teaspoons lemon juice
1 teaspoon dried parsley flakes
½ teaspoon salt
¼ teaspoon black pepper

Directions:

1. Season the salmon with lemon pepper then place it on a 12-inch square foil sheet. 2. Top the salmon with the remaining ingredients then seal the foil. 3. Plug the thermometer into the appliance. 4. Select the "Grill" Mode, set the temperature to MED then select the PRESET. 5. Use the right arrow keys on the display to select "FISH" and set the doneness to MED WELL. 6. Press the START/STOP button to initiate preheating. 7. Once preheated, place the fish fillets in the Ninja Foodi Smart XL grill. 8. Insert the thermometer probe into the thickest part of the fish. 9. Cover the hood and allow the grill to cook for 5 minutes per side. 10. Serve warm.

Serving Suggestion: Serve the Salmon Packets with lemon slices and fried rice.
Variation Tip: Use herbs to the seafood for a change of flavor.
Nutritional Information per Serving: Calories 378 | Fat 21g | Sodium 146mg | Carbs 7.1g | Fiber 0.1g | Sugar 0.4g | Protein 23g

Blackened Salmon

Prep time: 15 minutes | Cook Time: 20 minutes | Serves: 2

Ingredients:

1 pound salmon fillets
3 tablespoons melted butter
1 tablespoon lemon pepper
1 teaspoon seasoned salt
1½ tablespoon smoked paprika
1 teaspoon cayenne pepper
¾ teaspoon onion salt
½ teaspoon dry basil

½ teaspoon ground white pepper
½ teaspoon ground black pepper
¼ teaspoon dry oregano
¼ teaspoon Ancho chili powder
Olive oil cooking spray
Fresh dill sprigs, to serve
Lemon wedges

Directions:

1. Place the cooking pot in the Ninja Foodi Smart XL Grill then place the grill grate in the pot. 2. Liberally season the salmon fillets with butter and other ingredients. 3. Plug the thermometer into the appliance. 4. Select the "Bake" Mode, set the temperature to 300°F/150°C, then select the PRESET. 5. Use the right arrow keys on the display to select "FISH" and set the doneness to MED WELL. 6. Press the START/STOP button to initiate preheating. 7. Once preheated, place the fish fillets in the Ninja Foodi Smart XL Grill. 8. Insert the thermometer probe into the thickest part of the fish. 9. Cover the hood and allow the grill to cook for 10 minutes per side. 10. Serve warm.

Serving Suggestion: Serve the Blackened Salmon with fresh greens.
Variation Tip: Drizzle lemon juice on top for a rich taste.
Nutritional Information per Serving: Calories 351 | Fat 4g | Sodium 236mg | Carbs 19.1g | Fiber 0.3g | Sugar 0.1g | Protein 36g

Citrus-Soy Squid

Prep time: 15 minutes | Cook Time: 6 minutes | Serves: 6

Ingredients:

1 cup Mirin
1 cup soy sauce

⅓ cup Yuzu juice
2 pounds squid tentacles, cut crosswise 1 inch thick

Directions:

1. Place the cooking pot in the Ninja Foodi Smart XL Grill then place the grill grate in the pot. 2. Toss squid with Mirin, soy sauce, and water Yuzu juice in a bowl. 3. Cover and marinate the squid for 4 hours in the refrigerator. 4. Cover the Ninja Foodi Smart XL Grill's Hood, select the Grill mode and temperature to LO. 5. Place the squids in the Ninja Foodi Smart XL Grill. 6. Cover the hood and let the appliance cook for 3 minutes per side. 7. Serve warm.

Serving Suggestion: Serve the grilled squid with mashed potatoes.
Variation Tip: Coat the squid with breadcrumbs.
Nutritional Information per Serving: Calories 378 | Fat 7g | Sodium 316mg | Carbs 16.2g | Fiber 0.3g | Sugar 0.3g | Protein 26g

Clams with Horseradish-Tabasco Sauce

Prep time: 15 minutes | Cook Time: 4 minutes | Serves: 6

Ingredients:

4 tablespoons unsalted butter, softened
2 tablespoons drained Horseradish
1 tablespoon Tabasco
¼ teaspoon lemon zest, grated
1 tablespoon fresh lemon juice

¼ teaspoon Spanish smoked paprika
Salt, to taste
2 dozen littleneck clams, scrubbed
Grilled slices of crusty white bread for serving

Directions:

1. Blend butter with lemon zest, Tabasco, lemon juice, Pimento De La Vera, salt, and horseradish in a small bowl. 2. Place the clams in the Ninja Foodi Smart XL Grill. 3. Cover the Ninja Foodi Smart XL Grill's Hood, select the Grill mode, set the temperature to MED and cook for 2 minutes per side. 4. Serve the clams with a horseradish mixture.

Serving Suggestion: Serve the clams with roasted broccoli florets.
Variation Tip: Drizzle lemon garlic butter on top before cooking.
Nutritional Information per Serving: Calories 415 | Fat 15g | Sodium 634mg | Carbs 14.3g | Fiber 1.4g | Sugar 1g | Protein 23.3g

Grilled Shrimp Cocktail with Yellow Gazpacho Salsa

Prep time: 40 minutes | Cook Time: 60 minutes|Servings: 4

Ingredients

4 medium yellow tomatoes, seeded and finely chopped
1 stalk celery, finely chopped
½ small red onion, finely chopped
1 yellow bell pepper, finely chopped
1 medium cucumber, peeled, seeded and finely chopped
1 tablespoon Worcestershire sauce
½ tsp freshly ground pepper
2 tbsps. minced fresh chives

2 tbsps. white-wine vinegar
2 tbsps. lemon juice
¼ tsp salt
Several dashes hot sauce, to taste
1pound raw shrimp, peeled and deveined
2 cloves garlic, minced
2 tsp minced fresh thyme

Directions:

1. Preheat the grill for 8 minutes. 2. Mix the tomatoes, cucumber, celery, bell pepper, onion, vinegar, lemon juice, chives, Worcestershire sauce, salt and pepper, and hot sauce in a big bowl. Cover it and chill for at least twenty minutes or for a single day. 3. Mix the shrimp, garlic, and thyme in a medium bowl; cover it and refrigerate for twenty minutes. 4. Insert Grill Grate, select the option GRILL and set the temperature to LO heat. Grill the shrimps for 2 minutes on each side until done.

Serving Suggestion: Serve the shrimp with salsa in martini glasses.
Variation Tip: use chicken chips with same method.
Nutritional Information per Serving: Calories 251.8 | Carbohydrates 33.7g | Protein 2.6g | Fat 12.3g | Sodium 185.7mg| Fiber 0.6g

Grilled Seafood Platter

Prep time: 30 minutes | Cook Time: 10 minutes|Servings: 6

Ingredients

1 cup extra virgin olive oil
2 garlic cloves, finely chopped
2 tbsps. chopped basil
Zest and juice of 2 lemons
4 blue swimmer crabs, halved, claws cracked
4 lobster tails or small whole lobsters, halved, cleaned
Avocado Cream
2 ripe avocados, peeled, stoned, roughly chopped
½ cup thickened cream
Seafood Sauce
200ml whole-egg mayonnaise
1 small lime, zest grated, juiced

24 scampi, peeled (tails intact), deveined
32 green prawns, peeled (tails intact), deveined
350g clams
12 scallops in the half shell
2 tbsps. chopped flat-leaf parsley

1 garlic clove, chopped
Juice of 1 lime

1 tbsps. sweet chili sauce
1 tbsps. tomato sauce

Directions:

1. Combine the oil, garlic, basil, lemon juice and zest in a bowl, and then season. Brush the marinade over the seafood. 2. Preheat the Ninja Foodi Smart XL Grill for 5 minutes at the "GRILL" function at "MED" temperature setting. 3. Place the crab on cooking pot and cook the crab and lobster for 2 minutes, then add the scampi and cook for a further 2 minutes. Add the prawns and clams, and cook for 3-4 minutes, then add the scallops. When the clams open and the prawns and scallops are opaque, transfer all seafood to a platter. Serve with parsley, avocado and seafood sauces. 4. To make the avocado cream: Pulse ingredients in a food processor until smooth. Season to taste with sea salt and freshly ground black pepper. 5. To make the seafood sauce: Whisk the ingredients together. Season with salt and pepper.

Serving Suggestion: Serve the platter with yummy sauce.
Variation Tip: use your favorite fish.
Nutritional Information per Serving: Calories 664 | Carbohydrates 11g | Protein 68g | Fat 38g | Sodium 1459mg| Fiber 0.6g

Teriyaki-Marinated Salmon

Prep time: 5 minutes | Cook Time: 8 minutes|Servings: 4

Ingredients

4 uncooked skinless salmon fillets (6 ounces each)	1 cup teriyaki marinade

Directions:

1. Put the fish fillets and teriyaki sauce in a big resalable plastic bag. Move the fillets around to coat everywhere with sauce. Refrigerate it for one to twelve hours as per your need. 2. Insert the grill grate in the unit and close the hood. Select the "GRILL" function of the Ninja Foodi Smart XL Grill, set the temperature to "MAX" for 8 minutes. Select START/STOP to begin preheating. 3. When the unit signals that it has preheated, put fillets on the grill, gently press them to maximize the grill marks. Close the hood and cook it for 6 minutes. There isn't a need to flip the fish while cooking. 4. After 6 minutes, check the fillets if done; the internal temperature should come at least 140°F/60°C. If necessary, close the hood and continue to cook for 2 more minutes. 5. After cooking, serve the fillets immediately.

Serving Suggestion: Serve with lemon wedges.
Variation Tip: use chopped dill for garnish.
Nutritional Information per Serving: Calories 190 | Carbohydrates 26g | Protein 4g | Fat 9g | Sodium 105mg| Fiber 3g

Grilled Salmon with Mustard & Herbs

Prep time: 15 minutes | Cook Time: 40 minutes|Servings: 4

Ingredients

2 lemons, thinly sliced,	1 pound center-cut salmon, skinned
20-30 sprigs mixed fresh herbs, plus 2 tbsps. chopped, divided	1 clove garlic
1 tablespoon Dijon mustard	¼ tsp salt

Directions:

1. Preheat the grill for 8 minutes. 2. Lay the 2 9-inch pieces of heavy-duty foil on top of one another and place it on a baking sheet. Arrange the lemon slices in 2 layers in the center of the foil. Spread the herb sprigs on the lemons. With the chef's knife, mash the garlic with salt and form a paste. Transfer it to a small dish and then stir in mustard and the remaining two tsp of chopped herbs. Spread the mixture on double sides of the salmon. Place the salmon on top of the herb sprigs. 3. Slide off the foil and salmon from the baking sheet onto the grill. Insert Grill Grate in the unit and close the hood. 4. Select the option GRILL, set the temperature to MAX heat and time to 24 minutes. Select the option START/STOP to begin cooking. 5. Cook the fish for 20 minutes from each side. Work in batches.

Serving Suggestion: Divide the salmon into four portions and serve it with lemon wedges.
Variation Tip: use chopped dill for garnish.
Nutritional Information per Serving: Calories 197.3 | Carbohydrates 21.5g | Protein 2.5g | Fat 11.6g | Sodium 59.8mg| Fiber 1 g

Grilled Fish Tacos

Prep time: 30 minutes | Cook Time: 50minutes|Servings: 6

Ingredients

4 tsp chili powder	¼ cup reduced-fat sour cream
2 tbsps. lime juice	¼ cup low-fat mayonnaise
2 tbsps. extra-virgin olive oil	2 tbsps. chopped fresh cilantro
1 tsp ground cumin	1 tsp lime zest
1 tsp onion powder	Freshly ground pepper
1 tsp garlic powder	3 cups finely shredded red or green cabbage
1 tsp salt	2 tbsps. lime juice
½ tsp freshly ground pepper	1 tsp sugar
2 pounds mahi-mahi, ¾ inch thick, skinned and cut into 4 portions	⅛ tsp salt
	12 corn tortillas, warmed

Directions:

1. To prepare the fish: Combine lime juice, chili powder, oil, cumin, onion powder, salt and pepper, garlic powder in a bowl. Rub the adobo over all the fish. Let it stand 20 to 30 minutes for the fish to absorb the flavor. 2. To prepare the coleslaw: Add lime juice, sour cream, mayonnaise, cilantro, lime zest, salt and pepper, sugar, in a medium bowl; mix them until smooth and creamy. Add the cabbage and toss it to combine. Refrigerate until ready to use. 3. Select the "GRILL" function of the Ninja Foodi Smart XL Grill, adjust temperature to "LO" and set the time to 15 minutes. Preheat the grill for 8 minutes before use. 4. Insert Grill Grate in the unit and close the hood. Select the option START/STOP to begin preheating. 5. Cook fish on Grill Grate for 15 minutes flipping halfway. 6. Transfer the fish to a plate and then separate it into large chunks.

Serving Suggestion: Serve the tacos by passing the fish, tortillas, coleslaw and taco garnishes separately.
Variation Tip: use chopped dill for garnish.
Nutritional Information per Serving: Calories 215.3 | Carbohydrates 19.4g | Protein 3.7g | Fat 14.7g | Sodium 83.8mg| Fiber 1.1g

Ninja Foodi Breaded Shrimp

Prep time: 5 minutes | Cook Time: 16 minutes | Serves: 2

Ingredients:

1 egg
¼ cup bread crumbs
½ teaspoon garlic powder
½ pound shrimp, peeled and deveined

½ teaspoon ginger
¼ cup diced onion
Salt and black pepper, to taste

Directions:

1. Press the "Air Crisp" button in a Ninja Foodi Smart XL Grill and set the temperature to 350°F/175°C. Adjust time to 16 minutes. 2. Press START/STOP to begin preheating. 3. Meanwhile, combine bread crumbs, onions, garlic powder, ginger, salt and pepper in a large bowl. Mix well. 4. Whisk egg in another bowl and set aside. 5. Now, dip shrimps in egg mixture and then in bread crumbs mixture. Set aside. 6. When the Ninja Foodi Smart XL Grill shows "Add Food", place shrimps in it and cook for about 16 minutes. 7. Dish out and serve warm.
Serving Suggestions: Top with chopped mint leaves before serving.
Variation Tip: You can also use onion powder to enhance taste.
Nutritional Information per Serving: Calories: 229 |Fat: 4.9g|Sat Fat: 1.4g|Carbohydrates: 13.8g|Fiber: 1.1g|Sugar: 1.8g|Protein: 30.7g

Ninja Foodi Cajun Salmon

Prep time: 10 minutes | Cook Time: 8 minutes | Serves: 4

Ingredients:

4 tablespoons Cajun seasoning

4 salmon steaks

Directions:

1. Rub salmon steaks with Cajun seasoning and set aside for about 10 minutes. 2. Arrange "Crisper Basket" in a Ninja Foodi Smart XL Grill and press the "Air Crisp" button. 3. Set the temperature to 390°F/200°C and adjust the time to 8 minutes. 4. Press START/STOP to begin preheating. 5. When it shows "Add Food", place salmon steaks in it and cook for 8 minutes at 390°F/200°C. 6. Flip halfway through and dish out. 7. Serve and enjoy!
Serving Suggestions: Serve with coleslaw.
Variation Tip: You can add some sesame seeds to enhance taste.
Nutritional Information per Serving: Calories: 235 |Fat: 11g|Sat Fat: 1.6g|Carbohydrates: 0g|Fiber: 0g|Sugar: 0g|Protein: 34.7g

Ninja Foodi Simple Cod Fillets

Prep time: 10 minutes | Cook Time: 10 minutes | Serves: 4

Ingredients:

4 cod fillets

Salt and black pepper, to taste

Directions:

1. Season cod fillets with salt and pepper. Set aside. 2. Now, place the "Grill Grate" in a Ninja Foodi Smart XL Grill and press the "Grill" button. 3. Set the time to 12 minutes and temperature to MED heat. 4. Press START/STOP to begin preheating. 5. When it shows "Add Food", place salmon fillets in it and cook for about 12 minutes. 6. Take out and serve hot.
Serving Suggestions: You can add melted butter on the top.
Variation Tip: You can also use cayenne pepper to enhance taste.
Nutritional Information per Serving: Calories: 90 |Fat: 1g|Sat Fat: 0g|Carbohydrates: 0g|Fiber: 0g|Sugar: 0g|Protein: 20g

Ninja Foodi Buttered Scallops

Prep time: 10 minutes | Cook Time: 4 minutes | Serves: 4

Ingredients:

1½ pounds sea scallops
1 tablespoon fresh thyme, minced

2 tablespoons melted butter
Salt and black pepper, to taste

Directions:

1. Add scallops, thyme, butter, salt and pepper in a large bowl. Mix well. 2. Arrange the "Crisper Basket" in a Ninja Foodi Smart XL Grill and press the "Air Crisp" button. 3. Set the temperature to 390°F/200°C and adjust the time to 4 minutes. 4. Press START/STOP to begin preheating. 5. When it shows "Add Food", add in sea scallops and cook for 4 minutes at 390°F/200°C. 6. Dish out and serve warm.
Serving Suggestions: Serve with chopped parsley on the top.
Variation Tip: You can also add lemon juice to enhance taste.
Nutritional Information per Serving: Calories: 602 |Fat: 10.6g|Sat Fat: 4.2g|Carbohydrates: 15.2g|Fiber: 0.3g|Sugar: 0g|Protein: 104.8g

Honey Garlic Salmon

Prep time: 10 minutes | Cook Time: 10 minutes | Serves: 2

Ingredients:

2 salmon fillets
2 tablespoon lemon juice
2 tablespoon honey
3 tablespoon brown mustard

1 tablespoon garlic, minced
1 Serrano pepper, diced
¼ cup olive oil
¼ teaspoon red pepper flakes, crushed

Directions:

1. Place the cooking pot in the Ninja Foodi Smart XL Grill then place the grill grate in the pot. 2. Add fish fillets and remaining ingredients into the zip-lock bag. Seal bag and place in the refrigerator for 30 minutes. 3. Plug the thermometer into the appliance. 4. Select the "Grill" Mode, set the temperature to HI then select the PRESET. 5. Use the right arrow keys on the display to select "FISH" and set the doneness to MED WELL. 6. Press the START/STOP button to initiate preheating. 7. Once preheated, place the fish fillets in the Ninja Foodi Smart XL Grill. 8. Insert the thermometer probe into the thickest part of the fish. 9. Cover the hood and allow the grill to cook. 10. Turn fish fillets halfway through. 11. Serve, when done.

Serving Suggestion: Serve warm.

Variation Tip: Add one teaspoon dried oregano.

Nutritional Information per Serving: Calories 529 | Fat 36.5g |Sodium 204mg | Carbs 21.3g | Fiber 0.7g | Sugar 17.8g | Protein 35.1g

Thai Fish Fillets

Prep time: 10 minutes | Cook Time: 10 minutes | Serves: 4

Ingredients:

1½ pounds Tilapia fillets
2 teaspoons soy sauce
1 tablespoon fish sauce
1 tablespoon olive oil

¼ cup cilantro, chopped
½ teaspoon red pepper flakes
2 teaspoons garlic, minced
2 lime juice

Directions:

1. Place the cooking pot in the Ninja Foodi Smart XL Grill then place the grill grate in the pot. 2. Add fish fillets and remaining ingredients into the zip-lock bag. Seal bag and place in the refrigerator for 30 minutes. 3. Plug the thermometer into the appliance. 4. Insert the thermometer probe into the thickest part of the fish and connect it to the appliance. 5. Select the "Grill" Mode, set the temperature to HI then select the PRESET. 6. Use the right arrow keys on the display to select "FISH" and set the doneness to MED WELL. 7. Press the START/STOP button to initiate preheating. 8. Once preheated, place the fish fillets in the Ninja Foodi Smart XL Grill. 9. Insert the thermometer probe into the thickest part of the fish. 10. Cover the hood and allow the grill to cook. 11. Serve, when done.

Serving Suggestion: Serve warm.

Variation Tip: None

Nutritional Information per Serving: Calories 176 | Fat 5.1g |Sodium 558mg | Carbs 1g | Fiber 0.1g | Sugar 0.3g | Protein 32.2g

Baked Cajun Salmon

Prep time: 10 minutes | Cook Time: 12 minutes | Serves: 4

Ingredients:

4 salmon fillets
4 tablespoons brown sugar

2 teaspoons Cajun seasoning
Salt

Directions:

1. Place the cooking pot in the Ninja Foodi Smart XL Grill then set a grill grate inside. 2. In a small bowl, mix brown sugar, Cajun seasoning and salt and rub over fish fillets. 3. Plug the thermometer into the appliance. 4. Select the "Bake" Mode, set the temperature to 400°F/200°C then select the PRESET. 5. Use the right arrow keys on the display to select "FISH" and set the doneness to MED WELL. 6. Press the START/STOP button to initiate preheating. 7. Once preheated, place the fish fillets in the Ninja Foodi Smart XL Grill. 8. Insert the thermometer probe into the thickest part of the fish. 9. Cover the hood and allow the grill to cook. 10. Serve, when done.

Serving Suggestion: Serve warm.

Variation Tip: None

Nutritional Information per Serving: Calories 270 | Fat 11g |Sodium 145mg | Carbs 8.8g | Fiber 0g | Sugar 8.7g | Protein 34.6g

Grilled Shrimp with Miso Butter

Prep time: 15 minutes | Cook Time: 8 minutes | Serves: 6

Ingredients:

1 stick unsalted butter, softened

2 tablespoons white miso

½ teaspoon lemon zest, grated

1 tablespoon lemon juice

1 tablespoon scallion, sliced

1 pound large shrimp, shelled and deveined

2 tablespoons canola oil

1 large garlic clove, minced

1 teaspoon Korean chili powder

1 teaspoon salt

1½ teaspoons mustard seeds, pickled

Directions:

1. Place the cooking pot in the Ninja Foodi Smart XL Grill then place the grill grate in the pot. 2. Blend butter with lemon juice, lemon zest, miso, one tablespoon scallion in a bowl. 3. Toss in shrimp, chili powder, salt and garlic then mix well. 4. Place shrimps in the Ninja Foodi Smart XL Grill. 5. Cover the Ninja Foodi Smart XL Grill's Hood, select the Grill mode, set the temperature to LO and cook for 4 minutes per side. 6. Serve warm.

Serving Suggestion: Serve the shrimp with potato salad.

Variation Tip: Add garlic salt to the sauce for more taste.

Nutritional Information per Serving: Calories 251 | Fat 17g | Sodium 723mg | Carbs 21g | Fiber 2.5g | Sugar 2g | Protein 7.3g

Ninja Foodi Southern Catfish

Prep time: 15 minutes | Cook Time: 10 minutes | Serves: 8

Ingredients:

4 pounds catfish fillets

2 cups milk

1 cup cornmeal

½ cup all-purpose flour

½ teaspoon chili powder

½ teaspoon cayenne pepper

2 lemons, sliced

1 cup yellow mustard

4 tablespoons dried parsley

½ teaspoon onion powder

½ teaspoon garlic powder

Salt and black pepper, to taste

Directions:

1. Press the "Air Crisp" button in a Ninja Foodi Smart XL Grill and set the temperature to 400°F/200°C. Adjust the time to 10 minutes. 2. Press START/STOP to begin preheating. 3. Meanwhile, add lemon juice, milk and catfish in a bowl. Mix well and refrigerate for about 15 minutes. 4. Now, add cornmeal, parsley, all-purpose flour, salt, chili powder, onion powder, black pepper, garlic powder, and cayenne pepper in a large bowl. Mix well. 5. Rub catfish fillets with mustard and coat them with cornmeal mixture. 6. When the Ninja Foodi Smart XL Grill shows "Add Food", place catfish fillets in it and cook for 10 minutes. 7. Flip halfway through and dish out. 8. Serve and enjoy!

Serving Suggestions: Serve with chopped mint leaves on the top.

Variation Tip: You can omit parsley.

Nutritional Information per Serving: Calories: 448 |Fat: 20.5g|Sat Fat: 4.1g|Carbohydrates: 24.2g|Fiber: 2.9g|Sugar: 3.6g|Protein: 41g

Herb Salmon

Prep time: 10 minutes | Cook Time: 15 minutes | Serves: 4

Ingredients:

1 pound salmon, cut into 4 pieces

1 tablespoon olive oil

¼ teaspoon dried basil

½ tablespoon dried rosemary

Pepper

Salt

Directions:

1. Place the cooking pot in the Ninja Foodi Smart XL Grill then set a Crisper Basket inside. 2. In a small bowl, mix olive oil, basil, chives and rosemary. 3. Brush salmon with oil mixture. 4. Plug the thermometer into the appliance. 5. Select the "Air Crisp" Mode, set the temperature to 400°F/200°C then select the PRESET. 6. Use the right arrow keys on the display to select "FISH" and set the doneness to MED WELL. 7. Press the START/STOP button to initiate preheating. 8. Once preheated, place the salmon fillets in the Ninja Foodi Smart XL Grill. 9. Insert the thermometer probe into the thickest part of the fish. 10. Cover the hood and allow the grill to cook. 11. Serve, when done.

Serving Suggestion: Serve warm.

Variation Tip: Add ¼ teaspoon of mix dried herbs.

Nutritional Information per Serving: Calories 181 | Fat 10.6g |Sodium 89mg | Carbs 0.3g | Fiber 0.2g | Sugar 0g | Protein 22g

Shrimp Casserole

Prep time: 10 minutes | Cook Time: 8 minutes | Serves: 4

Ingredients:

1 pound shrimp, peeled and deveined
2 tablespoons white wine
1 tablespoon garlic, minced
2 tablespoons fresh parsley, chopped

½ cup breadcrumbs
¼ cup butter, melted
Pepper
Salt

Directions:

1. Place the cooking pot in the Ninja Foodi Smart XL Grill. 2. Add shrimp and remaining ingredients into the bowl and toss well. 3. Pour shrimp mixture into the baking dish. 4. Select the "Bake" Mode, set the temperature to 350°F/175°C. 5. Press the START/STOP button to initiate preheating. 6. Once preheated, place the baking dish in the Ninja Foodi Smart XL Grill. 7. Cover the hood and cook for 8 minutes. 8. Serve, when done.

Serving Suggestion: Serve warm.
Variation Tip: Add your choice of seasonings.
Nutritional Information per Serving: Calories 300 | Fat 14.2g |Sodium 498mg | Carbs 12.5g | Fiber 0.7g | Sugar 1g | Protein 28g

Garlic Rosemary Shrimp

Prep time: 10 minutes | Cook Time: 10 minutes | Serves: 4

Ingredients:

1 pound shrimp, peeled and deveined
2 garlic cloves, minced
1 tablespoon olive oil

½ tablespoon fresh rosemary, chopped
Pepper
Salt

Directions:

1. Place the cooking pot in the Ninja Foodi Smart XL Grill. 2. Add shrimp and remaining ingredients into the bowl and toss well. 3. Transfer shrimp mixture into the baking dish. 4. Select the "Bake" Mode, set the temperature to 400°F/200°C. 5. Press the START/STOP button to initiate preheating. 6. Once preheated, place the baking dish in the Ninja Foodi Smart XL Grill. 7. Cover the hood and let the appliance cook. 8. Serve, when done.

Serving Suggestion: Serve warm.
Variation Tip: Add ¼ teaspoon of crushed red pepper flakes.
Nutritional Information per Serving: Calories 168 | Fat 5.5g |Sodium 316mg | Carbs 2.5g | Fiber 0.2g | Sugar 0g | Protein 26g

Ginger Salmon with Cucumber Lime Sauce

Prep time: 30 minutes | Cook Time: 10 minutes|Servings: 10

Ingredients

1 tablespoon grated lime zest
4 tsp. sugar
½ tsp. salt
¼ cup lime juice
2 tbsps. olive oil
2 tbsps. rice vinegar or white wine vinegar
½ tsp. ground coriander

½ tsp. freshly ground pepper
2 tsp. minced fresh ginger root
2 garlic cloves, minced
2 medium cucumbers, peeled, seeded and chopped
⅓ cup chopped fresh cilantro
1 tablespoon finely chopped onion

Salmon

1 tablespoon olive oil
½ tsp. salt
⅓ cup minced fresh ginger root

1 tablespoon lime juice
½ tsp freshly ground pepper
10 salmon fillets (6 ounces each)

Directions:

1. Place the first 13 Ingredients of the list in a blender. Cover and process until pureed. 2. In a bowl, combine ginger, oil, salt, lime juice, and pepper. Rub over flesh side of salmon fillets. 3. Select the "Grill" function of the Ninja Foodi Smart XL Grill at the "MED" temperature. Preheat for 5 minutes before use. 4. Lightly oil the Grill Grate. Place salmon on grill, skin side down. Grill while covered over MED heat for 10-12 minutes or until fish just begins to flake easily with a fork.

Serving Suggestion: Serve with sauce.
Variation Tip: use chopped dill for garnish.
Nutritional Information per Serving: Calories 248 | Carbohydrates 40.7g | Protein 2.5g | Fat 10.8g | Sodium 120.4mg| Fiber 0.7g

Spicy Shrimp

Prep time: 10 minutes | Cook Time: 6 minutes | Serves: 2

Ingredients:

½ pound shrimp, peeled and deveined
½ teaspoon Cayenne
1 tablespoon olive oil

½ teaspoon Old bay seasoning
¼ teaspoon paprika
Pinch of salt

Directions:

1. Place the cooking pot in the Ninja Foodi Smart XL Grill then place the Crisper Basket in the pot. 2. Add shrimp and remaining ingredients into the bowl and toss well. 3. Select the "Air Crisp" Mode, set the temperature to 390°F/200°C. 4. Press the START/STOP button to initiate preheating. 5. Once preheated, place the shrimp in the Ninja Foodi Smart XL Grill. 6. Cover the hood and let the appliance cook for 6 minutes. 7. Serve, when done.

Serving Suggestion: Serve warm.
Variation Tip: None
Nutritional Information per Serving: Calories 197 | Fat 9g |Sodium 514mg | Carbs 2.1g | Fiber 0.2g | Sugar 0.1g | Protein 25.9g

Grill Cod

Prep time: 10 minutes | Cook Time: 10 minutes | Serves: 4

Ingredients:

1 pound cod fillets, boneless & skinless
1 fresh lemon juice
¼ cup butter, melted

¼ teaspoon dried parsley
Pepper
Salt

Directions:

1. Place the cooking pot in the Ninja Foodi Smart XL Grill then place the grill grate in the pot. 2. In a small bowl, mix butter, lemon juice, parsley, pepper and salt. 3. Brush fish fillets with melted butter mixture. 4. Plug the thermometer into the appliance. 5. Select the "Grill" Mode, set the temperature to HI then select the PRESET. 6. Use the right arrow keys on the display to select "FISH" and set the doneness to MED WELL. 7. Press the START/STOP button to initiate preheating. 8. Once preheated, place the fish fillets in the Ninja Foodi Smart XL Grill. 9. Insert the thermometer probe into the thickest part of the fish. 10. Cover the hood and allow the grill to cook. 11. Turn fish fillets halfway through. 12. Serve, when done.

Serving Suggestion: Serve warm.
Variation Tip: None
Nutritional Information per Serving: Calories 193 | Fat 12.5g |Sodium 191mg | Carbs 0g | Fiber 0g | Sugar 0g | Protein 20.4g

Paprika Grilled Shrimp

Prep time: 5-10 minutes | Cook Time: 6 minutes|Servings: 4

Ingredients

1-pound jumbo shrimps, peeled and deveined
2 tbsps. brown sugar
1 tablespoon paprika
1 tablespoon garlic powder

2 tbsps. olive oil
1 tsp garlic salt
½ tsp black pepper

Directions:

1. Add listed Ingredients into a mixing bowl. 2. Mix them well. 3. Let it chill and marinate for 30-60 minutes. 4. Pre-heat Ninja Foodi Smart XL Grill by selecting the "GRILL" function and temperature setting to "MED" to 6 minutes. 5. Let it pre-heat until you hear a beep. 6. Arrange prepared shrimps over the Grill Grate. 7. Lock lid and cook for 3 minutes. 8. Then flip and cook for 3 minutes more. 9. Serve and enjoy!

Serving Suggestion: Serve with dill garnishing or enjoy as it is.
Variation Tip: use hot chili powder for spicier.
Nutritional Information per Serving: Calories: 370| Fat: 27 g| Carbohydrates: 23 g| Fiber: 8 g| Sodium: 182 mg| Protein: 6 g

Apricot-Chile Glazed Salmon

Prep time: 25 minutes | Cook Time: 25 minutes | Servings: 4

Ingredients

2 tbsps. red chili powder
3 tbsps. apricot jam

½ tsp salt
1¼-1½ pounds center-cut wild salmon, skinned

Directions:

1. Preheat the grill for 8 minutes. 2. Combine the salt and chili powder in a bowl. Rub them onto both sides of salmon. 3. Place the jam in a saucepan; heat it over medium heat, keep stirring it until melted. 4. Insert Grill Grate in the unit and close the hood. 5. Select the option GRILL, set the temperature to MED and time to 10 minutes. Use a pastry brush, coat the top of the salmon with the jam. Close the grill; cook until the salmon easily flakes with a fork, 3 to 5 minutes more. To serve, cut into 4 portions.

Serving Suggestion: Serve with chilled drink.

Variation Tip: use any jam of your liking for glaze.

Nutritional Information per Serving: Calories 151 | Carbohydrates 19.46g | Protein 1.85g | Fat 7.54g | Sodium 95mg | Fiber 0.4g

Greek Salmon

Prep time: 10 minutes | Cook Time: 20 minutes | Serves: 4

Ingredients:

4 salmon fillets
1 onion, chopped
½ cup Feta cheese, crumbled
½ cup basil pesto

2 cups cherry tomatoes, halved
Pepper
Salt

Directions:

1. Place the cooking pot in the Ninja Foodi Smart XL Grill then set a grill grate inside. 2. Place fish fillets in a baking dish and top with tomatoes, onion, pesto, cheese, pepper and salt. 3. Plug the thermometer into the appliance. 4. Select the "Bake" Mode, set the temperature to 350°F/175°C then select the PRESET. 5. Use the right arrow keys on the display to select "FISH" and set the doneness to MED WELL. 6. Press the START/STOP button to initiate preheating. 7. Once preheated, place the fish fillets in the Ninja Foodi Smart XL Grill. 8. Insert the thermometer probe into the thickest part of the fish. 9. Cover the hood and allow the grill to cook. 10. Serve, when done.

Serving Suggestion: Serve warm.

Variation Tip: Add your choice of seasonings.

Nutritional Information per Serving: Calories 313 | Fat 15.2g | Sodium 332mg | Carbs 6.9g | Fiber 1.7g | Sugar 4.3g | Protein 38.4g

Grilled Lemon-Garlic Salmon

Prep time: 10 minutes | Cook Time: 15-20 minutes | Servings: 4

Ingredients

2 garlic cloves, minced
½ tsp. minced fresh rosemary
2 tsps. grated lemon zest

½ tsp. salt
½ tsp. pepper
4 salmon fillets (6 ounces each)

Directions:

1. Take a small bowl, mix the first five Ingredients, and rub over fillets. Let it stand for 15 minutes. Coat the grill with cooking oil. 2. Preheat the grill for 8 minutes before use. 3. Place salmon on the grill with the skin side up. Grill while covered over MED heat or broil 4 in. 4. From heat 4 minutes. Turn and grill 3 to 6 minutes longer or until fish just begins to flake easily with a fork.

Serving Suggestion: Serve with lemon wedges.

Variation Tip: use chopped dill for garnish.

Nutritional Information per Serving: Calories 280 | Carbohydrates 40g | Protein 4g | Fat 12g | Sodium 200mg | Fiber 1g

Dijon Fish Fillets

Prep time: 10 minutes | Cook Time: 12 minutes | Serves: 4

Ingredients:

4 salmon fillets

2 tablespoons ground Dijon mustard

3 tablespoons maple syrup

Directions:

1. Place the cooking pot in the Ninja Foodi Smart XL Grill then set a baking dish inside. 2. In a small bowl, mix mustard and maple syrup and brush over salmon fillets. 3. Plug the thermometer into the appliance. 4. Select the "Bake" Mode, set the temperature to 390°F/200°C then select the PRESET. 5. Use the right arrow keys on the display to select "FISH" and set the doneness to MED WELL. 6. Press the START/STOP button to initiate preheating. 7. Once preheated, place the salmon fillets in the Ninja Foodi Smart XL Grill. 8. Insert the thermometer probe into the thickest part of the fish. 9. Cover the hood and allow the grill to cook. 10. Serve, when done.

Serving Suggestion: Serve warm.

Variation Tip: None

Nutritional Information per Serving: Calories 282 | Fat 11g |Sodium 207mg | Carbs 10.1g | Fiber 0g | Sugar 8.9g | Protein 34.5g

Grilled Halibut

Prep time: 5 minutes | Cook Time: 10 minutes|Servings: 4

Ingredients

For the Halibut

4 (4-6-oz.) halibut steaks

2 tbsp. extra-virgin olive oil

Kosher salt

Freshly ground black pepper

For the Mango Salsa

1 mango, diced

1 red pepper, finely chopped

½ red onion, diced

1 jalapeno, minced

1 tbsp. freshly chopped cilantro

Juice of 1 lime

Kosher salt

Freshly ground black pepper

Directions:

1. Select the "Grill" function and adjust temperature to "HI" and preheat Ninja Foodi Smart XL Grill. 2. Brush halibut with oil on both sides then season with salt and pepper. 3. Grill halibut until cooked through, about 5 minutes per side. 4. Make salsa: Mix together all ingredients in a medium bowl and season with salt and pepper. Serve salsa over halibut.

Serving Suggestion: Serve the fish with yummy mango salsa.

Variation Tip: Go for regular lime and tomato salsa for fun.

Nutritional Information per Serving: Calories 248 | Carbohydrates 40.7g | Protein 2.5g | Fat 10.8g | Sodium 120.4mg| Fiber 0.7g

Grilled Salmon Packets

Prep time: 5 minutes | Cook Time: 15-20 minutes|Servings: 4

Ingredients

4 salmon steaks (6 ounces each)

1 tsp lemon-pepper seasoning

1 cup shredded carrots

1 tsp dried parsley flakes

½ cup julienned sweet yellow pepper

½ cup julienned green pepper

4 tsp lemon juice

½ tsp salt

¼ tsp pepper

Directions:

1. Preheat the Ninja Foodi Smart XL Grill for 5 minutes after setting. 2. Sprinkle the salmon with a lemon-pepper. Place each of the salmon steaks on a double thickness of heavy-duty foil (about 12 in. square). Top with carrots and peppers. Sprinkle with remaining Ingredients. 3. Fold foil around fish and seal them tightly. Select GRILL mode, covered, grill over MED heat for 15-20 minutes or until fish flakes easily with a fork.

Serving Suggestion: Serve with dill garnishing or enjoy as it is.

Variation Tip: use chopped dill for garnish.

Nutritional Information per Serving: Calories 98 | Carbohydrates 7.1g | Protein 1.3g | Fat 6.5g | Sodium 154.6mg| Fiber 0g

Grilled Salmon Soft Tacos

Prep time: 20 minutes | Cook Time: 20 minutes | Servings: 4

Ingredients

2 tbsps. extra-virgin olive oil
1 tablespoon ancho or New Mexico chili powder
4 4-ounce wild salmon fillets, about 1-inch thick, skin on
1 tablespoon fresh lime juice
¼ tsp kosher salt

⅛ tsp freshly ground pepper
8 6-inch corn or flour tortillas, warmed
Cabbage Slaw
Citrus Salsa
Cilantro Crema

Directions:

1. Select the "GRILL" function and adjust temperature to "LO" and preheat the Ninja Foodi Smart XL Grill for 8 minutes before use. 2. Combine chili powder, oil, lime juice, salt, and pepper in a bowl. Rub the spice mixture over salmon. 3. Cut each of the fillets lengthwise into two pieces and then remove the skin. 4. Insert Grill Grate in the unit and close the hood. Select the option START/STOP to begin preheating. 5. Cook fish for 10 minutes from each side. Serve.
Serving Suggestion: To serve, place two tortillas on each plate. Divide the fish, Citrus Salsa, Cabbage Slaw, and Cilantro Crema among the tortillas.
Variation Tip: use chopped dill for garnish.
Nutritional Information per Serving: Calories 199.8 | Carbohydrates 25.6g | Protein 3.6g | Fat 2.2g | Sodium 147.6mg| Fiber 4.8g

Easy BBQ Roast Shrimp

Prep time: 5-10 minutes | Cook Time: 7 minutes | Servings: 2

Ingredients

½ pound shrimps, large
3 tbsps. chipotle in adobo sauce, minced
½ orange, juiced

¼ cup BBQ sauce
¼ tsp salt

Directions:

1. Add listed Ingredients into a mixing bowl. 2. Mix them well. 3. Keep it aside. 4. Pre-heat Ninja Foodi Smart XL Grill by selecting the "ROAST" function and temperature setting to "400°F/200°C" for 7 minutes. 5. Let it pre-heat until you hear a beep. 6. Arrange shrimps over Grill Grate and lock lid. 7. Cook for 7 minutes. 8. Serve and enjoy!
Serving Suggestion: Serve with dill garnishing.
Variation Tip: use chopped dill for garnish.
Nutritional Information per Serving: Calories: 173|Fat: 2 g| Carbohydrates: 21 g| Fiber: 2 g| Sodium: 1143 mg| Protein: 17 g

Ninja Foodi Crispy Salmon

Prep time: 10 minutes | Cook Time: 8 minutes | Serves: 4

Ingredients:

4 salmon fillets
8 teaspoons paprika

8 teaspoons avocado oil
Salt and black pepper, to taste

Directions:

1. In a Ninja Foodi Smart XL Grill, press the "Air Crisp" button and set the temperature to 390°F/200°C. Adjust the time to 8 minutes. 2. Press START/STOP to begin preheating. 3. Rub salmon fillets with salt, pepper, paprika and avocado oil and place them in the Ninja Foodi Smart XL Grill when it shows "Add Food". 4. Cook for 8 minutes and flip halfway through. 5. Dish out and serve hot.
Serving Suggestions: Serve with lemon wedges.
Variation Tip: You can also add parsley.
Nutritional Information per Serving: Calories: 260 |Fat: 12.7g|Sat Fat: 1.9g|Carbohydrates: 2.9g|Fiber: 2g|Sugar: 0.5g|Protein: 35.3g

Ninja Foodi Spicy Salmon Fillets

Prep time: 5 minutes | Cook Time: 8 minutes | Serves: 1

Ingredients:

1 salmon fillet
2 teaspoons paprika
½ teaspoon red chili powder
½ teaspoon onion powder
½ teaspoon garlic powder

2 teaspoons avocado oil
1 teaspoon dried parsley
½ teaspoon cayenne pepper
Salt and black pepper, to taste

Directions:

1. Combine salmon fillet with paprika, red chili powder, onion powder, garlic powder, parsley, cayenne pepper, avocado oil, salt and black pepper in a bowl. Mix well and set aside. 2. Meanwhile, press the "Air Crisp" button in a Ninja Foodi Smart XL Grill and set the temperature to 390°F/200°C. Adjust the time to 8 minutes. 3. Press START/STOP to begin preheating. 4. When it shows "Add Food", place the salmon fillet in it and cook for 8 minutes, flipping halfway through. 5. Dish out and serve hot.

Serving Suggestions: Serve with melted butter.

Variation Tip: Lemon juice can also be added.

Nutritional Information per Serving: Calories: 276 |Fat: 13.1g|Sat Fat: 2g|Carbohydrates: 6.2g|Fiber: 2.9g|Sugar: 1.4g|Protein: 36g

Ninja Foodi Broiled Tilapia

Prep time: 5 minutes | Cook Time: 8 minutes | Serves: 4

Ingredients:

2 pounds tilapia fillets
2 teaspoons lemon pepper
4 teaspoons melted butter

2 teaspoons old bay seasoning
Salt, to taste

Directions:

1. Add tilapia fillets, old bay seasoning, lemon pepper, melted butter and salt in a bowl. Mix well. 2. Meanwhile, press the "Broil" button in a Ninja Foodi Smart XL Grill and set the time to 8 minutes at 350°F/175°C. 3. Press START/STOP to begin preheating. 4. When it shows "Add Food", place tilapia fillets and cook for 8 minutes. 5. Dish out and serve hot.

Serving Suggestions: Serve with lemon wedges.

Variation Tip: You can add lemon juice to enhance taste.

Nutritional Information per Serving: Calories: 223 |Fat: 5.9g|Sat Fat: 3.3g|Carbohydrates: 0.7g|Fiber: 0.3g|Sugar: 0g|Protein: 42.3g

Ninja Foodi Lime Chili Tilapia

Prep time: 10 minutes | Cook Time: 10 minutes | Serves: 4

Ingredients:

2 cups bread crumbs
1 cup all-purpose flour
2 limes, squeezed
2 pounds tilapia fillets

2 tablespoons chili powder
4 eggs
Salt and black pepper, to taste

Directions:

1. Press the "Grill" button in a Ninja Foodi Smart XL Grill and set the time to 10 minutes and temperature to MED heat. 2. Press START/STOP to begin preheating. 3. Meanwhile, add bread crumbs, salt, black pepper and chili powder in a large bowl. Mix well. 4. Now, beat eggs in one bowl and flour in another. Set aside. 5. Cover tilapia fillets with flour, then dip them in eggs and then in bread crumbs mixture. 6. When the Ninja Foodi Smart XL Grill shows "Add Food", place tilapia fillets in it and cook for 10 minutes. 7. Dish out and drizzle with lime juice. 8. Serve and enjoy!

Serving Suggestions: Serve with lemon slices.

Variation Tip: Black pepper can be replaced with cayenne pepper.

Nutritional Information per Serving: Calories: 599 |Fat: 10.3g|Sat Fat: 3.1g|Carbohydrates: 68.7g|Fiber: 5.5g|Sugar: 4.6g|Protein: 58.9g

Ninja Foodi Tuna Patties

Prep time: 10 minutes | Cook Time: 10 minutes | Serves: 8

Ingredients:

3 tablespoons almond flour
3 tablespoons mayo
1 teaspoon onion powder
1½ pounds tuna

2 teaspoons garlic powder
2 teaspoons dried dill
1 lemon, squeezed
Salt and black pepper, to taste

Directions:

1. Press the "Grill" button in a Ninja Foodi Smart XL Grill and set the time to 10 minutes and temperature to MED heat. 2. Press START/STOP to begin preheating. 3. Meanwhile, add tuna, almond flour, mayo, onion powder, garlic powder, dill, salt, black pepper and lemon in a bowl. Mix well. 4. Make tuna patties out of the mixture and set aside. 5. When the Ninja Foodi Smart XL Grill shows "Add Food", place the tuna patties in it and cook for 10 minutes. 6. Flip halfway through and dish out. 7. Serve and enjoy!

Serving Suggestions: Before serving, garnish with red chili flakes.
Variation Tip: You can add chopped mint leaves in the mixture.
Nutritional Information per Serving: Calories: 623 |Fat: 28.3g|Sat Fat: 5.5g|Carbohydrates: 3.5g|Fiber: 0.6g|Sugar: 0.8g|Protein: 83.6g

Ninja Foodi Seasoned Catfish

Prep time: 5 minutes | Cook Time: 12 minutes | Serves: 2

Ingredients:

2 tablespoons Louisiana fish seasoning
2 catfish fillets

½ tablespoon parsley
½ tablespoon olive oil

Directions:

1. Press the "Grill" button in a Ninja Foodi Smart XL Grill and set the time to 12 minutes and temperature to MED heat. 2. Press START/STOP to begin preheating. 3. Meanwhile, combine catfish fillets with Louisiana fish seasoning, parsley and olive oil. Set aside. 4. When the Ninja Foodi Smart XL Grill shows "Add Food", place the fillets in it and cook for 12 minutes. 5. Dish out and serve hot.

Serving Suggestions: Serve with butter topping.
Variation Tip: You can use oregano to enhance taste.
Nutritional Information per Serving: Calories: 266 |Fat: 15.7g|Sat Fat: 2.7g|Carbohydrates: 5.1g|Fiber: 0g|Sugar: 0g|Protein: 24.9g

Grill Tuna Patties

Prep time: 10 minutes | Cook Time: 12 minutes | Serves: 12

Ingredients:

2 eggs, lightly beaten
2 cans tuna, drained
¼ cup mayonnaise
½ cup breadcrumbs

½ onion, diced
2 tablespoons fresh lemon juice
Pepper
Salt

Directions:

1. Place the cooking pot in the Ninja Foodi Smart XL Grill then set a Crisper Basket inside. 2. Add all ingredients into the bowl and mix until well combined. 3. Make patties from the mixture. 4. Select the Air Crisp mode, set the temperature to 375°F/190°C. 5. Press the START/STOP button to initiate preheating. 6. Once preheated, place the patties in the Ninja Foodi Smart XL Grill. 7. Cover the hood and allow the grill to cook for 12 minutes. 8. Turn patties halfway through. 9. Serve, when done.

Serving Suggestion: Serve with dip.
Variation Tip: Add your choice of seasonings.
Nutritional Information per Serving: Calories 105 | Fat 5g |Sodium 105mg | Carbs 5g | Fiber 0.3g | Sugar 0.9g | Protein 9.5g

Ninja Foodi Teriyaki Salmon

Prep time: 5 minutes | Cook Time: 8 minutes | Serves: 2

Ingredients:

½ cup teriyaki marinade

2 skinless salmon fillets

Directions:

1. Add teriyaki marinade and salmon fillets in a bowl. Mix well and refrigerate for about 3 hours. 2. Meanwhile, arrange "Grill Grate" in a Ninja Foodi Smart XL Grill and press the "Grill" button. Adjust the time to 8 minutes and temperature to MED heat. 3. Press START/STOP to begin preheating. 4. When it shows "Add Food", place the salmon fillets and cook for 8 minutes. 5. Dish out and serve warm.

Serving Suggestions: Serve with tomato sauce.

Variation Tip: You can also use sesame seeds to enhance taste.

Nutritional Information per Serving: Calories: 280 |Fat: 12g|Sat Fat: 2.5g|Carbohydrates: 16g|Fiber: 0g|Sugar: 12g|Protein: 22g

Shrimp and Vegetables

Prep time: 10 minutes | Cook Time: 15 minutes | Serves: 4

Ingredients:

1 pound shrimp, peeled & deveined

1 tablespoon olive oil

1 bell pepper, sliced

1 zucchini, sliced

¼ cup Parmesan cheese, grated

1 tablespoon Italian seasoning

1 tablespoon garlic, minced

Pepper

Salt

Directions:

1. Place the cooking pot in the Ninja Foodi Smart XL Grill then place the Crisper Basket in the pot. 2. Add shrimp and remaining ingredients into the bowl and toss well. 3. Select the "Air Crisp" Mode, set the temperature to 350°F/175°C. 4. Press the START/STOP button to initiate preheating. 5. Once preheated, place the shrimp mixture in the Ninja Foodi Smart XL Grill. 6. Cover the hood and cook for 15 minutes, flipping halfway through. 7. Serve, when done.

Serving Suggestion: Serve warm.

Variation Tip: Add your choice of seasonings.

Nutritional Information per Serving: Calories 346 | Fat 15.6g |Sodium 923mg | Carbs 6.7g | Fiber 1g | Sugar 2.7g | Protein 38.9g

Chapter 6 Snack and Side Recipes

Volcano Potatoes

Prep time: 15 minutes | Cook Time: 15 minutes | Serves: 4

Ingredients:

4 russet potatoes
8 strips bacon
Filling
2 cups cream cheese

1 cup cheddar cheese shredded

½ green onion diced

Directions:

1. Wrap the potatoes in a foil sheet. 2. Place the cooking pot in the Ninja Foodi Smart XL Grill then set a grill grate inside. 3. Select the "Bake" Mode, set the temperature to 400°F/200°C. 4. Use the arrow keys to set the cooking time to 10 minutes. 5. Press the START/STOP button to initiate preheating. 6. Once preheated, place the potatoes in the Ninja Foodi Smart XL Grill. 7. Cover the hood and allow the grill to cook. 8. Allow the potatoes to cool, unwrap and scoop out the flesh from their center. 9. Mash the scooped out flesh in a bowl and stir in the rest of the ingredients except the bacon. 10. Stuff each potato shell with the mashed filling and wrap them with 2 bacon strips. 11. Once preheated, place the mixtures in the Ninja Foodi Smart XL Grill. 12. Cover the Ninja Foodi Smart XL Grill's hood, set the temperature to 350°F/175°C and cook on the "BAKE Mode" for 10 minutes. 13. Drizzle cheese over the potatoes and broil for 5 minutes. 14. Serve warm.
Serving Suggestion: Serve the potatoes with tomato sauce.
Variation Tip: Drizzle lemon garlic butter on top before cooking.
Nutritional Information per Serving: Calories 56 | Fat 4g |Sodium 634mg | Carbs 43g | Fiber 1.4g | Sugar 1g | Protein 13g

Bison Sliders

Prep time: 10 minutes | Cook Time: 12 minutes | Serves: 4

Ingredients:

1 lb. ground buffalo meat
3 garlic cloves minced
2 tbsp. Worcestershire sauce
For Serving
Green onion thinly sliced
Yellow mustard
Tomato ketchup

1 tsp. kosher salt
1 tsp. black pepper
Cheese slices

Lettuce
Pickles

Directions:

1. Mix meat with black pepper, salt and Worcestershire sauce in a large bowl. 2. Make 8 patties out of this mixture. 3. Place the cooking pot in the Ninja Foodi Smart XL Grill then set a grill grate inside. 4. Select the "Grill" Mode, set the temperature to MED. 5. Use the arrow keys to set the cooking time to 10 minutes. 6. Press the START/STOP button to initiate preheating. 7. Once preheated, place the patties in the Ninja Foodi Smart XL Grill. 8. Cover the hood and allow the grill to cook. 9. Grill the buns for 2 minutes per side. 10. Add each patty in between the two sides of the buns and add other veggies to the buns. 11. Serve warm.
Serving Suggestion: Serve the sliders with fresh greens.
Variation Tip: Add chopped spinach to the filling.
Nutritional Information per Serving: Calories 24 | Fat 1g |Sodium 236mg | Carbs 22g | Fiber 0.3g | Sugar 0.1g | Protein 31g

Chicken Salad with Blueberry Vinaigrette

Prep time: 15 minutes | Cook Time: 14 minutes | Serves: 4

Ingredients:

Salads:
1 package (10 ounces) salad greens
1 cup fresh blueberries
Chicken:
2 boneless chicken breasts, halves
1 tablespoon olive oil
1 garlic clove, minced
Vinaigrette:
¼ cup olive oil
¼ cup blueberry preserves
2 tablespoons Balsamic vinegar
2 tablespoons maple syrup

½ cup canned oranges
1 cup Goat cheese, crumbled

¼ teaspoon salt
¼ teaspoon black pepper

¼ teaspoon ground mustard
⅛ teaspoon salt
Dash pepper

Directions:

1. Place the cooking pot in the Ninja Foodi Smart XL Grill then place the grill grate in the pot. 2. First, season the chicken liberally with garlic, salt, pepper and oil in a bowl. 3. Cover to refrigerate for 30 minutes' margination. 4. Select the "Grill" Mode, set the temperature to MED. 5. Press the START/STOP button to initiate preheating. 6. Place the chicken in the Ninja Foodi Smart XL Grill. 7. Cover the hood and allow the grill to cook for 7 minutes per side. 8. Toss the remaining ingredients for salad and vinaigrette in a bowl. 9. Slice the grilled chicken and serve with salad.
Serving Suggestion: Serve the chicken salad with fresh berries on top.
Variation Tip: Add shredded cheese and strawberries to the salad.
Nutritional Information per Serving: Calories 140 | Fat 5g | Sodium 244mg | Carbs 16g | Fiber 1g | Sugar 1g | Protein 17g

Grilled Stuffed Mushrooms

Prep time: 10 minutes | Cook Time: 10 minutes | Serves: 8

Ingredients:

8 Portobello mushrooms	cheddar cheese grated or shredded

Filling

4 slices bacon	1 large red onion sliced
½ lb. cream cheese	1 jalapeño peppers liked

Directions:

1. Sear bacon slices in a skillet until crispy and keep them aside. 2. Mix jalapenos, cream cheese, bacon, and onion in a small bowl. 3. Stuff each mushroom with this cream cheese mixture. 4. Place the cooking pot in the Ninja Foodi Smart XL Grill then set a grill grate inside. 5. Select the "Grill" Mode, set the temperature to MED. 6. Use the arrow keys to set the cooking time to 10 minutes. 7. Press the START/STOP button to initiate preheating. 8. Once preheated, place the mushrooms in the Ninja Foodi Smart XL Grill. 9. Cover the hood and allow the grill to cook. 10. Drizzle cheese on top of the mushrooms and bake for 5 minutes. 11. Serve warm.

Serving Suggestion: Serve the mushrooms with crispy bacon crumbled on top.

Variation Tip: Add garlic salt on top for more taste.

Nutritional Information per Serving: Calories 449 | Fat 31g |Sodium 723mg | Carbs 22g | Fiber 2.5g | Sugar 2g | Protein 26g

Figs Stuffed with Cheese

Prep time: 10 minutes | Cook Time: 10 minutes | Serves: 10

Ingredients:

20 ripe figs	2 tbsp. balsamic vinegar
4 oz. soft goat cheese	1 tbsp. fresh rosemary, chopped
2 tbsp. olive oil	

Directions:

1. Cut a cross on top (about ¾ way down) of each fig. 2. Mix goat cheese, oil, vinegar and rosemary in a bowl. 3. Stuff each fig with the goat cheese mixture. 4. Place the cooking pot in the Ninja Foodi Smart XL Grill then set a grill grate inside. 5. Select the "Grill" Mode, set the temperature to LOW. 6. Use the arrow keys to set the cooking time to 10 minutes. 7. Press the START/STOP button to initiate preheating. 8. Once preheated, place the figs in the Ninja Foodi Smart XL Grill. 9. Cover the hood and allow the grill to cook. 10. Serve.

Serving Suggestion: Serve the figs with your favorite entrée.

Variation Tip: Drizzle crushed pork rind on top before grilling.

Nutritional Information per Serving: Calories 38 | Fat 7g |Sodium 316mg | Carbs 24g | Fiber 0.3g | Sugar 0.3g | Protein 3g

Grilled Kimchi

Prep time: 20 minutes | Cook Time: 6 minutes | Serves: 4

Ingredients:

½ cup kochukaru	4 medium scallions end trimmed, cut into 1-inch-long pieces
2 tsp. sauejeot	¼ cup fish sauce
1 Napa cabbage, cut into 2 inch pieces	¼ cup minced ginger
8 oz. daikon radish	1 tbsp. of minced garlic cloves
½ cup kosher salt	1½ tsp. granulated sugar

Directions:

1. Toss cabbage with salt and soak in water for 12 hours then drain. 2. Place the cooking pot in the Ninja Foodi Smart XL Grill then set a Crisper Basket inside. 3. Plug the thermometer into the unit and place it inside the pot. 4. Select the "Air Crisp" Mode, set the temperature to 400°F/200°C. 5. Use the arrow keys to set the cooking time to 6 minutes. 6. Press the START/STOP button to initiate preheating. 7. Once preheated, place the cabbage in the Ninja Foodi Smart XL Grill. 8. Mix other ingredients in a bowl and stir in cabbage pieces then cover and refrigerate for 12 hours. 9. Serve.

Serving Suggestion: Serve the kimchi with bread.

Variation Tip: Add crushed red pepper on top.

Nutritional Information per Serving: Calories 132 | Fat 10g |Sodium 994mg | Carbs 13g | Fiber 0.4g | Sugar 3g | Protein 8g

Lemon Herb Carrots

Prep time: 10 minutes | Cook Time: 15 minutes | Serves: 2

Ingredients:

2 carrots, cut into fries' shape

2 tablespoons olive oil

2 tablespoons lemon-herb seasoning

Directions:

1. Place the cooking pot in the Ninja Foodi Smart XL Grill then place the Crisper Basket in the pot. 2. In a bowl, toss carrot fries with seasoning and oil. 3. Select the Air Crisp Mode, set the temperature to 350°F/175°C. 4. Use the Arrow keys to set the time to 15 minutes. 5. Press the START/STOP button to initiate preheating. 6. Once preheated, place the baking dish in the Ninja Foodi Smart XL Grill. 7. Cover the hood and allow the grill to cook. 8. Serve, when done.

Serving Suggestion: Allow to cool completely then serve.

Variation Tip: Once done sprinkle some grated Parmesan cheese.

Nutritional Information per Serving: Calories 145 | Fat 14g |Sodium 42mg | Carbs 6g | Fiber 1.5g | Sugar 3g | Protein 0.5g

Pesto Cheese Dip

Prep time: 10 minutes | Cook Time: 12 minutes | Serves: 8

Ingredients:

⅓ cup basil pesto

1 cup Mozzarella cheese, shredded

8 ounces of cream cheese, softened

¼ cup Parmesan cheese, grated

½ cup roasted peppers

Directions:

1. Place the cooking pot in the Ninja Foodi Smart XL Grill. 2. Add all ingredients into the bowl and mix until well-combined. 3. Pour mixture into the greased baking dish. 4. Select the Bake Mode and set the temperature to 350°F/175°C. 5. Use the Arrow keys to set the time to 12 minutes. 6. Press the START/STOP button to initiate preheating. 7. Once preheated, place the baking dish in the Ninja Foodi Smart XL Grill. 8. Cover the hood and allow the grill to cook. 9. Serve, when done.

Serving Suggestion: Serve warm.

Nutritional Information per Serving: Calories 112 | Fat 10.6g |Sodium 133mg | Carbs 1.6g | Fiber 0.2g | Sugar 0.6g | Protein 3.3g

Grilled Sweet Honey Carrot

Prep time: 10 minutes | Cook Time: 10 minutes|Servings: 6

Ingredients

1 tsp salt

1 tablespoon honey

1 tablespoon rosemary, chopped

1 tablespoon parsley, chopped

6 carrots, cut lengthwise

2 tbsps. butter, melted

Directions:

1. Pre-heat your Ninja Foodi Smart XL Grill by selecting "Grill" function to "MAX" temperature setting for 10 minutes. 2. Once you hear the beep, arrange carrots over the grill grate. 3. Spread remaining Ingredients and drizzle honey. 4. Lock lid and cook for 5 minutes, flip and cook for 5 minutes more.

Serving Suggestion: Serve and enjoy.

Variation Tip: use chopped dill for garnish.

Nutritional Information per Serving: Calories: 80| Fat: 4 g| Carbohydrates: 10 g| Fiber: 3 g| Sodium: 186 mg| Protein: 0.5 g

Crispy Brussels

Prep time: 5-10 minutes | Cook Time: 12 minutes|Servings: 4

Ingredients

1 pound Brussels sprouts, halved

6 slices bacon, chopped

2 tbsps. olive oil, extra virgin

1 tsp salt

½ tsp ground black pepper

Directions:

1. Add Brussels, bacon, olive oil, salt, and pepper into a mixing bowl. 2. Pre-heat Ninja Foodi Smart XL Grill by selecting the "AIR CRISP" function and temperature setting to "390°F/200°C" for 12 minutes. 3. Let it pre-heat until you hear a beep. 4. Arrange Brussels over Crisper basket and lock lid. 5. Cook for 6 minutes. 6. Shake it generously and cook for 6 minutes more.

Serving Suggestion: Serve warm and crispy.

Variation Tip: use chopped dill for flavor.

Nutritional Information per Serving: Calories: 279| Fat: 18 g| Carbohydrates: 12 g| Fiber: 4 g| Sodium: 874 mg| Protein: 14 g

Grilled Butternut Squash

Prep time: 15 minutes | Cook Time: 16 minutes | Serves: 4

Ingredients:

1 medium butternut squash
1 tablespoon olive oil
1½ teaspoons dried oregano

1 teaspoon dried thyme
½ teaspoon salt
¼ teaspoon black pepper

Directions:

1. Place the cooking pot in the Ninja Foodi Smart XL Grill then place the grill grate in the pot. 2. Peel and slice the squash into ½ inch thick slices. 3. Remove the center of the slices to discard the seeds. 4. Toss the squash slices with the remaining ingredients in a bowl. 5. Plug the thermometer into the appliance. 6. Select the "Grill" Mode, set the temperature to MED. 7. Use the arrow keys to set the time to 16 minutes. 8. Press the START/STOP button to initiate preheating. 9. Place the squash in the Ninja Foodi Smart XL Grill. 10. Cover the hood and allow the grill to cook. 11. Serve warm.

Serving Suggestion: Serve the squash with chili sauce or mayonnaise dip.
Variation Tip: Added shredded cheese on top of the grilled squash.
Nutritional Information per Serving: Calories 180 | Fat 9g | Sodium 318mg | Carbs 19g | Fiber 5g | Sugar 3g | Protein 7g

Grilled Potato Wedges

Prep time: 10 minutes | Cook Time: 20 minutes | Serves: 6

Ingredients:

6 russet potatoes medium-sized, cut into wedges
½ cup cooking oil
2 tbsp. paprika

¼ cup salt
1 tbsp. black pepper
⅔ cup potato flakes

Directions:

1. Toss potato wedges with black pepper and other ingredients in a bowl. 2. Place the cooking pot in the Ninja Foodi Smart XL Grill then set a grill grate inside. 3. Select the "Grill" Mode, set the temperature to MED. 4. Use the arrow keys to set the cooking time to 10 minutes. 5. Press the START/STOP button to initiate preheating. 6. Once preheated, place the mushrooms in the Ninja Foodi Smart XL Grill. 7. Cover the hood and allow the grill to cook. 8. Serve warm.

Serving Suggestion: Serve the potatoes with ketchup.
Variation Tip: Add a drizzle of taco seasoning.
Nutritional Information per Serving: Calories 218 | Fat 14g |Sodium 220mg | Carbs 22g | Fiber 2.4g | Sugar 1.2g | Protein 2.5g

Creamed Potato Corns

Prep time: 5-10 minutes | Cook Time: 30-40 minutes|Servings: 4

Ingredients

1 and ½ tsp garlic salt
½ cup sour cream
1 jalapeno pepper, seeded and minced
1 tablespoon lime juice
1 tsp ground cumin
½ cup milk

2 pobiano pepper
¼ tsp cayenne pepper
2 sweet corn years
1 tablespoon cilantro, minced
3 tbsps. olive oil

Directions:

1. Drain potatoes and rub them with oil. 2. Pre-heat your Ninja Foodi Smart XL Grill at the "Grill" function to "MED" temperature setting. 3. Once you hear the beep, arrange poblano peppers over the grill grate. 4. Let them cook for 5 minutes, flip and cook for 5 minutes more. 5. Grill remaining veggies in the same way, giving 7 minutes to each side. 6. Take a bowl and whisk in the remaining Ingredients and prepare your vinaigrette. 7. Peel grilled corn and chop them. 8. Divide ears into small pieces and cut the potatoes.

Serving Suggestion: Serve grilled veggies with vinaigrette.
Variation Tip: use chopped dill for garnish.
Nutritional Information per Serving: Calories: 344| Fat: 5 g| Carbohydrates: 51 g| Fiber: 3 g| Sodium: 600 mg| Protein: 5 g

Pig Candy

Prep time: 10 minutes | Cook Time: 20 minutes | Serves: 4

Ingredients:

½ cup dark brown sugar

⅛ tsp. cayenne pepper

1 lb. thick cut bacon strips

¼ cup maple syrup

Directions:

1. Mix cayenne pepper and brown sugar in a small bowl. 2. Drizzle this mixture over the bacon strips. 3. Place the cooking pot in the Ninja Foodi Smart XL Grill then set a grill grate inside. 4. Select the "Grill" Mode, set the temperature to MED. 5. Use the arrow keys on the display to select the cooking time to 10 minutes. 6. Press the START/STOP button to initiate preheating. 7. Once preheated, place the bacon in the Ninja Foodi Smart XL Grill. 8. Cover the hood and allow the grill to cook. 9. Brush the bacon with maple syrup and cook for 10 minutes more. 10. Serve.

Serving Suggestion: Serve the candy with zucchini chips.

Variation Tip: Drizzle maple syrup over the candy before serving.

Nutritional Information per Serving: Calories 85 | Fat 8g |Sodium 146mg | Carbs 25g | Fiber 0.1g | Sugar 0.4g | Protein 1g

Lovely Seasonal Broccoli

Prep time: 10 minutes | Cook Time: 10 minutes|Servings: 4

Ingredients

½ tsp salt

½ tsp red chili powder

¼ tsp spice mix

2 tbsps. yogurt

1 tablespoon chickpea flour

¼ tsp turmeric powder

1pound broccoli, cut into florets

Directions:

1. Take your florets and wash them thoroughly. 2. Take a bowl and add listed Ingredients, except the florets. 3. Add broccoli and combine the mix well; let the mixture sit for 30 minutes. 4. Pre-heat your Ninja Foodi Smart XL Grill to "AIR CRISP" mode at 390°F/200°C and set the timer to 10 minutes. 5. Once you hear a beep, add florets to Crisper Basket and crisp for 10 minutes.

Serving Suggestion: Serve warm.

Variation Tip: use shredded cheese for taste.

Nutritional Information per Serving: Calories: 111|Fat: 2 g| Carbohydrates: 12 g| Fiber: 1 g| Sodium: 024 mg| Protein: 7 g

Pineapple with Cream Cheese Dip

Prep time: 15 minutes | Cook Time: 8 minutes | Serves: 4

Ingredients:

Pineapple

1 fresh pineapple

¼ cup packed brown sugar

Dip

3 ounces cream cheese, softened

¼ cup yogurt

2 tablespoons honey

3 tablespoons honey

2 tablespoons lime juice

1 tablespoon brown sugar

1 tablespoon lime juice

1 teaspoon lime zest, grated

Directions:

1. Place the cooking pot in the Ninja Foodi Smart XL Grill then place the grill grate in the pot. 2. First, slice the peeled pineapple into 8 wedges, then cut each wedge into 2 spears. 3. Toss the pineapple with sugar, lime juice and honey in a bowl, then refrigerate for one hour. 4. Meanwhile, prepare the lime dip by whisking all its ingredients together in a bowl. 5. Remove the pineapple from its marinade. 6. Select the "Grill" Mode, set the temperature to MED. 7. Use the arrow keys to set the time to 8 minutes. 8. Press the START/STOP button to initiate preheating. 9. Place the asparagus in the Ninja Foodi Smart XL grill. 10. Cover the hood and allow the grill to cook. 11. Press the START/STOP button to initiate preheating. 12. Place the pineapple in the Ninja Foodi Smart XL Grill. 13. Cover the hood and allow the grill to cook, flipping halfway through. 14. Serve with lime dip.

Serving Suggestion: Serve the pineapple with cream cheese dip.

Variation Tip: Toss the grilled pineapples with berries.

Nutritional Information per Serving: Calories 282 | Fat 4g | Sodium 232mg | Carbs 47g | Fiber 1g | Sugar 0g | Protein 4g

Ninja Foodi Potato Croquettes

Prep time: 20 minutes | Cook Time: 23 minutes | Serves: 8

Ingredients:

4 potatoes, peeled and cubed
1 cup grated parmesan cheese
4 tablespoons chives, minced
1 cup bread crumbs
4 tablespoons all-purpose flour

2 egg yolks
4 eggs
4 tablespoons vegetable oil
Salt and black pepper, to taste

Directions:

1. Add potatoes in boiling water and cook for about 15 minutes. 2. Mash them in a large bowl and set aside to cool. 3. Add egg yolk, chives, flour, parmesan cheese, salt and black pepper in mashed potatoes. Mix properly. 4. Make cylindrical shapes out of the mixture and set aside. 5. Now, crack eggs in a shallow dish and beat well. 6. Add bread crumbs in another bowl and set aside. 7. Dip croquettes first in egg mixture and then in bread crumbs. 8. Meanwhile, arrange the "Crisper Basket" in the Ninja Foodi Smart XL Grill cooking pot and press the "Air Crisp" button. Set the heat to 390°F/200°C and set the time to 8 minutes. 9. Press START/STOP to begin preheating. Put croquettes in the "Crisper Basket" when the Ninja Foodi Smart XL Grill shows "Add Food". 10. Put Cook for 8 minutes and take out. 11. Serve and enjoy!

Serving Suggestions: Serve with tomato sauce.
Variation Tip: You can add chopped cilantro to enhance taste.
Nutritional Information per Serving: Calories: 258 |Fat: 11.8g|Sat Fat: 3.1g|Carbohydrates: 30g|Fiber: 3.3g|Sugar: 2.3g|Protein: 8.6g

Tarragon Asparagus

Prep time: 15 minutes | Cook Time: 8 minutes | Serves: 4

Ingredients:

2 pounds fresh asparagus, trimmed
2 tablespoons olive oil
1 teaspoon salt

½ teaspoon black pepper
¼ cup honey
4 tablespoons fresh tarragon, minced

Directions:

1. Place the cooking pot in the Ninja Foodi Smart XL Grill then place the grill grate in the pot. 2. Liberally season the asparagus by tossing it with oil, salt, pepper, honey and tarragon. 3. Select the "Grill" Mode, set the temperature to MED. 4. Press the START/STOP button to initiate preheating. 5. Place the asparagus in the Ninja Foodi Smart XL Grill. 6. Cover the hood and allow the grill to cook for 4 minutes per side. 7. Serve warm.

Serving Suggestion: Serve the asparagus with crispy bacon.
Variation Tip: Coat the asparagus with breadcrumbs before cooking.
Nutritional Information per Serving: Calories 104 | Fat 3g | Sodium 216mg | Carbs 17g | Fiber 3g | Sugar 4g | Protein 1g

Grilled Oysters with Chorizo Butter

Prep time: 15 minutes | Cook Time: 10 minutes | Serves: 6

Ingredients:

4 ounces Mexican chorizo
1½ sticks butter, cut into cubes
2 tablespoons fresh lime juice

Salt, to taste
18 Louisiana oysters, scrubbed
Cilantro leaves and lime zest for garnish

Directions:

1. Sauté chorizo with butter and lime juice and salt in a skillet for eight minutes until brown. 2. Transfer the sautéed chorizo to a plate. 3. Place the cooking pot in the Ninja Foodi Smart XL Grill then place the grill grate in the pot. 4. Select the "Grill" Mode, set the temperature to MED. 5. Press the START/STOP button to initiate preheating. 6. Place the oysters in the Ninja Foodi Smart XL grill. 7. Cover the hood and allow the grill to cook. 8. Press the START/STOP button to initiate preheating. 9. Place the chicken in the Ninja Foodi Smart XL Grill. 10. Cover the hood and allow the grill to cook for 4 minutes. 11. Divide the chorizo on top of the grilled oysters. 12. Serve warm.

Serving Suggestion: Serve the oysters with garlic butter.
Variation Tip: Drizzle paprika on top for more spice.
Nutritional Information per Serving: Calories 201 | Fat 7g | Sodium 269mg | Carbs 15g | Fiber 4g | Sugar 12g | Protein 26g

Honey Glazed Bratwurst

Prep time: 15 minutes | Cook Time: 20 minutes | Serves: 4

Ingredients:

4 bratwurst links, uncooked
¼ cup Dijon mustard
¼ cup honey

2 tablespoons mayonnaise
1 teaspoon steak sauce
4 brat buns, split

Directions:

1. Place the cooking pot in the Ninja Foodi Smart XL Grill then place the grill grate in the pot. 2. First, mix the mustard with steak sauce and mayonnaise in a bowl. 3. Select the "Grill" Mode, set the temperature to MED. 4. Press the START/STOP button to initiate preheating. 5. Place the bratwurst in the Ninja Foodi Smart XL Grill. 6. Cover the hood and allow the grill to cook for 5 minutes per side. 7. Serve with buns and mustard sauce on top.

Serving Suggestion: Serve the bratwurst with crumbled nacho chips on top and a cream cheese dip on the side.

Variation Tip: Toss bratwurst with shredded parmesan before serving.

Nutritional Information per Serving: Calories 173 | Fat 8g | Sodium 146mg | Carbs 18g | Fiber 5g | Sugar 1g | Protein 7g

Cheese-Stuffed Grilled Peppers

Prep time: 15 minutes | Cook Time: 7 minutes | Serves: 4

Ingredients:

1 cup Ricotta cheese
1 cup cream cheese
½ cup Parmigiano-Reggiano cheese, grated
Salt and black pepper, to taste

4 Anaheim or Cubanelle peppers
4 baby bell peppers
4 small Poblano chilies
Olive oil, for rubbing

Directions:

1. Mix cream cheese, Ricotta, black pepper, salt and Parmigiano-Reggiano in a bowl. 2. Remove the top of the peppers and stuff them with Ricotta mixture. 3. Place the cooking pot in the Ninja Foodi Smart XL Grill then place the grill grate in the pot. 4. Select the "Grill" Mode, set the temperature to MED. 5. Press the START/STOP button to initiate preheating. 6. Place the peppers in the Ninja Foodi Smart XL Grill. 7. Cover the hood and allow the grill to cook for 7 minutes, rotating after 4 minutes. 8. Serve warm.

Serving Suggestion: Serve the peppers with chili garlic sauce.

Variation Tip: Add pepperoni and sliced olives to the filling.

Nutritional Information per Serving: Calories 148 | Fat 12g | Sodium 710mg | Carbs 14g | Fiber 5g | Sugar 3g | Protein 11g

Grilled Zucchini with Fresh Mozzarella

Prep time: 15 minutes | Cook Time: 10 minutes | Serves: 6

Ingredients:

3 zucchinis, cut into slices
2 tablespoons olive oil
Salt, to taste
Black pepper, to taste

¼ teaspoon wine vinegar
1 garlic clove, minced
1 tablespoon parsley, chopped
½ pound fresh Mozzarella, cut into thick slices

Directions:

1. Toss zucchini with olive oil, black pepper, salt, wine vinegar, garlic and parsley in a bowl. 2. Place the cooking pot in the Ninja Foodi Smart XL Grill then place the grill grate in the pot. 3. Select the "Grill" Mode, set the temperature to MED. 4. Use the arrow keys to set the time to 10 minutes. 5. Press the START/STOP button to initiate preheating. 6. Place the zucchini in the Ninja Foodi Smart XL Grill. 7. Cover the hood and allow the grill to cook, flipping halfway through. 8. Serve the zucchini slices with the cheese. 9. Enjoy.

Serving Suggestion: Serve the zucchini with yogurt dip.

Variation Tip: Coat the zucchini with breadcrumbs before cooking.

Nutritional Information per Serving: Calories 175 | Fat 16g | Sodium 255mg | Carbs 31g | Fiber 1.2g | Sugar 5g | Protein 24.1g

Tasty Cauliflower Tots

Prep time: 10 minutes | Cook Time: 20 minutes | Serves: 6

Ingredients:

1 egg
2 cups cauliflower florets
1 small onion, minced
¼ cup breadcrumbs
½ cup Cheddar cheese, shredded

¼ cup bell pepper, minced
¼ cup Parmesan cheese, shredded
Pepper
Salt

Directions:

1. Place the cooking pot in the Ninja Foodi Smart XL Grill. 2. Boil cauliflower florets for five minutes. Drain well. 3. Add cauliflower florets into the food processor and blend. 4. Add blended cauliflower and remaining ingredients in a mixing bowl and mix until well combined. 5. Make small tots from cauliflower mixture. 6. Select the Bake Mode and set the temperature to 375°F/190°C. 7. Use the Arrow keys to set the time to 20 minutes. 8. Press the START/STOP button to initiate preheating. 9. Once preheated, place the tots in the Ninja Foodi Smart XL Grill. 10. Cover the hood and allow the grill to cook. 11. Serve, when done.

Serving Suggestion: Serve with ketchup.
Variation Tip: Add ¼ teaspoon of crushed red pepper flakes.
Nutritional Information per Serving: Calories 81 | Fat 4g |Sodium 139mg | Carbs 6g | Fiber 1.4g | Sugar 1.9g | Protein 4.7g

Eggplant and Tomato Meal

Prep time: 10 minutes | Cook Time: 14 minutes|Servings: 4

Ingredients

1 eggplant, sliced and ¼ inch thick
½ pound buffalo mozzarella, sliced into ¼ inch thick
2 heirloom tomatoes, cut into ¼ inch thick

12 large basil leaves
2 tablespoons canola oil
Salt to taste

Directions:

1. Add eggplant, oil into a large-sized bowl. 2. Toss them well. 3. Pre-heat Ninja Foodi Smart XL Grill by selecting the "GRILL" function and temperature setting to "MAX" for 15 minutes. 4. Let it pre-heat until you hear a beep. 5. Transfer eggplants to Grill Plant and lock lid. 6. Cook for 8-12 minutes. 7. Once done, top eggplant with one slice of tomato and mozzarella. 8. Lock lid and cook for 2 minutes more until cheese melts. 9. Once done, remove eggplant from the Grill. 10. Place 2-3 basil leaves on top of half stack. 11. Place remaining eggplant stacks on top with basil. 12. Season with salt and garnish with remaining basil. 13. Serve and enjoy!

Serving Suggestion: serve with basil.
Variation Tip: use chives for taste.
Nutritional Information per Serving: Calories: 100| Fat: 19 g| Carbohydrates: 11 g| Fiber: 4 g| Sodium: 1555 mg| Protein: 32 g

Delicious Corn Dip

Prep time: 10 minutes | Cook Time: 20 minutes | Serves: 6

Ingredients:

14 ounce can corn kernel, drained
1 teaspoon smoked paprika
¼ cup sour cream
⅓ cup mayonnaise

1 tablespoon green chilies, diced
½ bell pepper, diced
½ cup Cheddar cheese, shredded

Directions:

1. Place the cooking pot in the Ninja Foodi Smart XL Grill. 2. Add all ingredients into the bowl and mix until well combined. 3. Pour mixture into the greased baking dish. 4. Select the Bake Mode and set the temperature to 350°F/175°C. 5. Use the Arrow keys to set the time to 20 minutes. 6. Press the START/STOP button to initiate preheating. 7. Once preheated, place the baking dish in the Ninja Foodi Smart XL Grill. 8. Cover the hood and allow the grill to cook. 9. Serve, when done.

Serving Suggestion: Serve with tortilla chips.
Variation Tip: Add ¼ cup of chopped green onion.
Nutritional Information per Serving: Calories 168 | Fat 10.2g |Sodium 354mg | Carbs 17.3g | Fiber 1.6g | Sugar 3.6g | Protein 4.7g

Ninja Foodi Lemon Tofu

Prep time: 10 minutes | Cook Time: 20 minutes | Serves: 4

Ingredients:

2 tablespoons tamari

3 tablespoons arrowroot powder

2 tablespoons lemon zest

2 pounds extra-firm tofu, drained, pressed and cubed

¾ cup lemon juice

1 cup water

4 tablespoons organic sugar

Directions:

1. In a Ninja Foodi Smart XL Grill, press the "Grill" button and set the time to 15 minutes and temperature to MED heat. 2. Press START/STOP to begin preheating. 3. Meanwhile, add two tablespoons arrowroot powder, tofu, and tamari in a Ziploc bag. 4. Seal the Ziploc bag, shake it properly and set aside for about 30 minutes. 5. When the Ninja Foodi Smart XL Grill shows "Add Food", place the tofu mixture and cook for 15 minutes. 6. Take out and set aside. 7. Now, add remaining arrowroot powder, lemon juice, lemon zest, water and sugar in a skillet. 8. Cook for about 5 minutes on medium-low heat and add in tofu mixture in the sauce. 9. Dish out and serve.

Serving Suggestions: Top with oregano before serving.

Variation Tip: You can also add brown sugar in the sauce.

Nutritional Information per Serving: Calories: 296 |Fat: 13.6g|Sat Fat: 1.6g|Carbohydrates: 24.6g|Fiber: 1.4g|Sugar: 14.4g|Protein: 23.8g

Bacon Hot Dogs

Prep time: 15 minutes | Cook Time: 6 minutes | Serves: 8

Ingredients:

12 bacon strips

8 beef hot dogs

8 hot dog buns, split and toasted

¼ cup chopped red onion

2 cups sauerkraut, rinsed and drained

Directions:

1. Sear the bacon in a skillet until crispy from both sides. 2. Wrap a bacon strip around each hot dog and secure it by inserting a toothpick. 3. Plug the thermometer into the appliance. 4. Place the cooking pot in the Ninja Foodi Smart XL Grill then place the grill grate in the pot. 5. Select the "Grill" Mode, set the temperature to MED. 6. Press the START/STOP button to initiate preheating. 7. Place the hot dogs in the Ninja Foodi Smart XL Grill. 8. Cover the hood and allow the grill to cook for 6 minutes, rotate after 3 minutes. 9. Serve warm in a hotdog bun with sauerkraut and onion. 10. Enjoy.

Serving Suggestion: Serve the hotdogs with tomato sauce or mayo dip.

Variation Tip: Add mustard sauce to hotdogs.

Nutritional Information per Serving: Calories 229 | Fat 5g | Sodium 510mg | Carbs 37g | Fiber 5g | Sugar 4g | Protein 11g

Ninja Foodi Mac n' Cheese

Prep time: 15 minutes | Cook Time: 25 minutes | Serves: 8

Ingredients:

2 teaspoons cornstarch

4 cups dry macaroni

4 cups shredded cheddar cheese

4 cups heavy whipping cream

Directions:

1. Place three cups of cheese and cornstarch in a bowl. Mix well and set aside. 2. Add remaining cheese, macaroni and whipping cream in another bowl. Mix well. 3. Pour the macaroni mixture in a baking pan and cover it with a piece of foil. Set aside. 4. Meanwhile, arrange a "Crisper Basket" in a Ninja Foodi Smart XL Grill and press the "Air Crisp" button. Set the temperature to 310°F/155°C and the time to 25 minutes. 5. Press START/STOP to begin preheating. 6. When it shows "Add Food", place the baking pan in the "Crisper Basket" and cook for 15 minutes at 310°F/155°C. 7. Remove the foil and top with cornstarch mixture. 8. Cook for 10 minutes and take out. 9. Serve and enjoy!

Serving Suggestions: Top with chopped mint leaves before serving.

Variation Tip: You can also mozzarella cheese to enhance taste.

Nutritional Information per Serving: Calories: 593 |Fat: 41.6g|Sat Fat: 25.9g|Carbohydrates: 34.4g|Fiber: 1.4g|Sugar: 1.5g|Protein: 20.8g

Spicy Cashews

Prep time: 10 minutes | Cook Time: 10 minutes | Serves: 6

Ingredients:

3 cups cashews

1 teaspoon ground coriander

2 tablespoons olive oil

1 teaspoon ground cumin

1 teaspoon paprika

1 teaspoon salt

Directions:

1. Place the cooking pot in the Ninja Foodi Smart XL Grill then place the Crisper Basket in the pot. 2. Add cashews and remaining ingredients into the bowl and toss well. 3. Select the Air Crisp Mode, set the temperature to 330°F/165°C. 4. Use the Arrow keys to set the time to 10 minutes. 5. Press the START/STOP button to initiate preheating. 6. Once preheated, place the cashews in the Ninja Foodi Smart XL Grill. 7. Cover the hood and allow the grill to cook. 8. Serve, when done.

Serving Suggestion: Allow to cool completely then serve.

Variation Tip: Add your choice of seasonings.

Nutritional Information per Serving: Calories 436 | Fat 36.6g |Sodium 399mg | Carbs 22.7g | Fiber 2.2g | Sugar 3.5g | Protein 10.6g

Cheesy Chicken Dip

Prep time: 10 minutes | Cook Time: 25 minutes | Serves: 8

Ingredients:

2 chicken breasts, cooked and shredded

½ cup hot sauce

8 ounces of cream cheese, softened

1 cup Mozzarella cheese, shredded

¼ cup Blue cheese, crumbled

½ cup ranch dressing

1 cup Cheddar cheese, shredded

Directions:

1. Place the cooking pot in the Ninja Foodi Smart XL Grill. 2. In a mixing bowl, add all ingredients and mix well. 3. Pour bowl mixture into the greased baking dish. 4. Select the Bake Mode and set the temperature to 350°F/175°C. 5. Use the Arrow keys to set the time to 25 minutes. 6. Press the START/STOP button to initiate preheating. 7. Once preheated, place the baking dish in the Ninja Foodi Smart XL Grill. 8. Cover the hood and allow the grill to cook. 9. Serve, when done.

Serving Suggestion: Serve with tortilla chips.

Variation Tip: Add ¼ cup of cooked and chopped bacon.

Nutritional Information per Serving: Calories 256 | Fat 19.2g |Sodium 748mg | Carbs 2.2g | Fiber 0.1g | Sugar 0.7g | Protein 18.4g

Chicken Stuff Jalapenos

Prep time: 10 minutes | Cook Time: 25 minutes | Serves: 12

Ingredients:

6 Jalapenos, cut in half and remove seeds

¼ teaspoon dried basil

½ cup chicken, cooked and shredded

¼ teaspoon garlic powder

¼ cup green onion, sliced

¼ cup Monterey jack cheese, shredded

4 ounces of cream cheese

¼ teaspoon dried oregano

¼ teaspoon salt

Directions:

1. Place the cooking pot in the Ninja Foodi Smart XL Grill. 2. Add all ingredients except Jalapeno pepper into the bowl and mix until well combined. 3. Spoon tablespoon mixture into each Jalapeno half and place into the baking dish. 4. Select the Bake Mode and set the temperature to 390°F/200°C. 5. Use the Arrow keys to set the time to 25 minutes. 6. Press the START/STOP button to initiate preheating. 7. Once preheated, place the baking dish in the Ninja Foodi Smart XL Grill. 8. Cover the hood and allow the grill to cook. 9. Serve, when done.

Serving Suggestion: Serve warm.

Variation Tip: Add ¼ teaspoon of Italian seasoning.

Nutritional Information per Serving: Calories 52 | Fat 4g |Sodium 95mg | Carbs 0.5g | Fiber 0.1g | Sugar 0.1g | Protein 3g

Savory Roasted Almonds

Prep time: 10 minutes | Cook Time: 12 minutes | Serves: 6

Ingredients:

2 cups almonds
½ teaspoon garlic powder
1 tablespoon olive oil

1 teaspoon Italian seasoning
2 teaspoons rosemary, chopped
Salt

Directions:

1. Place the cooking pot in the Ninja Foodi Smart XL Grill. 2. In a bowl, toss almonds with remaining ingredients. 3. Select the Bake Mode and set the temperature to 350°F/175°C. 4. Use the Arrow keys to set the time to 12 minutes. 5. Press the START/STOP button to initiate preheating. 6. Once preheated, place the almonds in the Ninja Foodi Smart XL Grill. 7. Cover the hood and allow the grill to cook. 8. Serve, when done.
Serving Suggestion: Allow to cool completely then serve.
Variation Tip: Add your choice of seasonings.
Nutritional Information per Serving: Calories 208 | Fat 18.5g |Sodium 28mg | Carbs 7.3g | Fiber 4.2g | Sugar 1.5g | Protein 6.8g

Crispy Potato Wedges

Prep time: 10 minutes | Cook Time: 15 minutes | Serves: 4

Ingredients:

2 potatoes, cut into wedges
½ teaspoon paprika
1½ tablespoon olive oil
⅛ teaspoon Cayenne

¼ teaspoon garlic powder
¼ teaspoon pepper
1 teaspoon sea salt

Directions:

1. Place the cooking pot in the Ninja Foodi Smart XL Grill then place the Crisper Basket in the pot. 2. In a bowl, toss potato wedges with the remaining ingredients. 3. Select the Air Crisp Mode, set the temperature to 400°F/200°C. 4. Use the Arrow keys to set the time to 15 minutes. 5. Press the START/STOP button to initiate preheating. 6. Once preheated, place the potato wedges in the basket in the Ninja Foodi Smart XL Grill. 7. Cover the hood and allow the grill to cook. 8. Serve, when done.
Serving Suggestion: Serve with your choice of dip.
Variation Tip: Add your choice of seasonings.
Nutritional Information per Serving: Calories 120 | Fat 5.4g |Sodium 475mg | Carbs 17.1g | Fiber 2.7g | Sugar 1.3g | Protein 1.9g

Delicious Grilled Honey Fruit Salad

Prep time: 5-10 minutes | Cook Time: 5 minutes|Servings: 4

Ingredients

1 tablespoon lime juice, freshly squeezed
6 tbsps. honey, divided
2 peaches, pitted and sliced

1 can (9 ounces) pineapple chunks, drained and juiced reserved
½ pound strawberries washed, hulled, and halved

Directions:

1. Take a shallow mixing bowl, then add respectively soy sauce, balsamic vinegar, oil, maple syrup and whisk well. 2. Then add broccoli and keep it aside. 3. Select the "GRILL" function of the Ninja Foodi Smart XL Grill and set temperature to "MAX" with 10 minutes' timer. 4. Keep it in the preheating process. 5. When you hear a beep, add broccoli over the grill grate. 6. After then lock the lid and cook until the timer shows 0. 7. Lastly, garnish the food with pepper flakes and sesame seeds. 8. Enjoy!
Serving Suggestion: Serve topped with sesame seeds and pepper flakes.
Variation Tip: use chopped dill for garnish.
Nutritional Information per Serving: Calories: 141| Fat: 7 g| Carbohydrate: 14 g| Fiber: 4 g| Sodium: 853 mg| Protein: 4 g

Grilled Honey Carrots

Prep time: 15 minutes | Cook Time: 10 minutes|Servings: 4

Ingredients

6 carrots, cut lengthwise

1 tablespoon rosemary, chopped

2 tbsps. melted butter

1 tablespoon parsley, chopped

1 tablespoon honey

1 tsp salt

Directions:

1. Take your Ninja Foodi Smart XL Grill and open the lid. 2. Arrange grill grate and close top. 3. Pre-heat Ninja Foodi Smart XL Grill by selecting the "GRILL" function and temperature setting it to "MAX" for 10 minutes. 4. Let it pre-heat until you hear a beep. 5. Arrange carrots over grill grate and spread the remaining Ingredients, and drizzle honey. 6. Lock lid and cook for 5 minutes. 7. Flip sausages and cook for 5 minutes more.

Serving Suggestion: Serve with dill garnishing or enjoy as it is.

Variation Tip: use chopped dill for garnish.

Nutritional Information per Serving: Calories: 80| Fat: 4 g| Carbohydrates: 10 g| Fiber: 3 g| Sodium: 186 mg| Protein: 0.5 g

Mammamia Banana Boats

Prep time: 19 minutes | Cook Time: 6 minutes|Servings: 4

Ingredients

½ cup peanut butter chips

½ cup of chocolate chips

1 cup mini marshmallows

4 ripe bananas

Directions:

1. With the peel, slice a banana lengthwise and remember that not to cut all the way through. 2. Onward, reveal the inside of the banana by using your hand. 3. Select the "GRILL" function and set temperature setting to "MED" to pre-heat Ninja Foodi Smart XL Grill with a 6 minutes' timer. 4. Until you hear a beep, keep it in the pre-heat process. 5. Put the banana over the Grill Grate and lock the lid, let it cook for 4-6 minutes until chocolate melts and bananas are toasted. 6. Serve and Enjoy!

Serving Suggestion: Serve with melted chocolate.

Variation Tip: Uses condense milk as topping.

Nutritional Information per Serving: Calories: 505| Fat: 18 g| Carbohydrates: 82 g| Fiber: 6 g | Sodium: 166 mg| Protein: 10 g

Ninja Foodi Buffalo Chicken Wings

Prep time: 20 minutes | Cook Time: 16 minutes | Serves: 10

Ingredients:

4 pounds frozen chicken wings

4 tablespoons buffalo sauce

4 tablespoons olive oil

1 teaspoon red pepper flakes

Salt, to taste

Directions:

1. Arrange the "Crisper Basket" in a Ninja Foodi Smart XL Grill and press the "Air Crisp" button. Set the temperature to 390°F/200°C and set the time to 12 minutes. 2. Press START/STOP to begin preheating. 3. Coat chicken wings with olive oil and place them in the "Crisper Basket". 4. Cook for about 12 minutes at 390°F/200°C and take out. 5. Meanwhile, add buffalo sauce, red pepper flakes and salt in a large bowl. Mix well. 6. Dip the wings in buffalo sauce mixture and serve.

Serving Suggestions: Top with chopped mint leaves before serving.

Variation Tip: Barbeque sauce can also be used to enhance taste.

Nutritional Information per Serving: Calories: 410 |Fat: 31.6g|Sat Fat: 8.1g|Carbohydrates: 0.9g|Fiber: 0.5g|Sugar: 0g|Protein: 29.2g

Complete Italian Squash

Prep time: 5-10 minutes | Cook Time: 16 minutes|Servings: 4

Ingredients

¼ tsps. black pepper
1 and ½ tsp dried oregano
1 tablespoon olive oil
½ tsp salt

1 tsp dried thyme
1 medium butternut squash, peeled, seeded, and cut into ½ inch slices

Directions:

1. Take a mixing bowl and add slices and other Ingredients and mix well. 2. Pre-heat your Ninja Foodi Smart XL Grill by selecting the "Grill" function to "MED" temperature setting for 16 minutes. 3. Once you hear the beep, arrange squash slices over the grill grate. 4. Cook for 8 minutes, flip and cook for another 8 minutes.
Serving Suggestion: Serve warm.
Variation Tip: use shredded cheese for extra taste.
Nutritional Information per Serving: Calories: 238| Fat: 12 g| Carbohydrates: 36 g| Fiber: 3 g| Sodium: 128 mg| Protein: 15 g

Grilled Peach Salsa

Prep time: 15 minutes | Cook Time: 10 minutes | Serves: 4

Ingredients:

4 peaches, halved and pitted
4 heirloom tomatoes diced
1 bunch cilantro
2 limes juiced

2 garlic cloves minced
2 tbsp. olive oil
Sea salt to taste
Black pepper to taste

Directions:

1. Brush the peaches with oil. 2. Place the cooking pot in the Ninja Foodi Smart XL Grill then set a grill grate inside. 3. Select the "Grill" Mode, set the temperature to MED. 4. Use the arrow keys to set the cooking time to 10 minutes. 5. Press the START/STOP button to initiate preheating. 6. Once preheated, place the fruits in the Ninja Foodi Smart XL Grill. 7. Cover the hood and allow the grill to cook. 8. Dice the grilled peaches and mix with rest of the ingredients in a bowl. 9. Serve.
Serving Suggestion: Serve the salsa with the skewers.
Variation Tip: Add hot sauce to season for a tangy taste.
Nutritional Information per Serving: Calories 82 | Fat 6g |Sodium 620mg | Carbs 25g | Fiber 2.4g | Sugar 1.2g | Protein 12g

Cob with Pepper Butter

Prep time: 15 minutes | Cook Time: 15 minutes | Serves: 8

Ingredients:

8 medium ears sweet corn
1 cup butter, softened

2 tablespoons lemon-pepper seasoning

Directions:

1. Place the cooking pot in the Ninja Foodi Smart XL Grill then place the grill grate in the pot. 2. Season the corn cob with butter and lemon pepper liberally. 3. Place the corn cob in the Ninja Foodi Smart XL Grill. 4. Cover the Ninja Foodi Smart XL Grill's Hood, select the Grill mode, select the Low setting and grill for 15 minutes with grilling after every 5 minutes. 5. Grill the corn cobs in batches. 6. Serve warm.
Serving Suggestion: Serve the corn with parsley on top.
Variation Tip: Coat the corn with crushed cornflakes after grilling.
Nutritional Information per Serving: Calories 218 | Fat 22g | Sodium 350mg | Carbs 32.2g | Fiber 0.7g | Sugar 1g | Protein 4.3g

Creamy Chicken Dip

Prep time: 10 minutes | Cook Time: 25 minutes | Serves: 6

Ingredients:

2 cups chicken, cooked and shredded

4 tablespoons hot sauce

¼ teaspoon garlic powder

½ cup sour cream

8 ounces of cream cheese, softened

Directions:

1. Place the cooking pot in the Ninja Foodi Smart XL Grill. 2. Add all ingredients to a bowl and mix until well combined. 3. Transfer mixture in a greased baking dish. 4. Select the Bake Mode and set the temperature to 350°F/175°C. 5. Use the Arrow keys to set the time to 25 minutes. 6. Press the START/STOP button to initiate preheating. 7. Once preheated, place the baking dish in the Ninja Foodi Smart XL Grill. 8. Cover the hood and allow the grill to cook. 9. Serve, when done.

Serving Suggestion: Serve with tortilla chips.

Variation Tip: Add one tablespoon of dried parsley flakes.

Nutritional Information per Serving: Calories 245 | Fat 18.7g |Sodium 405mg | Carbs 2.1g | Fiber 0g | Sugar 0.3g | Protein 17.1g

Chapter 7 Vegetarian Recipes

Veggie Kabobs

Prep time: 10 minutes | Cook Time: 12 minutes | Serves: 4

Ingredients:

2 medium zucchinis, cut into 1" thick half-moons
1 (10-oz.) package baby bella mushrooms, cleaned and halved
1 medium red onion, cut into wedges
2 small lemons, cut into eighths
3 tbsp. olive oil

1 garlic clove, grated
1 tsp. thyme, chopped
Pinch of crushed red pepper flakes
Kosher salt, to taste
Black pepper, to taste

Directions:

1. Toss all the veggies with other ingredients in a bowl. 2. Place the cooking pot in the Ninja Foodi Smart XL Grill. 3. Select the Bake Mode and set the temperature to 350°F/175°C. 4. Use the Arrow keys to set the time to 6 minutes. 5. Press the Start/Stop button to initiate preheating. 6. Once preheated, place the skewers in the Ninja Foodi Smart XL Grill. 7. Cover the hood and allow the grill to cook. 8. Flip the skewers and cook again for 6 minutes. 9. Serve warm.
Serving Suggestion: Serve the kabobs with mashed cauliflower.
Variation Tip: Add crispy fried onions on top for a crunchier taste.
Nutritional Information Per Serving: Calories 304 | Fat 31g |Sodium 834mg | Carbs 14g | Fiber 0.2g | Sugar 0.3g | Protein 4.6g

Mushroom Tomato Roast

Prep time: 10 minutes | Cook Time: 15 minutes|Servings: 4

Ingredients

2 cups cherry tomatoes
2 cups cremini button mushrooms
¼ cup of vinegar or ¼ cup of red wine
2 garlic cloves, finely chopped
½ cup extra-virgin olive oil

3 tbsps. chopped thyme
Pinch of crushed red pepper flakes
1 tsp kosher salt
½ tsp black pepper
6 scallions, cut crosswise into 2-inch pieces

Directions:

1. Take a zip-lock bag; add black pepper, salt, red pepper flakes, thyme, vinegar, oil, and garlic. Add mushrooms, tomatoes, and scallions. 2. Shake well and refrigerate for 30-40 minutes to marinate. 3. Take Ninja Foodi Smart XL Grill, arrange it over your kitchen stage, and open the top. 4. Select the "ROAST" function of the Ninja Foodi Smart XL Grill and temperature to 400°F/200°C for 12 minutes and afterward Select "START/STOP." Ninja Foodi Smart XL Grill will begin preheating. 5. Ninja Foodi Smart XL Grill is preheated and prepared to cook when it begins to beep. After you hear a beep, open the top. 6. Arrange the mushroom mixture directly inside the Cooking Pot. 7. Close the top lid and allow it to roast the veggies until the timer reads zero.
Serving Suggestion: Serve warm with chilled wine.
Variation Tip: use chopped dill for garnish.
Nutritional Information per Serving: Calories: 253| Fat: 24g| Carbohydrates: 7g| Fiber: 2g| Sodium: 546mg| Protein: 1g

Vegetable Orzo Salad

Prep time: 15 minutes | Cook Time: 14 minutes | Serves: 4

Ingredients:

1¼ cups Orzo, uncooked
½ pound fresh asparagus, trimmed
1 zucchini, sliced
Salad:
½ teaspoon salt
1 cup grape tomatoes, halved
1 tablespoon minced fresh parsley
Dressing:
4 garlic cloves, minced
⅓ cup olive oil
¼ cup Balsamic vinegar

1 sweet yellow, halved
1 Portobello mushroom, stem removed
½ red onion, halved

1 tablespoon minced fresh basil
¼ teaspoon black pepper
1 cup (4 ounces) Feta cheese, crumbled

3 tablespoons lemon juice
1 teaspoon lemon-pepper seasoning

Directions:

1. Cook the Orzo as per the given instructions on the package, then drain. 2. Toss all the salad and dressing ingredients in a bowl until well coated. 3. Place the mushrooms, pepper and onion in the Ninja Foodi Smart XL Grill. 4. Cover the Ninja Foodi Smart XL Grill's Hood, select the Grill mode, set the temperature to MED and cook for 5 minutes per side. 5. Now grill zucchini and asparagus for 2 minutes per side. 6. Dice the grilled veggies and add them to the salad bowl. 7. Mix well, then stir in Orzo. 8. Give it a toss, then serve.
Serving Suggestion: Serve the Orzo Salad with guacamole on top.
Variation Tip: Add olives or sliced mushrooms to the salad.
Nutritional Information per Serving: Calories 246 | Fat 15g | Sodium 220mg | Carbs 40.3g | Fiber 2.4g | Sugar 1.2g | Protein 12.4g

Apple Salad

Prep time: 15 minutes | Cook Time: 10 minutes | Serves: 4

Ingredients:

6 tablespoons olive oil
¼ cup cilantro, minced
¼ cup vinegar
2 tablespoons honey
1 garlic clove, minced
¼ cup orange juice

½ teaspoon salt
½ teaspoon Sriracha chili sauce
2 large apples, wedged
1 pack (5 ounces) salad greens
1 cup walnut halves, toasted
½ cup crumbled Blue cheese

Directions:

1. Place the cooking pot in the Ninja Foodi Smart XL Grill then place the grill grate in the pot. 2. Whisk the first eight ingredients in a bowl and add ¼ cup of this dressing to the apples. 3. Toss well and let them sit for 10 minutes. 4. Place the apples in the Ninja Foodi Smart XL Grill. 5. Cover the Ninja Foodi Smart XL Grill's Hood, select the Grill mode, set the temperature to LO and grill for 5 minutes per side. 6. Toss the rest of the salad ingredients together in a salad bowl. 7. Add grilled apples and serve.
Serving Suggestion: Serve the Apple Salad with lemon wedges.
Variation Tip: Add breadcrumbs to the salad for a crispy texture.
Nutritional Information per Serving: Calories 93 | Fat 3g | Sodium 510mg | Carbs 12g | Fiber 3g | Sugar 4g | Protein 4g

Sweet Grilled Pickles

Prep time: 15 minutes | Cook Time: 10 minutes | Serves: 4

Ingredients:

Brine:
1¼ cup distilled white vinegar
1¼ cup water
1 cup sugar
Pickles
5 large cucumbers, cut into 4 to 5-inch spears
1 white onion, sliced
6 sprigs dill

2 tbsp. Kosher salt
2 tsp. crushed red pepper

3 tsp. minced garlic
3 sanitized canning jars with lids

Directions:

1. Place the cooking pot in the Ninja Foodi Smart XL Grill then set a grill grate inside. 2. Select the "Grill" Mode, set the temperature to MED. 3. Use the arrow keys to set the cooking time to 6 minutes. 4. Press the START/STOP button to initiate preheating. 5. Once preheated, place the cucumber in the Ninja Foodi Smart XL Grill. 6. Cover the hood and allow the grill to cook. 7. Flip the cucumber once cooked halfway through. 8. Mix the brine ingredients in a saucepan and divide into 2 canning jars. 9. Add 1 tsp. garlic and 2 dill sprigs to each jar. 10. Repeat the same steps with the onion. 11. Add cucumbers to one jar and onions to the other. 12. Close the lids and refrigerate them overnight. 13. Serve.
Serving Suggestion: Serve the grilled pickles with zucchini noodles.
Variation Tip: Add green beans to the pickles before serving.
Nutritional Information per Serving: Calories 318 | Fat 15.7g |Sodium 124mg | Carbs 27g | Fiber 0.1g | Sugar 0.3g | Protein 4.9g

Grilled Veggies with Vinaigrette

Prep time: 15 minutes | Cook Time: 16 minutes | Serves: 4

Ingredients:

Vinaigrette:
¼ cup red wine vinegar
1 tablespoon Dijon mustard
1 tablespoon honey
½ teaspoon salt
Vegetables:
2 large sweet onions, diced
2 medium zucchinis, diced
2 yellow summer squash, diced

⅛ teaspoon black pepper
¼ cup canola oil
¼ cup olive oil

2 red peppers, seeded and cut in half
1 bunch green onions, trimmed
Cooking spray

Directions:

1. Place the cooking pot in the Ninja Foodi Smart XL Grill then place the grill grate in the pot. 2. Start by whisking the first five ingredients in a small bowl. 3. Gradually add oil while mixing the vinaigrette thoroughly. 4. Place the onion quarters in the Ninja Foodi Smart XL Grill. 5. Cover the Ninja Foodi Smart XL Grill's Hood, select the Grill mode, set the temperature to LO and grill for 5 minutes per side. 6. Grill squash, peppers and zucchini for 7 minutes per side in the same grill. 7. Finally, grill the green onions for 1 minute per side. 8. Dice the grilled veggies and mix with vinaigrette. 9. Serve.
Serving Suggestion: Serve the vegetables with boiled rice or pasta.
Variation Tip: Top the veggies with Feta cheese before serving.
Nutritional Information per Serving: Calories 341 | Fat 24g | Sodium 547mg | Carbs 36.4g | Fiber 1.2g | Sugar 1g | Protein 10.3g

Grilled Greens and Cheese on Toast

Prep time: 15 minutes | Cook Time: 36 minutes | Serves: 4

Ingredients:

2 tablespoons olive oil
1 bunch, kale, stems removed
½ teaspoons Kosher salt
½ teaspoons black pepper
6 ounces cherry tomatoes

½ pound Halloumi cheese, sliced
1 lemon, halved crosswise
4 thick slices of country-style bread
1 large garlic clove, peeled, halved

Directions:

1. Place the cooking pot in the Ninja Foodi Smart XL Grill then place the grill grate in the pot. 2. Toss kale with olive oil, salt, black pepper, tomatoes, lemon juice and garlic. 3. Place the tomatoes and kale in the Ninja Foodi Smart XL Grill. 4. Cover the Ninja Foodi Smart XL Grill's Hood, select the Grill mode, set the temperature to LO and grill the tomatoes for 5 minutes per side. 5. Grill the kale leaves for 2 to 3 minutes per side. 6. Transfer the veggies to a bowl. 7. Grill the bread slices for 4 to 5 minutes per side. 8. Grill the cheese slices for 3 to 5 minutes per side. 9. Divide the veggies and cheese on top of the bread slices. 10. Serve warm.

Serving Suggestion: Serve the bread slices with roasted mushrooms.
Variation Tip: Add lemon zest and lemon juice on top for better taste.
Nutritional Information per Serving: Calories 324 | Fat 5g | Sodium 432mg | Carbs 13.1g | Fiber 0.3g | Sugar 1g | Protein 5.7g

Tomato Salsa

Prep time: 5-10 minutes | Cook Time: 10 minutes|Servings: 4

Ingredients

1 red onion, peeled, cut in quarters
1 jalapeño pepper, cut in half, seeds removed
5 Roma tomatoes, cut in half lengthwise
1 tablespoon kosher salt
2 tsp ground black pepper

2 tbsps. canola oil
1 bunch cilantro, stems trimmed
Juice and zest of 3 limes
3 cloves garlic, peeled
2 tbsps. ground cumin

Directions:

1. In a blending bowl, join the onion, tomatoes, jalapeño pepper, salt, dark pepper, and canola oil. 2. Take Ninja Foodi Smart XL Grill, place it over your kitchen stage, and open the top. Place the Grill Grate and close the top cover. 3. Select the "Grill" function and temperature setting to the "MAX" for 10 minutes. Ninja Foodi Smart XL Grill is preheated and prepared to cook when it begins to beep. After you hear a signal, open the top cover. 4. Arrange the vegetables over the Grill Grate. 5. Close the top lid and cook for 5 minutes. Now open the top lid, flip the vegetables. 6. Close the top lid and cook for 5 more minutes. 7. Blend the mixture in a blender and serve as needed.

Serving Suggestion: Serve with dill garnishing or enjoy as it is.
Variation Tip: use chopped dill for garnish.
Nutritional Information per Serving: Calories: 169| Fat: 9g|Carbohydrates: 12g| Fiber: 3g| Sodium: 321mg| Protein: 2.5g

Ninja Foodi Tofu with Orange Sauce

Prep time: 20 minutes | Cook Time: 20 minutes | Serves: 8

Ingredients:

2 pounds extra-firm tofu, pressed and cubed
2 tablespoons tamari
¾ cup fresh orange juice
2 teaspoons orange zest, grated
2 teaspoons fresh ginger, minced

½ teaspoon red pepper flakes
4 tablespoons cornstarch
1 cup water
2 tablespoons honey
2 teaspoons garlic, minced

Directions:

1. Add two tablespoons cornstarch, tofu and tamari in a bowl. Mix well and set aside for 15 minutes. 2. Arrange the "Crisper Basket" in a Ninja Foodi Smart XL Grill. Press the "Air Crisp" button. Set the temperature to 390°F/200°C and adjust the time to 10 minutes. 3. Press START/STOP to begin preheating. 4. Place tofu mixture in the "Crisper Basket" when it shows "Add Food" and cook for 10 minutes. Take out and set aside. 5. Meanwhile, add water, orange juice, honey, orange zest, garlic, ginger, remaining cornstarch and red pepper flakes in a pan and cook for 10 minutes. Stir continuously. 6. Pour the sauce on tofu mixture and serve.

Serving Suggestions: Serve with sesame seeds on the top.
Variation Tip: You can omit red pepper flakes.
Nutritional Information per Serving: Calories: 151 |Fat: 6.7g|Sat Fat: 0.6g|Carbohydrates: 13.7g|Fiber: 0.7g|Sugar: 7g|Protein: 12g

Ninja Foodi Mushroom Steak

Prep time: 10 minutes | Cook Time: 10 minutes | Serves: 8

Ingredients:

2 pounds beef sirloin steak, cubed
2 cups sliced mushrooms
2 teaspoons parsley flakes
2 teaspoons chili flakes, crushed

½ cup Worcestershire sauce
2 tablespoons olive oil
2 teaspoons paprika

Directions:

1. Add steak, olive oil, paprika, mushrooms, chili flakes and Worcestershire sauce in a large bowl. Toss to coat properly. 2. Cover with foil and refrigerate for about 3 hours. 3. Meanwhile, press the "Air Crisp" button in a Ninja Foodi Smart XL Grill and set the temperature to 400°F/200°C. Adjust the time to 10 minutes. 4. Press START/STOP to begin preheating. 5. When it shows "Add Food", place the mixture and cook for 10 minutes. 6. Dish out and serve hot.

Serving Suggestions: Serve with chopped mint leaves on the top.
Variation Tip: Canola oil can also be used.
Nutritional Information per Serving: Calories: 261 |Fat: 10.7g|Sat Fat: 3.2g|Carbohydrates: 3.9g|Fiber: 0.4g|Sugar: 3.4g|Protein: 35.1g

Grilled Potato Rounds

Prep time: 15 minutes | Cook Time: 14 minutes | Serves: 4

Ingredients:

4 large potatoes, baked and cooled
¼ cup butter, melted
¼ teaspoon salt
¼ teaspoon black pepper

1 cup sour cream
1½ cups Cheddar cheese, shredded
8 bacon strips, cooked and crumbled
3 tablespoons chives, minced

Directions:

1. Place the cooking pot in the Ninja Foodi Smart XL Grill then place the grill grate in the pot. 2. First, cut the potatoes into 1-inch thick rounds. 3. Rub them with butter, salt and black pepper. 4. Place the potatoes slices in the Ninja Foodi Smart XL Grill. 5. Cover the Ninja Foodi Smart XL Grill's Hood, select the Grill mode, set the temperature to LO and grill for 7 minutes per side. 6. Serve warm with bacon, chives, cheese and sour cream on top. 7. Enjoy.

Serving Suggestion: Serve the potatoes with tomato sauce.
Variation Tip: Add green beans around the potatoes before serving.
Nutritional Information per Serving: Calories 318 | Fat 15.7g | Sodium 124mg | Carbs 27g | Fiber 0.1g | Sugar 0.3g | Protein 4.9g

Grilled Cauliflower with Miso Mayo

Prep time: 15 minutes | Cook Time: 20 minutes | Serves: 6

Ingredients:

1 head of cauliflower, cut into florets
½ teaspoons Kosher salt
4 tablespoons unsalted butter
¼ cup hot sauce
1 tablespoon ketchup
1 tablespoon soy sauce

½ cup mayonnaise
2 tablespoons white miso
1 tablespoon fresh lemon juice
½ teaspoons black pepper
2 scallions, sliced

Directions:

1. Mix salt, butter, hot sauce, ketchup, soy sauce, miso, mayonnaise, lemon juice and black pepper in a bowl. 2. Season the cauliflower florets with the marinade and mix well. 3. Place the florets in the Ninja Foodi Smart XL Grill. 4. Cover the Ninja Foodi Smart XL Grill's Hood, set the temperature to 350°F/175°C and bake the florets on the Bake mode for 5 to 10 minutes per side. 5. Serve warm.

Serving Suggestion: Serve the cauliflower steaks with tomato sauce or guacamole.
Variation Tip: Add cheese on top of the grilled cauliflower.
Nutritional Information per Serving: Calories 391 | Fat 2.2g | Sodium 276mg | Carbs 27.7g | Fiber 0.9g | Sugar 1.4g | Protein 8.8g

Baked Apple and Sweet Potatoes

Prep time: 5 minutes | Cook Time: 30 minutes | Serves: 2

Ingredients:

2 sweet potatoes, diced
2 apples, diced

1 tablespoon olive oil
2 tablespoons honey

Directions:

1. Place the cooking pot in the Ninja Foodi Smart XL Grill. 2. In a bowl, add sweet potatoes, oil and apples and toss well. 3. Pour sweet potato and apple mixture into the baking dish. 4. Select the Bake Mode and set the temperature to 400°F/200°C. 5. Use the Arrow keys to set the time to 30 minutes. 6. Press the START/STOP button to initiate preheating. 7. Once preheated, place the baking dish in the Ninja Foodi Smart XL Grill. 8. Cover the hood and allow the grill to cook. 9. Once preheated, place the baking dish in the Ninja Foodi Smart XL Grill. 10. Serve, when done.

Serving Suggestion: Drizzle with honey and serve.
Variation Tip: Add ¼ teaspoon of ground cinnamon.
Nutritional Information per Serving: Calories 240 | Fat 7.4g |Sodium 3mg | Carbs 48.1g | Fiber 5.4g | Sugar 40.5g | Protein 0.7g

Jalapeño Poppers with Smoked Gouda

Prep time: 15 minutes | Cook Time: 10 minutes | Serves: 6

Ingredients:

12 large Jalapeño chilies
4 ounces cream cheese
1 cup smoked Gouda, shredded

Salt, to taste
Chopped fresh cilantro for serving

Directions:

1. Cut the Jalapenos chilies in half and remove the seeds. 2. Mix cream cheese, gouda and salt in a bowl. 3. Stuff this cheese mixture in the chilies. 4. Place the chilies in the Ninja Foodi Smart XL Grill. 5. Cover the Ninja Foodi Smart XL Grill's Hood, set the temperature to 350°F/175°C and cook them on the Bake mode for 5 minutes. 6. Garnish with cilantro and serve warm.

Serving Suggestion: Serve the peppers with crispy bacon.
Variation Tip: Add shredded chicken to the filling.
Nutritional Information per Serving: Calories 136 | Fat 10g | Sodium 249mg | Carbs 8g | Fiber 2g | Sugar 3g | Protein 4g

Mustard Green Veggie Meal

Prep time: 10 minutes | Cook Time: 30-40 minutes|Servings: 4

Ingredients

Vinaigrette
2 tbsps. Dijon mustard
1 tsp salt
¼ tsp black pepper
½ cup avocado oil
½ olive oil
½ cup red wine vinegar
2 tbsps. honey

Veggies
4 sweet onions, quartered
4 yellow squash, cut in half
4 red peppers, seeded and halved
4 zucchinis, halved
2 bunches green onions, trimmed

Directions:

1. Take a small bowl and whisk mustard, pepper, honey, vinegar, and salt. 2. Add oil to make a smooth mixture. 3. Place Pre-heat Ninja Foodi Smart XL Grill by selecting the "GRILL" function and temperature setting to "MED". 4. Let it pre-heat until you hear a beep. 5. Arrange the onion quarters over the grill grate, lock lid and cook for 5 minutes. 6. Flip the peppers and cook for 5 minutes more. 7. Grill the other vegetables in the same manner with 7 minutes each side for zucchini, pepper, and squash and 1 minute for onion. 8. Prepare the vinaigrette by mixing all the Ingredients under vinaigrette in a bowl.

Serving Suggestion: Serve the grilled veggies with vinaigrette on top.
Variation Tip: use your favorite veggies for fun.
Nutritional Information per Serving: Calories: 326| Fat: 4.5 g| Carbohydrates: 35 g| Fiber: 4 g| Sodium: 543 mg| Protein: 8 g

Grilled Watermelon, Feta, and Tomato Salad

Prep time: 15 minutes | Cook Time: 10 minutes | Serves: 8

Ingredients:

1 tablespoon olive oil

1 (4 pounds) watermelon, cut into slices

1 teaspoon salt

4 heirloom tomatoes, sliced

½ teaspoon black pepper

6 ounces Feta, sliced

Directions:

1. Place the cooking pot in the Ninja Foodi Smart XL Grill then place the grill grate in the pot. 2. Season the tomatoes and watermelon with olive oil, salt and black pepper. 3. Place the watermelons in the Ninja Foodi Smart XL Grill. 4. Cover the Ninja Foodi Smart XL Grill's Hood, select the Grill mode, set the temperature to MED and grill for 2 minutes per side. 5. Transfer the watermelons to a plate and grill the tomatoes for 3 minutes per side. 6. Transfer the tomatoes to the watermelon plate. 7. Add Feta cheese on top. 8. Serve.

Serving Suggestion: Serve the salad with fresh herbs on top.

Variation Tip: Add canned corn to the salad.

Nutritional Information per Serving: Calories 351 | Fat 19g | Sodium 412mg | Carbs 43g | Fiber 0.3g | Sugar 1g | Protein 23g

Balsamic Vegetables

Prep time: 10 minutes | Cook Time: 30 minutes | Serves: 3

Ingredients:

1 cup sweet potato, cut into chunks

1 cup broccoli, cut into chunks

1 cup beet, cut into chunks

1 tablespoon Balsamic vinegar

1 cup mushrooms, sliced

1 tablespoon olive oil

1 tablespoon honey

Pepper

Salt

Directions:

1. Place the cooking pot in the Ninja Foodi Smart XL Grill. 2. In a bowl, toss vegetables with oil, pepper and salt. 3. Transfer vegetables into the baking dish. 4. Select the Bake Mode and set the temperature to 390°F/200°C. 5. Use the Arrow keys to set the time to 25 minutes. 6. Press the START/STOP button to initiate preheating. 7. Once preheated, place the baking dish in the Ninja Foodi Smart XL Grill. 8. Cover the hood and allow the grill to cook. 9. Once veggies are baked then mix honey and vinegar and drizzle over vegetables and bake for five minutes more. 10. Serve, when done.

Serving Suggestion: Allow to cool completely then serve.

Variation Tip: Add your choice of seasonings.

Nutritional Information per Serving: Calories 163 | Fat 5.1g | Sodium 130mg | Carbs 28.1g | Fiber 4.4g | Sugar 15.5g | Protein 3.9g

Parmesan Zucchini and Squash

Prep time: 10 minutes | Cook Time: 30 minutes | Serves: 6

Ingredients:

2 medium zucchinis, sliced

2 yellow squash, sliced

¾ cup Parmesan cheese, shredded

3 tomatoes, sliced

1 tablespoon olive oil

Pepper

Salt

Directions:

1. Place the cooking pot in the Ninja Foodi Smart XL Grill. 2. Arrange sliced tomatoes, squash and zucchinis alternately in the baking dish. 3. Sprinkle cheese on top of vegetables and drizzle with oil. Season with pepper and salt. 4. Select the Bake Mode and set the temperature to 350°F/175°C. 5. Use the Arrow keys to set the time to 30 minutes. 6. Press the START/STOP button to initiate preheating. 7. Once preheated, place the baking dish in the Ninja Foodi Smart XL Grill. 8. Cover the hood and allow the grill to cook. 9. Serve, when done.

Serving Suggestion: Allow to cool completely then serve.

Variation Tip: Add your choice of seasonings.

Nutritional Information per Serving: Calories 97 | Fat 6g | Sodium 263mg | Carbs 5g | Fiber 1.5g | Sugar 2.8g | Protein 6.4g

Crispy Cauliflower Florets

Prep time: 10 minutes | Cook Time: 10 minutes | Serves: 4

Ingredients:

1 small cauliflower head, cut into florets
2 tablespoons olive oil
1 tablespoon curry powder

Pepper
Salt

Directions:

1. Place the cooking pot in the Ninja Foodi Smart XL Grill then place the Crisper Basket in the pot. 2. In a bowl, toss cauliflower florets with oil, curry powder, pepper and salt. 3. Select the Air Crisp Mode and set the temperature to 350°F/175°C. 4. Use the Arrow keys to set the time to 10 minutes. 5. Press the START/STOP button to initiate preheating. 6. Once preheated, place the florets in the Ninja Foodi Smart XL Grill. 7. Cover the hood and allow the grill to cook. 8. Serve, when done.

Serving Suggestion: Allow to cool completely then serve.

Variation Tip: Add paprika for more spiciness.

Nutritional Information per Serving: Calories 82 | Fat 7.3g |Sodium 59mg | Carbs 4.5g | Fiber 2.2g | Sugar 1.6g | Protein 1.5g

Rosemary Potatoes

Prep time: 10 minutes | Cook Time: 15 minutes | Serves: 4

Ingredients:

4 cups of baby potatoes, cut into four pieces each
2 teaspoons dried rosemary, minced
1 tablespoon garlic, minced
3 tablespoons olive oil

¼ cup fresh parsley, chopped
1 tablespoon fresh lemon juice
Pepper
Salt

Directions:

1. Place the cooking pot in the Ninja Foodi Smart XL Grill then place the Crisper Basket in the pot. 2. In a bowl, toss potatoes with garlic, rosemary, oil, pepper and salt. 3. Select the Air Crisp Mode and set the temperature to 400°F/200°C. 4. Use the Arrow keys to set the time to 15 minutes. 5. Press the START/STOP button to initiate preheating. 6. Once preheated, place the baking dish in the Ninja Foodi Smart XL Grill. 7. Cover the hood and allow the grill to cook. 8. Transfer potatoes to a large bowl and toss with parsley and lemon juice. 9. Serve.

Serving Suggestion: Allow to cool completely then serve.

Variation Tip: You can use vegetable oil instead of olive oil.

Nutritional Information per Serving: Calories 201 | Fat 10.8g |Sodium 51mg | Carbs 25g | Fiber 4.1g | Sugar 1.9g | Protein 2.8g

Baked Parmesan Zucchini

Prep time: 10 minutes | Cook Time: 10 minutes | Serves: 4

Ingredients:

2 zucchinis, cut into ½-inch slices
2 tablespoons olive oil
⅓ cup Parmesan cheese, grated
¼ cup breadcrumbs

1 teaspoon Italian seasoning
Pepper
Salt

Directions:

1. Place the cooking pot in the Ninja Foodi Smart XL Grill. 2. In a bowl, toss zucchini with remaining ingredients until well coated. 3. Add zucchini slices into the baking dish. 4. Select the Bake Mode and set the temperature to 400°F/200°C. 5. Use the Arrow keys to set the time to 5 minutes. 6. Press the START/STOP button to initiate preheating. 7. Once preheated, place the baking dish in the Ninja Foodi Smart XL Grill. 8. Cover the hood and allow the grill to cook. 9. Serve, when done.

Serving Suggestion: Allow to cool completely then serve.

Variation Tip: Add ¼ teaspoon of crushed red pepper flakes.

Nutritional Information per Serving: Calories 156 | Fat 10.9g |Sodium 298mg | Carbs 8.3g | Fiber 1.4g | Sugar 2.2g | Protein 6.1g

Baked Zucchini and Eggplant

Prep time: 10 minutes | Cook Time: 35 minutes | Serves: 6

Ingredients:

3 medium zucchini, sliced

1 medium eggplant, sliced

1 tablespoon olive oil

1 tablespoon garlic, minced

1 cup cherry tomatoes, halved

3 ounces of Parmesan cheese, grated

4 tablespoons parsley, chopped

4 tablespoons basil, chopped

Pepper

Salt

Directions:

1. Place the cooking pot in the Ninja Foodi Smart XL Grill. 2. In a bowl, mix cherry tomatoes, eggplant, zucchini, oil, garlic, cheese, basil, pepper and salt. 3. Pour veggie mixture into the baking dish. 4. Select the Bake Mode and set the temperature to 350°F/175°C. 5. Use the Arrow keys to set the time to 35 minutes. 6. Press the START/STOP button to initiate preheating. 7. Once preheated, place the baking dish in the Ninja Foodi Smart XL Grill. 8. Cover the hood and allow the grill to cook. 9. Serve, when done.

Serving Suggestion: Garnish with parsley and serve.

Variation Tip: You can use vegetable oil instead of olive oil.

Nutritional Information per Serving: Calories 109 | Fat 5.8g |Sodium 173mg | Carbs 10.1g | Fiber 4.3g | Sugar 4.8g | Protein 7g

Baked Mushrooms

Prep time: 10 minutes | Cook Time: 15 minutes | Serves: 4

Ingredients:

1½ pound mushrooms, sliced

¼ cup Parmesan cheese, grated

¼ cup fresh lemon juice

3 tablespoons olive oil

1½ teaspoon dried thyme

1 tablespoon garlic, minced

1 lemon zest

Pepper

Salt

Directions:

1. Place the cooking pot in the Ninja Foodi Smart XL Grill. 2. Add mushrooms and remaining ingredients into the bowl and toss well. 3. Transfer mushroom mixture into the baking dish. 4. Select the Bake Mode and set the temperature to 375°F/190°C. 5. Use the Arrow keys to set the time to 15 minutes. 6. Press the START/STOP button to initiate preheating. 7. Once preheated, place the baking dish in the Ninja Foodi Smart XL Grill. 8. Cover the hood and allow the grill to cook. 9. Serve, when done.

Serving Suggestion: Allow to cool completely then serve.

Variation Tip: Add your choice of seasonings.

Nutritional Information per Serving: Calories 284 | Fat 20.2g |Sodium 652mg | Carbs 6.9g | Fiber 2g | Sugar 3.3g | Protein 17.6g

Cheesy Cauliflower Casserole

Prep time: 10 minutes | Cook Time: 15 minutes | Serves: 6

Ingredients:

1 cauliflower head, cut into florets &boil

2 ounces of cream cheese

1 cup heavy cream

2 cups Cheddar cheese, shredded

2 teaspoon Dijon mustard

1 teaspoon garlic powder

Pepper

Salt

Directions:

1. Place the cooking pot in the Ninja Foodi Smart XL Grill. 2. Add all ingredients into the bowl and mix until well combined. 3. Pour cauliflower mixture into the baking dish. 4. Select the Bake Mode and set the temperature to 375°F/190°C. 5. Use the Arrow keys to set the time to 15 minutes. 6. Press the START/STOP button to initiate preheating. 7. Once preheated, place the baking dish in the Ninja Foodi Smart XL Grill. 8. Cover the hood and allow the grill to cook. 9. Serve, when done.

Serving Suggestion: Serve warm and enjoy.

Variation Tip: None

Nutritional Information per Serving: Calories 268 | Fat 23.3g |Sodium 329mg | Carbs 4.1g | Fiber 1.2g | Sugar 1.4g | Protein 11.5g

Zucchini Carrot Patties

Prep time: 10 minutes | Cook Time: 15 minutes | Serves: 2

Ingredients:

1 egg
1 zucchini, grated & squeezed
1 carrot, grated & squeezed
¼ cup Parmesan cheese, grated

¼ cup breadcrumbs
Pepper
Salt

Directions:

1. Place the cooking pot in the Ninja Foodi Smart XL Grill then place the Crisper Basket in the pot. 2. Add all ingredients into the bowl and mix until well combined. 3. Make patties from the mixture. 4. Select the Air Crisp Mode, set the temperature to 350°F/175°C. 5. Usc the Arrow keys to set the time to 15 minutes. 6. Press the START/STOP button to initiate preheating. 7. Once preheated, place the patties in the Ninja Foodi Smart XL Grill. 8. Cover the hood and allow the grill to cook. 9. Flip the patties once cooked halfway through. 10. Serve, when done.

Serving Suggestion: Serve warm.

Variation Tip: Add your choice of seasonings.

Nutritional Information per Serving: Calories 188 | Fat 7.6g |Sodium 538mg | Carbs 16.2g | Fiber 2.5g | Sugar 4.2g | Protein 12g

Garlic Flavored Artichoke Meal

Prep time: 10 minutes | Cook Time: 10 minutes | Servings: 4

Ingredients

2 large artichokes, trimmed and halved
3 garlic cloves, chopped
½ a lemon, juiced

½ cup canola oil
Salt and pepper to taste

Directions:

1. Select the "GRILL" function and set your Ninja Foodi Smart XL Grill to "MAX" temperature for 10 minutes. 2. Let it pre-heat until you hear a beep. 3. Add lemon juice, oil, garlic into a medium-sized bowl. 4. Season with salt and pepper. 5. Brush artichoke halves with lemon garlic mix. 6. Once ready, transfer artichokes to Grill. 7. Press them down to maximize grill mark. 8. Grill for 8-10 minutes; make sure to blister on all sides.

Serving Suggestion: Serve with dill garnishing or enjoy as it is.

Variation Tip: use chopped dill for garnish.

Nutritional Information per Serving: Calories: 285| Fat: 28 g| Fat: 8 g Carbohydrates: 10 g| Fiber: 3 g| Sodium: 137 mg| Protein: 3 g

Ninja Foodi Crispy Chicken with Potatoes

Prep time: 10 minutes | Cook Time: 15 minutes | Serves: 8

Ingredients:

2 teaspoons olive oil
1½ cups shredded cheddar cheese
½ teaspoon paprika
2 pounds potatoes, drained and sliced

2 pounds chicken breasts, cubed
8 bacon slices, cooked and cut into strips
Salt and black pepper, to taste

Directions:

1. Add chicken, olive oil, salt, pepper and potato slices in a large bowl. Toss to coat well. 2. Meanwhile, press the "Broil" button in a Ninja Foodi Smart XL Grill and set the time to 20 minutes at 350°F/175°C. 3. Press START/STOP to begin preheating. 4. When it shows "Add Food", place the potato mixture and top it with bacon and cheese. 5. Flip halfway through and dish out. 6. Top with paprika and serve.

Serving Suggestions: Top with chopped mint leaves before serving.

Variation Tip: You can also mozzarella cheese to enhance taste.

Nutritional Information per Serving: Calories: 720 |Fat: 43.4g|Sat Fat: 21.5g|Carbohydrates: 19.2g|Fiber: 2.8g|Sugar: 1.7g|Protein: 61.1g

Cajun Green Beans

Prep time: 15 minutes | Cook Time: 11 minutes | Serves: 4

Ingredients:

1 pound fresh green beans, trimmed

½ teaspoon Cajun seasoning

1 tablespoon butter

Directions:

1. Add green beans to an 18-inch square sheet. 2. Drizzle Cajun seasoning and butter on top. 3. Cover and seal the foil over the green beans. 4. Place the green bean pockets in the Ninja Foodi Smart XL Grill. 5. Cover the Ninja Foodi Smart XL Grill's Hood, set the temperature to 350°F/175°C and cook on the Bake mode for 11 minutes. 6. Serve warm

Serving Suggestion: Serve the green beans with crispy nachos and mashed potatoes.

Variation Tip: Add crispy dried onion for better taste.

Nutritional Information per Serving: Calories 304 | Fat 31g | Sodium 834mg | Carbs 21.4g | Fiber 0.2g | Sugar 0.3g | Protein 4.6g

Hearty Spinach Olive

Prep time: 5-10 minutes | Cook Time: 15 minutes|Servings: 3

Ingredients

2 pounds spinach, chopped and boiled

1 and ½ cups feta cheese, grated

4 tbsps. butter

⅔ cup olives, halved and pitted

4 tsp lemon zest, grated

Pepper and salt to taste

Directions:

1. Add spinach, butter, salt, pepper into a mixing bowl, Mix them well. 2. Pre-heat your Ninja Foodi Smart XL Grill by selecting the "AIR CRISP" function and temperature setting to 340°F/170°C for 15 minutes. 3. Allow it to pre-heat until it beeps. 4. Arrange a cooking pot in the Ninja Foodi Smart XL Grill. 5. Arrange spinach mixture in a cooking pot and place pot in the appliance. 6. Let them crisp for 15 minutes. 7. Serve and enjoy!

Serving Suggestion: Serve with chilled drink.

Variation Tip: add honey for extra fun.

Nutritional Information per Serving: Calories: 250| Fat: 18 g| Carbohydrates: 8 g| Fiber: 4 g| Sodium: 339 mg| Protein: 10 g

Buttery Spinach Meal

Prep time: 10 minutes | Cook Time: 15 minutes|Servings: 4

Ingredients

⅔ cup olives, halved and pitted

1 and ½ cups feta cheese, grated

4 tbsps. butter

2 pounds spinach, chopped and boiled

Pepper and salt to taste

4 tsp lemon zest, grated

Directions:

1. Take a mixing bowl and add spinach, butter, salt, pepper and mix well. 2. Pre-heat Ninja Foodi Smart XL Grill by selecting the "AIR CRISP" function and temperature setting to "340°F/170°C" and timer to 15 minutes. 3. Let it pre-heat until you hear a beep. 4. Place the spinach mixture in a basket. 5. Let them cook until the timer runs out. 6. Serve and enjoy!

Serving Suggestion: Serve with your favorite dipping.

Variation Tip: use chopped cilantro for garnish.

Nutritional Information per Serving: Calories: 250|Fat: 18 g| Carbohydrates: 8 g| Fiber: 3 g| Sodium: 309 mg| Protein: 10 g

Italian Squash Meal

Prep time: 5-10 minutes | Cook Time: 16 minutes|Servings: 4

Ingredients

1 medium butternut squash, peeled, seeded and cut into ½ inch slices

1 and ½ tsp oregano, dried

1 tsp. dried thyme

1 tablespoon olive oil

½ tsp. salt

¼ tsp. black pepper

Directions:

1. Add slices alongside other Ingredients into a mixing bowl. 2. Mix them well. 3. Pre-heat your Ninja Foodi Smart XL Grill by selecting the "GRILL" function and temperature setting it to "MED" for 16 minutes. 4. Allow it to pre-heat until it beeps. 5. Arrange squash slices over the grill grate. 6. Cook for 8 minutes. 7. Flip and cook for 8 minutes more. 8. Serve and enjoy!

Serving Suggestion: Serve warm and enjoy.

Variation Tip: use chopped dill for garnish.

Nutritional Information per Serving: Calories: 238| Fat: 12 g| Carbohydrates: 36 g| Fiber: 3 g| Sodium: 128 mg| Protein: 15 g

Cheddar Cauliflower Meal

Prep time: 5-10 minutes | Cook Time: 15 minutes | Servings: 2

Ingredients

½ tsp garlic powder
½ tsp paprika
Ocean salt and ground dark pepper to taste
1 head cauliflower, stemmed and leaves removed
1 cup Cheddar cheese, shredded

Ranch dressing, for garnish
¼ cup canola oil or vegetable oil
2 tbsps. chopped chives
4 slices bacon, cooked and crumbled

Directions:

1. Cut the cauliflower into 2-inch pieces. 2. In a blending bowl, include the oil, garlic powder, and paprika. Season with salt and ground dark pepper; join well. Coat the florets with the blend. 3. Take Ninja Foodi Smart XL Grill, place it over your kitchen stage, and open the top cover. 4. Select GRILL function, set the temperature to MAX heat and timer to 15 minutes. Press START/STOP to begin preheating. 5. Ninja Foodi Smart XL Grill is preheated and prepared to cook when it begins to signal. After you hear a beep, open the top. 6. Organize the pieces over the Grill Grate. 7. Close the top lid and cook for 10 minutes. Now open the top lid, flip the pieces and top with the cheese. 8. Close the top lid and cook for 5 more minutes.

Serving Suggestion: Serve warm with the chives and ranch dressing on top.
Variation Tip: use chili flakes for spice.
Nutritional Information per Serving: Calories: 534| Fat: 34g |Carbohydrates: 14.5g| Fiber: 4g| Sodium: 1359mg| Protein: 31g

Delicious Broccoli and Arugula

Prep time: 10 minutes | Cook Time: 12 minutes | Servings: 4

Ingredients

Pepper as needed
½ tsp salt
Red pepper flakes
2 tbsps. extra virgin olive oil
1 tablespoon canola oil
½ red onion, sliced
1 garlic clove, minced

1 tsp Dijon mustard
1 tsp honey
1 tablespoon lemon juice
2 tbsps. parmesan cheese, grated
4 cups arugula, torn
2 heads broccoli, trimmed

Directions:

1. Pre-heat your Ninja Foodi Smart XL Grill by selecting the "Grill" function and temperature setting to "MAX" and set the timer to 12 minutes. 2. Take a large-sized bowl and add broccoli, sliced onion, and canola oil, toss the mixture well until coated. 3. Once you hear the beep, it is pre-heated. 4. Arrange your vegetables over the grill grate; let them grill for 8-12 minutes. 5. Take a medium-sized bowl and whisk in lemon juice, olive oil, mustard, honey, garlic, red pepper flakes, pepper, and salt. 6. Once done, add the prepared veggies and arugula in a bowl. 7. Drizzle the prepared vinaigrette on top, sprinkle a bit of parmesan. 8. Stir and mix. 9. Enjoy!

Serving Suggestion: Serve warm with favorite drink.
Variation Tip: use cheese for taste.
Nutritional Information per Serving: Calories: 168| Fat: 12 g| Carbohydrates: 13 g| Fiber: 1 g| Sodium: 392 mg| Protein: 6 g

Honey Dressed Asparagus

Prep time: 5-10 minutes | Cook Time: 15 minutes | Servings: 4

Ingredients

2pounds asparagus, trimmed
4 tbsps. tarragon, minced
¼ cup honey

2 tbsps. olive oil
1 tsp salt
½ tsp pepper

Directions:

1. Add asparagus, oil, salt, honey, pepper, tarragon into your bowl, Toss them well. 2. Pre-heat your Ninja Foodi Smart XL Grill by selecting the "GRILL" function and temperature setting to "MED" for 8 minutes. 3. Allow it pre-heat until it makes a beep sound. 4. Arrange asparagus over grill grate and lock lid. 5. Cook for 4 minutes. 6. Then flip asparagus and cook for 4 minutes more. 7. Serve and enjoy!

Serving Suggestion: Serve warm and enjoy.
Variation Tip: use chili flakes for extra spice.
Nutritional Information per Serving: Calories: 240| Fat: 15 g| Carbohydrates: 31 g| Fiber: 1 g| Sodium: 103 mg| Protein: 7 g

Ninja Foodi Cheesy Spinach

Prep time: 20 minutes | Cook Time: 15 minutes | Serves: 8

Ingredients:

2 pounds fresh spinach, chopped
2 teaspoons fresh lemon zest, grated
2 cups feta cheese, crumbled

½ cup melted butter
Salt and black pepper, to taste

Directions:

1. Add butter, spinach, salt and pepper in a large bowl. Mix well. 2. Meanwhile, arrange a "Crisper Basket" in the Ninja Foodi Smart XL Grill cooking pot and select "Air Crisp". 3. Set the temperature to 340°F/170°C and adjust the time to 15 minutes. 4. Press START/STOP to begin preheating. 5. When Ninja Foodi Smart XL Grill shows "Add Food", place the spinach mixture in "Crisper Basket" and cook for 15 minutes. 6. Take out the mixture in a bowl and stir in cheese and lemon zest. 7. Serve and enjoy!

Serving Suggestions: Top with chopped mint leaves before serving.

Variation Tip: Replace feta cheese with mozzarella cheese.

Nutritional Information per Serving: Calories: 227 |Fat: 19.9g|Sat Fat: 13g|Carbohydrates: 5.8g|Fiber: 2.5g|Sugar: 2.1g|Protein: 8.7g

Air Grilled Brussels

Prep time: 5-10 minutes | Cook Time: 12 minutes|Servings: 4

Ingredients

6 slices bacon, chopped
1 pound Brussel sprouts, halved
2 tbsps. olive oil, extra virgin

1 tsp salt
½ tsp black pepper, ground

Directions:

1. Add Brussels, olive oil, salt, pepper, and bacon into a mixing bowl. 2. Pre-heat Ninja Foodi Smart XL Grill by selecting the "AIR CRISP" function and temperature setting it to "390°F/200°C" for 12 minutes. 3. Allow it to pre-heat until it beeps. 4. Arrange Brussels over the Crisper Basket and lock lid. 5. Cook for 6 minutes. 6. Shake it and cook for 6 minutes more. 7. Serve and enjoy!

Serving Suggestion: Serve with chilled drink.

Variation Tip: use chopped dill for garnish.

Nutritional Information per Serving: Calories: 279| Fat: 18 g| Carbohydrates: 12 g| Fiber: 4 g| Sodium: 874 mg| Protein: 1 g

Ninja Foodi Stuffed Tomatoes

Prep time: 20 minutes | Cook Time: 15 minutes | Serves: 4

Ingredients:

4 tomatoes
1 cup shredded cheddar cheese
1 teaspoon dried thyme

1 cup chopped broccoli
2 tablespoons unsalted butter, melted

Directions:

1. Cut tomato from the top and scoop out the pulp. 2. Now, add broccoli and cheese in a bowl. Mix well. 3. Stuff tomatoes with the broccoli mixture and set aside. 4. Meanwhile, arrange the "Crisper Basket" in a Ninja Foodi Smart XL Grill and press the "Air Crisp" button. Set the temperature to 355°F/180°C and set the time to 15 minutes. 5. Press START/STOP to begin preheating. 6. Place the tomatoes in the "Crisper Basket" when the Ninja Foodi Smart XL Grill shows "Add Food". 7. Drizzle with butter and cook for 15 minutes at 355°F/180°C. 8. Take out and top with dried thyme. 9. Serve and enjoy!

Serving Suggestions: Top with chopped cilantro before serving.

Variation Tip: Mozzarella cheese can also be used.

Nutritional Information per Serving: Calories: 195 |Fat: 15.5g|Sat Fat: 9.7g|Carbohydrates: 6.8g|Fiber: 2.2g|Sugar: 3.8g|Protein: 8.8g

Ninja Foodi Potato Gratin

Prep time: 20 minutes | Cook Time: 20 minutes | Serves: 8

Ingredients:

4 potatoes, thinly sliced
4 eggs
1 cup grated cheddar cheese

¾ cup cream
2 tablespoons plain flour

Directions:

1. Arrange a "Crisper Basket" in a Ninja Foodi Smart XL Grill. Press the "Air Crisp" button. Set the temperature to 355°F/180°C and adjust the time to 10 minutes. 2. Place potato slices in the "Crisper Basket" and cook for 10 minutes. 3. Meanwhile, add eggs, flour, and cream in a bowl. Mix properly. 4. Now, take out the potato slices and arrange them in 8 ramekins. 5. Top them with egg mixture and place the ramekins in "Crisper Basket". 6. Press the "Air Crisp" button and cook for 10 minutes at 390°F/200°C. 7. Take out and serve hot.

Serving Suggestions: Top with chili flakes before serving.
Variation Tip: Replace cheddar cheese with mozzarella cheese.
Nutritional Information per Serving: Calories: 183 |Fat: 8.3g|Sat Fat: 4.5g|Carbohydrates: 19.3g|Fiber: 2.6g|Sugar: 1.9g|Protein: 8.5g

Ninja Foodi Glazed Vegetables

Prep time: 20 minutes | Cook Time: 25 minutes | Serves: 8

Ingredients:

½ cup cherry tomatoes, sliced
4 green bell peppers, seeded and chopped
4 tablespoons honey
2 teaspoons dried herbs
4 large zucchinis, chopped

1½ cups olive oil, divided
2 teaspoons Dijon mustard
2 teaspoons garlic paste
Salt, to taste

Directions:

1. Line a baking dish with parchment paper, place vegetables on it and drizzle with half of the olive oil. 2. Arrange a "Crisper Basket" in a Ninja Foodi Smart XL Grill and press the "Air Crisp" button. 3. Set the temperature to 350°F/175°C and the time to 20 minutes. 4. Press START/STOP to begin preheating. 5. When it shows "Add Food", place the baking dish in a "Crisper Basket". 6. Meanwhile, add remaining oil, mustard, honey, garlic, herbs, salt and pepper in a bowl. Mix well. 7. Pour the honey mixture on vegetables and cook for 5 minutes at 395°F/200°C. 8. Take out and serve hot.

Serving Suggestions: Serve with black cumin seeds on the top.
Variation Tip: Honey can be replaced with maple syrup.
Nutritional Information per Serving: Calories: 1296 |Fat: 139.1g|Sat Fat: 19.9g|Carbohydrates: 19.4g|Fiber: 2.9g|Sugar: 14.7g|Protein: 2.8g

Ninja Foodi Broccoli Chicken

Prep time: 10 minutes | Cook Time: 20 minutes | Serves: 8

Ingredients:

2 tablespoons olive oil
1 pound broccoli, cut into bite-sized pieces
4 teaspoons hot sauce
1 onion, sliced
2 tablespoons fresh minced ginger
4 teaspoons rice vinegar

2 pounds boneless chicken breast, chopped
2 tablespoons low-sodium soy sauce
1 teaspoon garlic powder
2 teaspoons sesame seed oil
Salt and black pepper, to taste

Directions:

1. Press the "Grill" button in a Ninja Foodi Smart XL Grill and set the time to 20 minutes at MED. 2. Press START/STOP to begin preheating. 3. Meanwhile, add chicken, broccoli and onion in a large bowl. Mix well. 4. Add in all the other ingredients and toss to coat well. 5. When the Ninja Foodi Smart XL Grill shows "Add Food", place the broccoli mixture and grill for 20 minutes. 6. Dish out and serve hot.

Serving Suggestions: Squeeze lemon juice on the top before serving.
Variation Tip: Soy sauce can be omitted.
Nutritional Information per Serving: Calories: 289 |Fat: 13.3g|Sat Fat: 3g|Carbohydrates: 6.6g|Fiber: 2g|Sugar: 2g|Protein: 35g

Ninja Foodi Spicy Cauliflower

Prep time: 5 minutes | Cook Time: 20 minutes | Serves: 2

Ingredients:

¼ cup sliced onion
2½ garlic cloves, thinly sliced
½ tablespoon sriracha sauce
¼ teaspoon coconut sugar

½ cauliflower head, cut into florets
½ tablespoon rice vinegar
¾ tablespoon tamari

Directions:

1. In a Ninja Foodi Smart XL Grill, press the "Grill" button and set the time to 20 minutes. Adjust the temperature to MED heat. 2. Press START/STOP to begin preheating. 3. When it shows "Add Food", place the cauliflowers and cook for 10 minutes. 4. Add in onion and garlic slices and cook for 5 minutes. 5. Meanwhile, add soy sauce, sugar, rice vinegar, salt, pepper and sriracha sauce in a large bowl. Mix well. 6. Pour this mixture on cauliflowers and cook for 5 minutes. 7. Take out and serve with a smile.
Serving Suggestions: Top with chopped scallion before serving.
Variation Tip: You can also add red chili flakes to enhance taste.
Nutritional Information per Serving: Calories: 64 |Fat: 0.2g|Sat Fat: 0g|Carbohydrates: 12.8g|Fiber: 2.4g|Sugar: 2.5g|Protein: 3.3g

Ninja Foodi Seasoned Asparagus

Prep time: 5 minutes | Cook Time: 5 minutes | Serves: 4

Ingredients:

¼ teaspoon cayenne pepper
1 teaspoon dried onion powder
2 pounds asparagus

1 teaspoon olive oil
1 teaspoon dried garlic powder
Salt and black pepper, to taste

Directions:

1. Add asparagus, cayenne pepper, onion powder, olive oil, garlic powder, salt and pepper in a large bowl. Mix well. 2. Meanwhile, arrange the "Crisper Basket" in a Ninja Foodi Smart XL Grill. Press the "Grill" button in the unit and set the time to 5 minutes at MAX. 3. Press START/STOP to begin preheating. 4. Place asparagus in it and cook for about 5 minutes. 5. Dish out and serve hot.
Serving Suggestions: Serve with lemon wedges.
Variation Tip: Cayenne pepper can be omitted.
Nutritional Information per Serving: Calories: 60 |Fat: 1.5g|Sat Fat: 0.3g|Carbohydrates: 9.9g|Fiber: 4.9g|Sugar: 4.7g|Protein: 5.2g

Cool Rosemary Potatoes

Prep time: 10 minutes | Cook Time: 20 minutes|Servings: 4

Ingredients

2 pounds baby red potatoes, quartered
½ tsp. parsley, dried
¼ tsp. celery powder
2 tbsps. extra virgin olive oil
¼ cup onion flakes, dried

½ tsp. garlic powder
½ tsp. onion powder
½ tsp. salt
¼ tsp. freshly ground black pepper

Directions:

1. Add all listed Ingredients into a large bowl. 2. Toss well and coat them well. 3. Pre-heat your Ninja Foodi Smart XL Grill by selecting the "AIR CRISP" function and temperature setting to 390°F/200°C for 20 minutes. 4. Allow it to pre-heat until it beeps. 5. Once preheated, add potatoes to the cooking basket. 6. Close the lid and cook for 10 minutes. 7. Shake the basket and cook for 10 minutes more. 8. Check the crispness if it is done or not. 9. Cook for 5 minutes more if needed. 10. Serve and enjoy!
Serving Suggestion: Serve with chilled beer.
Variation Tip: use shredded cheese for extra flavor.
Nutritional Information per Serving: Calories: 232| Fat: 7 g| Carbohydrates: 39 g| Fiber: 6 g| Sodium: 249 mg| Protein: 4 g

Honey Carrot Dish

Prep time: 15 minutes | Cook Time: 10 minutes|Servings: 4

Ingredients

6 carrots, cut lengthwise

1 tablespoon rosemary, chopped

1 tablespoon honey

2 tablespoons. butter, melted

1 tablespoon parsley, chopped

1 teaspoon salt

Directions:

1. Take your Ninja Foodi Smart XL Grill, open the lid. 2. Arrange grill grate and close top. 3. Pre-heat Ninja Foodi Smart XL Grill by selecting the "GRILL" function and temperature setting it to "MAX" for 10 minutes. 4. Allow it pre-heat until it sounds a beep. 5. Arrange carrots over the grill grate. 6. Take the remaining Ingredients and spread them. 7. Drizzle honey, lock lid and cook for 5 minutes. 8. Then flip sausages and cook for 5 minutes more. 9. Once done, serve and enjoy!

Serving Suggestion: Serve with dill garnishing or enjoy as it is.

Variation Tip: use chopped dill for garnish.

Nutritional Information per Serving: Calories: 80|, Fat: 4 g| Carbohydrates: 10 g| Fiber: 3 g| Sodium: 186 mg| Protein: 0.5 g

Chapter 8 Dessert Recipes

S'mores Pizza

Prep time: 15 minutes | Cook Time: 17 minutes | Serves: 6

Ingredients:

1 pizza crust dough
⅓ cup nutella
3 graham crackers, broken into large pieces

1 tbsp. honey
8 marshmallows

Directions:

1. Spread the dough in a baking pan. 2. Place the cooking pot in the Ninja Foodi Smart XL Grill. 3. Select the Bake Mode and set the temperature to 350°F/175°C. 4. Use the Arrow keys to set the time to 12 minutes. 5. Press the Start/Stop button to initiate preheating. 6. Once preheated, place the pan in the Ninja Foodi Smart XL Grill. 7. Cover the hood and allow the grill to cook. 8. Add nutella and rest of the ingredients on top of the crust. 9. Cover the hood and bake for 5 minutes. 10. Serve.

Serving Suggestion: Serve the pizza with chocolate sauce on top.

Variation Tip: Add chopped nuts to the toppings.

Nutritional Information per Serving: Calories 248 | Fat 16g |Sodium 95mg | Carbs 24g | Fiber 0.3g | Sugar 10g | Protein 14.1g

Grilled Pineapple Pizza

Prep time: 15 minutes | Cook Time: 20 minutes | Serves: 6

Ingredients:

1 pizza dough crust
3 tbsp. light brown sugar
⅛ tsp. ground cinnamon
1 fresh pineapple
1 (8-oz.) package cream cheese, softened

3 tbsp. light brown sugar
⅛ tsp. ground cinnamon
Caramel topping
Toasted pecans
Fresh mint sprigs

Directions:

1. Flour the pizza crust evenly in a baking pan. 2. Place the cooking pot in the Ninja Foodi Smart XL Grill. 3. Select the "Grill" Mode, set the temperature to MED. 4. Use the arrow keys to set the cooking time to 10 minutes. 5. Press the START/STOP button to initiate preheating. 6. Once preheated, place the pineapple in the Ninja Foodi Smart XL Grill. 7. Cover the hood and allow the grill to cook. 8. Meanwhile, mix rest of the ingredients in a bowl and spread over the pizza crust then top with pineapple. 9. Cover the hood and cook on "Bake Mode" for 10 minutes. 10. Serve.

Serving Suggestion: Serve the pizza with chocolate syrup on top.

Variation Tip: Add crushed cashews to the pizza.

Nutritional Information per Serving: Calories 153 | Fat 1g |Sodium 8mg | Carbs 26g | Fiber 0.8g | Sugar 56g | Protein 1g

Fruit Kabobs

Prep time: 15 minutes | Cook Time: 7 minutes | Serves: 4

Ingredients:

1 tablespoon butter
½ cup apricot preserves
1 tablespoon water
⅛ teaspoon ground cinnamon
⅛ teaspoon ground nutmeg

3 nectarines, quartered
3 peaches, quartered
3 plums, quartered
1 loaf (10-¾ ounces) pound cake, cubed

Directions:

1. Place the cooking pot in the Ninja Foodi Smart XL Grill then place the grill grate in the pot. 2. Take the first five ingredients in a small saucepan and stir cook for 3 minutes on medium heat. 3. Alternately thread the pound cake and fruits on the skewers. 4. Brush these skewers with the apricot mixture. 5. Place the skewers in the Ninja Foodi Smart XL Grill. 6. Cover the Ninja Foodi Smart XL Grill's Hood, select the Grill mode, set the temperature to LO and grill for 2 minutes per side. 7. Cook the skewers in batches. 8. Serve.

Serving Suggestion: Serve the fruits with cream cheese dip.

Variation Tip: Soak the cake cubes in orange juice before grilling.

Nutritional Information per Serving: Calories 159 | Fat 3g | Sodium 277mg | Carbs 21g | Fiber 1g | Sugar 9g | Protein 2g

Pumpkin Muffins

Prep time: 10 minutes | Cook Time: 35 minutes | Serves: 12

Ingredients:

2 eggs
2 cups all-purpose flour
1 cup pumpkin puree
½ cup olive oil
½ cup maple syrup

½ cup of chocolate chips
1 teaspoon pumpkin pie spice
1 teaspoon baking soda
½ teaspoon salt

Directions:

1. Place the cooking pot in the Ninja Foodi Smart XL Grill. 2. In a bowl, mix flour, baking soda, pumpkin pie spice and salt. 3. In a separate bowl, whisk eggs, pumpkin puree, oil and maple syrup. 4. Add flour mixture into the egg mixture and mix until well combined. 5. Add chocolate chips and fold well. Pour batter into the muffin molds. 6. Select the Bake Mode and set the temperature to 350°F/175°C. 7. Use the Arrow keys to set the time to 35 minutes. 8. Press the START/STOP button to initiate preheating. 9. Once preheated, place the baking dish in the Ninja Foodi Smart XL Grill. 10. Cover the hood and allow the grill to cook. 11. Serve, when done.

Serving Suggestion: Allow to cool completely then serve.

Variation Tip: None

Nutritional Information per Serving: Calories 237 | Fat 11.5g |Sodium 219mg | Carbs 30.7g | Fiber 1.4g | Sugar 12.2g | Protein 3.8g

Dessert Nachos

Prep time: 10 minutes | Cook Time: 9 minutes | Serves: 8

Ingredients:

8 flour tortillas
¼ cup sugar
1 tbsp. cinnamon
1 cup caramel sauce

6 oz. chocolate chips
6 oz. white chocolate, grated
½ cup heavy cream
1 cup pecans, chopped

Directions:

1. Cut tortillas in 8 wedges. 2. Place the cooking pot in the Ninja Foodi Smart XL Grill. 3. Select the Bake Mode and set the temperature to 350°F/175°C. 4. Use the Arrow keys to set the time to 10 minutes. 5. Press the Start/Stop button to initiate preheating. 6. Once preheated, place the wedges in the Ninja Foodi Smart XL Grill. 7. Cover the hood and allow the grill to cook. 8. Spread the rest of the ingredients on top of the tortilla wedges. 9. Cover the hood and bake for 3 minutes. 10. Serve.

Serving Suggestion: Serve the nachos with creamy frosting on top.

Variation Tip: Add crushed pecans to the muffins.

Nutritional Information per Serving: Calories 195 | Fat 3g |Sodium 355mg | Carbs 27g | Fiber 1g | Sugar 25g | Protein 1g

Delicious Chocolate Brownie

Prep time: 10 minutes | Cook Time: 20 minutes | Serves: 8

Ingredients:

2 eggs
½ cup chocolate chips
2 cup all-purpose flour
2 teaspoons baking powder

1 teaspoon vanilla
1¼ cup brown sugar
1 cup butter, melted
½ teaspoon salt

Directions:

1. Place the cooking pot in the Ninja Foodi Smart XL Grill. 2. In a bowl, mix butter and sugar. 3. Add vanilla and eggs and mix well. 4. Add flour, baking powder and salt and mix until well combined. 5. Add chocolate chips and stir well. 6. Pour batter into the greased baking dish. 7. Select the Bake Mode and set the temperature to 350°F/175°C. 8. Use the Arrow keys to set the time to 20 minutes. 9. Press the START/STOP button to initiate preheating. 10. Once preheated, place the baking dish in the Ninja Foodi Smart XL Grill. 11. Cover the hood and allow the grill to cook. 12. Serve, when done.

Serving Suggestion: Slice and serve.

Variation Tip: None

Nutritional Information per Serving: Calories 478 | Fat 27.5g |Sodium 343mg | Carbs 53.1g | Fiber 1.2g | Sugar 27.6g | Protein 5.7g

Grilled Pound Cake

Prep time: 15 minutes | Cook Time: 5 minutes | Serves: 4

Ingredients:

2 large peaches, sliced
2 tbsp. pomegranate molasses
2 tbsp. brandy

½ tsp. sugar
4 1-in.-thick pound cake slices
About ¼ cup whipped cream

Directions:

1. Mix peaches with sugar, brandy, and molasses in a bowl. 2. Place the cooking pot in the Ninja Foodi Smart XL Grill then set a grill grate inside. 3. Select the "Grill" Mode, set the temperature to MED. 4. Use the arrow keys to set the cooking time to 5 minutes. 5. Press the START/STOP button to initiate preheating. 6. Once preheated, place the cake slices in the Ninja Foodi Smart XL Grill. 7. Cover the hood and allow the grill to cook. 8. Flip the cake slices once cooked halfway through. 9. Top the cake slices with the peach mixture. 10. Garnish with almonds and whipped cream. 11. Serve.

Serving Suggestion: Serve the pound cake with melted chocolate on top.

Variation Tip: Add crushed nuts to the cake.

Nutritional Information per Serving: Calories 118 | Fat 20g |Sodium 192mg | Carbs 26g | Fiber 0.9g | Sugar 19g | Protein 5.2g

Pecan Kabobs

Prep time: 15 minutes | Cook Time: 10 minutes | Serves: 4

Ingredients:

1 loaf (10- ¾ oz.) pound cake, cubed
2 large bananas, cut into 1-inch slices
¼ cup butter, melted
2 tbsp. brown sugar
½ tsp. vanilla extract

⅛ tsp. ground cinnamon
4 cups butter pecan ice cream
½ cup butterscotch ice cream topping
½ cup chopped pecans, toasted

Directions:

1. Thread cake and banana pieces on the wooden skewers. 2. Mix butter with cinnamon, vanilla and brown sugar. 3. Brush this mixture over the skewers. 4. Place the cooking pot in the Ninja Foodi Smart XL Grill. 5. Select the Bake Mode and set the temperature to 350°F/175°C. 6. Use the Arrow keys to set the time to 10 minutes. 7. Press the Start/Stop button to initiate preheating. 8. Once preheated, place the skewers in the Ninja Foodi Smart XL Grill. 9. Cover the hood and allow the grill to cook. 10. Serve the skewers with ice cream and, butterscotch topping. 11. Garnish with pecans. 12. Serve.

Serving Suggestion: Serve the kabobs with whipped cream on top.

Variation Tip: Add crushed walnuts or pecans to the kebabs.

Nutritional Information per Serving: Calories 203 | Fat 8.9g |Sodium 340mg | Carbs 22g | Fiber 1.2g | Sugar 11.3g | Protein 5.3g

Grilled Fruit Skewers

Prep time: 15 minutes | Cook Time: 12 minutes | Serves: 6

Ingredients:

6 peaches, sliced
1 pint strawberries, sliced

1 pineapple, cut into cubes
Honey, for drizzling

Directions:

1. Thread the peaches and other fruits on the wooden skewers. 2. Place the cooking pot in the Ninja Foodi Smart XL Grill then set a grill grate inside. 3. Select the Grill Mode and set the temperature to 350°F/175°C. 4. Use the Arrow keys to set the time to 12 minutes. 5. Press the Start/Stop button to initiate preheating. 6. Once preheated, place the silicon molds in the Ninja Foodi Smart XL Grill. 7. Cover the hood and allow the grill to cook. 8. Flip the skewers once cooked halfway through. 9. Drizzle honey over the skewers and serve.

Serving Suggestion: Serve the skewers with chocolate sauce on top.

Variation Tip: Add crushed walnuts or pecans over the skewers.

Nutritional Information per Serving: Calories 217 | Fat 12g |Sodium 79mg | Carbs 28g | Fiber 1.1g | Sugar 18g | Protein 5g

Donut Ice Cream Sandwich

Prep time: 15 minutes | Cook Time: 14 minutes | Serves: 4

Ingredients:

4 whole donuts

2 cups fresh blueberries

1 cup fresh blackberries

¾ cup water

1 tsp. lemon zest

¼ cup honey

Directions:

1. Toss berries with water, honey, and lemon zest in a baking pan. 2. Place the cooking pot in the Ninja Foodi Smart XL Grill. 3. Select the Bake Mode and set the temperature to 350°F/175°C. 4. Use the Arrow keys to set the time to 10 minutes. 5. Press the Start/Stop button to initiate preheating. 6. Once preheated, place the pan in the Ninja Foodi Smart XL Grill. 7. Cover the hood and allow the grill to cook. 8. Slice the donuts in half and grill them in the Ninja Foodi Smart Grill for 2 minutes per side. 9. Add ice cream scoop and berries mixture to the donut halves. 10. Serve.

Serving Suggestion: Serve the donuts with chocolate syrup on top.

Variation Tip: Add crushed walnuts or pecans to the filling.

Nutritional Information per Serving: Calories 198 | Fat 14g |Sodium 272mg | Carbs 27g | Fiber 1g | Sugar 9.3g | Protein 1.3g

Grilled Apples a la Mode

Prep time: 10 minutes | Cook Time: 6 minutes | Serves: 4

Ingredients:

2 tart-sweet apples, sliced

2 tbsp. butter, melted

2 tbsp. brown sugar

2 tbsp. white sugar

1 tsp. cinnamon

¼ tsp. ginger

¼ tsp. nutmeg

For serving: Vanilla ice cream

Directions:

1. Mix sugars, butter, cinnamon, nutmeg and ginger in a suitable bowl. 2. Toss in butter, and apples mix well and leave for 5 minutes. 3. Place the cooking pot in the Ninja Foodi Smart XL Grill then set a grill grate inside. 4. Select the "Grill" Mode, set the temperature to MED. 5. Use the arrow keys to set the cooking time to 6 minutes. 6. Press the START/STOP button to initiate preheating. 7. Once preheated, place the apple in the Ninja Foodi Smart XL Grill. 8. Cover the hood and allow the grill to cook. 9. Flip the apple slices once cooked halfway through. 10. Serve with an ice-cream scoop on top.

Serving Suggestion: Serve the apples with fresh blueberries on top.

Variation Tip: Add crushed nuts on top of the apples.

Nutritional Information per Serving: Calories 255 | Fat 21g |Sodium 152mg | Carbs 36g | Fiber 2g | Sugar 15g | Protein 3.6g

Grilled Apples with Bourbon and Brown Sugar

Prep time: 20 minutes | Cook Time: 7 minutes | Serves: 4

Ingredients

1 packet Brown Sugar Bourbon Marinade

½ cup oil

½ cup water

2 tbsps. apple cider vinegar

4 apples

½ tsp cinnamon

1 cup vanilla ice cream

¼ cup granola

Directions:

1. Prepare the Brown Sugar Bourbon Marinade by whisking together the water, oil, and apple cider vinegar. Pour the marinade into a large pan or zip top bag. 2. Remove the cores from the four apples with an apple corer. 3. Cut the apples horizontally into thick ½-inch slices. Discard the top and bottom. You should get 2-3 apple slices per apple depending on the size of your apples. 4. Place the apple slices in the marinade and turn or toss to gently coat. Cover and allow marinating for 15 minutes, but no longer than 30 minutes. 5. Select the "Grill" function and adjust temperature to "MAX" and preheat your Ninja Foodi Smart XL Grill for 10 minutes. 6. Using tongs, place the apple slices onto the hot grill grate. Allow to grill for 2-3 minutes or until light brown grill marks appear on the bottoms. 7. Turn and grill an additional 2-3 minutes or until the apples are just fork-tender. 8. Remove to a plate and allow cooling a few minutes.

Serving Suggestion: Top the 2-3 slices of the warm apples with a sprinkle of cinnamon, a scoop of vanilla ice cream, and granola. Serve immediately.

Variation Tip: add pears and have unique deliciousness.

Nutritional Information per Serving: Calories 199 | Fat 5g | Carbohydrates 38g| Fiber 5g | Sodium 31mg | Protein 3g

Grilled Chocolate Sandwiches

Prep time: 15 minutes | Cook Time: 10 minutes | Serves: 4

Ingredients:

¼ cup seedless raspberry preserves

8 (¼ -inch) Portuguese bread slices

12 (.53-oz.) packages dark chocolate squares

8 tsp. butter

Directions:

1. Top each of the 4 bread slices with 2 chocolate squares, and ¼ raspberry preserves. 2. Place the other bread slices on top and brush the top with butter. 3. Place the cooking pot in the Ninja Foodi Smart XL Grill then set a grill grate inside. 4. Select the "Grill" Mode, set the temperature to MED. 5. Use the arrow keys to set the cooking time to 10 minutes. 6. Press the START/STOP button to initiate preheating. 7. Once preheated, place the sandwiches in the Ninja Foodi Smart XL Grill. 8. Cover the hood and allow the grill to cook. 9. Flip the sandwiches once cooked halfway through. 10. Serve.

Serving Suggestion: Serve the sandwiches with sliced strawberries on top.

Variation Tip: Add crushed nuts on top.

Nutritional Information per Serving: Calories 159 | Fat 3g |Sodium 277mg | Carbs 29g | Fiber 1g | Sugar 9g | Protein 2g

---

Cinnamon Grilled Peaches

Prep time: 15 minutes | Cook Time: 2 minutes | Serves: 4

Ingredients:

¼ cup salted butter

1 tablespoon, 1 teaspoon granulated sugar

¼ teaspoon cinnamon

4 ripe peaches, halved and pitted

Vegetable oil

Directions:

1. Place the cooking pot in the Ninja Foodi Smart XL Grill then place the grill grate in the pot. 2. Mix sugar with butter and cinnamon in a bowl until smooth. 3. Place the peaches in the Ninja Foodi Smart XL Grill. 4. Cover the Ninja Foodi Smart XL Grill's Hood, select the Grill mode, set the temperature to MED and grill for 1 minute per side. 5. Serve the peaches with cinnamon butter on top. 6. Enjoy.

Serving Suggestion: Serve the peaches with chocolate syrup on top.

Variation Tip: Add dried raisins to garnish the grilled peaches.

Nutritional Information per Serving: Calories 203 | Fat 8.9g | Sodium 340mg | Carbs 24.7g | Fiber 1.2g | Sugar 11.3g | Protein 5.3g

---

Moist Lemon Cupcakes

Prep time: 10 minutes | Cook Time: 15 minutes | Serves: 6

Ingredients:

1 egg

1 cup flour

¾ teaspoon baking powder

½ teaspoon vanilla

½ cup milk

2 tablespoons canola oil

¼ teaspoon baking soda

1 teaspoon lemon zest, grated

½ cup sugar

½ teaspoon salt

Directions:

1. Place the cooking pot in the Ninja Foodi Smart XL Grill. 2. In a bowl, whisk egg, vanilla, milk, oil and sugar until creamy. 3. Add remaining ingredients and stir until well combined. 4. Pour batter into the silicone muffin molds. 5. Select the Bake Mode and set the temperature to 350°F/175°C. 6. Use the Arrow keys to set the time to 15 minutes. 7. Press the START/STOP button to initiate preheating. 8. Once preheated, place the muffin molds in the Ninja Foodi Smart XL Grill. 9. Cover the hood and allow the grill to cook. 10. Serve, when done.

Serving Suggestion: Allow to cool completely then serve.

Variation Tip: Add melted butter if you don't have canola oil.

Nutritional Information per Serving: Calories 202 | Fat 6g |Sodium 267mg | Carbs 34g | Fiber 0.6g | Sugar 17.8g | Protein 3.8g

Grilled Pears with Cinnamon Drizzle

Prep time: 15 minutes | Cook Time: 14 minutes | Serves: 3

Ingredients:

3 ripe pears

2 tablespoons honey

1 tablespoon cinnamon

¼ cup pecans, chopped

Coconut oil

Sea salt

Directions:

1. Peel and cut the pears into quarters. 2. Toss pears with honey, cinnamon and coconut oil. 3. Place the pears in the Ninja Foodi Smart XL Grill. 4. Cover the Ninja Foodi Smart XL Grill's Hood, set the temperature to 375°F/190°C and cook them on the Bake mode for 7 minutes per side. 5. Garnish with pecans and sea salt. 6. Serve.

Serving Suggestion: Serve the pears with fresh berries on top.

Variation Tip: Add crushed nuts to give the pears a crunchy texture.

Nutritional Information per Serving: Calories 118 | Fat 20g | Sodium 192mg | Carbs 23.7g | Fiber 0.9g | Sugar 19g | Protein 5.2g

Marshmallow Roll-Up

Prep time: 15 minutes | Cook Time: 10 minutes | Serves: 2

Ingredients:

1 flour tortilla

1 handful mini marshmallows

1 handful of chocolate chips

2 graham crackers

Directions:

1. Spread a 12x12 inch foil on a working surface. 2. Place the tortilla over this sheet and top it with graham crackers, chocolate chips and marshmallows. 3. Roll the tortilla tightly by rolling the foil sheet. 4. Place the tortilla rolls in the Ninja Foodi Smart XL Grill. 5. Cover the Ninja Foodi Smart XL Grill's Hood, set the temperature to 350°F/175°C and select the Bake mode for 5 minutes per side. 6. Unwrap and slice in half. 7. Serve.

Serving Suggestion: Serve the rolls with chocolate syrup on top.

Variation Tip: Drizzle chocolate syrup on top of the rolls.

Nutritional Information per Serving: Calories 153 | Fat 1g | Sodium 8mg | Carbs 66g | Fiber 0.8g | Sugar 56g | Protein 1g

Berry Cobbler

Prep time: 15 minutes | Cook Time: 20 minutes | Serves: 8

Ingredients:

2 cans (21 ounces) blueberry pie filling

1¼ cups water

½ cup canola oil

1 (8 ounces) package cake mix

Vanilla ice cream

Directions:

1. First, mix the cake mix with oil and water in a bowl until smooth. 2. Place the foil packet on a working surface and add pie filling. 3. Spread the cake mix on top of the filling. 4. Cover the foil packet and seal it. 5. Place the packet in the Ninja Foodi Smart XL Grill. 6. Cover the Ninja Foodi Smart XL Grill's Hood, set the temperature to 350°F/175°C and cook on Bake mode for 20 minutes. 7. Serve fresh with vanilla ice cream on top.

Serving Suggestion: Serve the cobbler with blueberry syrup on top.

Variation Tip: Add crushed walnuts or pecans to the filling.

Nutritional Information per Serving: Calories 198 | Fat 14g | Sodium 272mg | Carbs 34g | Fiber 1g | Sugar 9.3g | Protein 1.3g

Ninja Foodi Grilled Pineapple Sundaes

Prep time: 5 minutes | Cook Time: 4 minutes | Serves: 2

Ingredients:

2 scoops vanilla ice cream

2 pineapple slices

1 tablespoon sweetened coconut, toasted and shredded

Directions:

1. Press "Grill" button in a Ninja Foodi Smart XL Grill and set the time to 4 minutes. Adjust the temperature to HI heat. 2. Press START/STOP to begin preheating. 3. When it shows "Add Food", place pineapple slices in it and cook for 4 minutes, flipping halfway through. 4. Dish out and top with vanilla ice cream and shredded coconut. 5. Serve and enjoy!

Serving Suggestions: Serve with pineapple syrup on the top.

Variation Tip: You can add vanilla extract.

Nutritional Information per Serving: Calories: 228 |Fat: 8g|Sat Fat: 5.3g|Carbohydrates: 38g|Fiber: 3g|Sugar: 30.4g|Protein: 3.3g

Grill Pineapple Slices

Prep time: 10 minutes | Cook Time: 8 minutes | Serves: 6

Ingredients:

6 pineapple slices
½ teaspoon ground cinnamon

¼ cup brown sugar

Directions:

1. Place the grill grate in the Ninja Foodi Smart XL Grill. 2. Toss pineapple slices with brown sugar and cinnamon. 3. Select the "Grill" Mode, set the temperature to HI. 4. Use the arrow keys on the display to select time to 8 minutes. 5. Press the START/STOP button to initiate preheating. 6. Once preheated, place the pineapple in the Ninja Foodi Smart XL Grill. 7. Cover the hood and allow the grill to cook. 8. Flip the halfway through. 9. Serve, when done.

Serving Suggestion: Allow to cool completely then serve.

Variation Tip: None

Nutritional Information per Serving: Calories 83 | Fat 0g |Sodium 2mg | Carbs 21g | Fiber 1g | Sugar 19g | Protein 0g

Banana Skewers

Prep time: 15 minutes | Cook Time: 6 minutes | Serves: 2

Ingredients:

1 loaf (10 ¾ ounces) cake, cubed
2 large bananas, 1-inch slices
¼ cup butter, melted
2 tablespoons brown sugar
½ teaspoon vanilla extract

⅛ teaspoon ground cinnamon
4 cups butter pecan ice cream
½ cup butterscotch ice cream topping
½ cup chopped pecans, toasted

Directions:

1. Place the cooking pot in the Ninja Foodi Smart XL Grill then place the grill grate in the pot. 2. Thread the cake and bananas over the skewers alternately. 3. Whisk butter with cinnamon, vanilla and brown sugar in a small bowl. 4. Brush this mixture over the skewers liberally. 5. Place the banana skewers in the Ninja Foodi Smart XL Grill. 6. Cover the Ninja Foodi Smart XL Grill's Hood, select the Grill mode, set the temperature to LO and grill for 3 minutes per side. 7. Serve with ice cream, pecan and butterscotch topping on top.

Serving Suggestion: Serve the skewers with maple syrup on top.

Variation Tip: Add crushed chocolate on top of the skewers.

Nutritional Information per Serving: Calories 245 | Fat 14g | Sodium 122mg | Carbs 23.3g | Fiber 1.2g | Sugar 12g | Protein 4.3g

Moist Carrot Muffins

Prep time: 10 minutes | Cook Time: 20 minutes | Serves: 6

Ingredients:

1 egg
¼ cup brown sugar
¼ cup sugar
1 cup all-purpose flour
¾ cup grated carrots
1 teaspoon vanilla

¼ cup applesauce
½ tablespoon canola oil
1½ teaspoon baking powder
¼ teaspoon nutmeg
1 teaspoon cinnamon
¼ teaspoon salt

Directions:

1. Place the cooking pot in the Ninja Foodi Smart XL Grill. 2. Add all ingredients into the bowl and mix until well combined. 3. Pour batter into the greased silicone muffin molds. 4. Select the Bake Mode and set the temperature to 350°F/175°C. 5. Use the Arrow keys to set the time to 20 minutes. 6. Press the START/STOP button to initiate preheating. 7. Once preheated, place the silicon molds in the Ninja Foodi Smart XL Grill. 8. Cover the hood and allow the grill to cook. 9. Serve, when done.

Serving Suggestion: Allow to cool completely then serve.

Variation Tip: Add melted butter if you don't have canola oil.

Nutritional Information per Serving: Calories 165 | Fat 2.2g |Sodium 120mg | Carbs 33.7g | Fiber 1.3g | Sugar 16.2g | Protein 3.2g

Chocolate Chip Bars

Prep time: 10 minutes | Cook Time: 30 minutes | Serves: 12

Ingredients:

2 eggs, lightly beaten
1½ cup all-purpose flour
1 teaspoon vanilla
1½ cups chocolate chips

½ teaspoon baking soda
½ cup sugar
½ cup brown sugar
1 stick butter

Directions:

1. Place the cooking pot in the Ninja Foodi Smart XL Grill. 2. In a bowl, beat butter with sugar, vanilla and brown sugar until fluffy. 3. Add eggs and vanilla and beat well. 4. In a separate bowl, mix flour and baking soda. 5. Add flour mixture into the egg mixture and mix until just combined. 6. Add 1 cup chocolate chips and fold well. 7. Pour batter into the greased baking dish. 8. Sprinkle remaining chocolate chips on top. 9. Select the Bake Mode and set the temperature to 350°F/175°C. 10. Use the Arrow keys to set the time to 30 minutes. 11. Press the START/STOP button to initiate preheating. 12. Once preheated, place the baking dish in the Ninja Foodi Smart XL Grill. 13. Cover the hood and allow the grill to cook. 14. Serve, when done.

Serving Suggestion: Slice and serve.
Variation Tip: None
Nutritional Information per Serving: Calories 302 | Fat 14g |Sodium 135mg | Carbs 38g | Fiber 1g | Sugar 25g | Protein 4g

Easy Scalloped Pineapple

Prep time: 10 minutes | Cook Time: 30 minutes | Serves: 6

Ingredients:

3 eggs, lightly beaten
8 ounces can pineapple, crushed
1½ cup sugar
4 cups of bread cubes

¼ cup milk
½ cup butter, melted
½ cup brown sugar

Directions:

1. Place the cooking pot in the Ninja Foodi Smart XL Grill. 2. In a bowl, mix eggs, milk, pineapple, butter, brown sugar and sugar. 3. Add bread cubes and stir until well coated. 4. Pour mixture into the greased baking dish. 5. Select the Bake Mode and set the temperature to 350°F/175°C. 6. Use the Arrow keys to set the time to 30 minutes. 7. Press the START/STOP button to initiate preheating. 8. Once preheated, place the baking dish in the Ninja Foodi Smart XL Grill. 9. Cover the hood and allow the grill to cook. 10. Serve, when done.

Serving Suggestion: Serve warm.
Variation Tip: None
Nutritional Information per Serving: Calories 492 | Fat 17g |Sodium 281mg | Carbs 80g | Fiber 0g | Sugar 66g | Protein 3.4g

Fudgy Brownie

Prep time: 10 minutes | Cook Time: 45 minutes | Serves: 16

Ingredients:

4 eggs
1 cup all-purpose flour
1¼ cups butter
1½ cups cocoa powder
2½ cups sugar

1 teaspoon vanilla
1 cup chocolate chips
2 teaspoons baking powder
½ tsp Kosher salt

Directions:

1. Place the cooking pot in the Ninja Foodi Smart XL Grill. 2. Add butter, cocoa powder and sugar in a microwave-safe bowl and microwave for one minute. Stir well. 3. Add eggs and stir until well combined. 4. Add flour, baking powder and salt and stir well. 5. Add chocolate chips and fold well. 6. Pour batter into the greased baking dish. 7. Select the Bake Mode and set the temperature to 325°F/160°C. 8. Use the Arrow keys to set the time to 45 minutes. 9. Press the START/STOP button to initiate preheating. 10. Once preheated, place the baking dish in the Ninja Foodi Smart XL Grill. 11. Cover the hood and allow the grill to cook. 12. Serve, when done.

Serving Suggestion: Slice and serve.
Variation Tip: None
Nutritional Information per Serving: Calories 364 | Fat 19.7g |Sodium 202mg | Carbs 48.3g | Fiber 3g | Sugar 36.9g | Protein 4.6g

Moist Raspberry Muffins

Prep time: 10 minutes | Cook Time: 20 minutes | Serves: 12

Ingredients:

1 egg
1 cup raspberries
1 ¾ cups all-purpose flour
1 teaspoon baking powder
⅓ cup sugar

½ cup canola oil
6 ounces of yogurt
½ teaspoon baking soda
½ teaspoon salt

Directions:

1. Place the cooking pot in the Ninja Foodi Smart XL Grill. 2. In a bowl, mix all dry ingredients. 3. In a small bowl, whisk egg, oil and yogurt. 4. Add egg mixture and raspberries into the dry mixture and mix until well combined. 5. Spoon mixture into the silicone muffin molds. 6. Select the Bake Mode and set the temperature to 400°F/200°C. 7. Use the Arrow keys to set the time to 20 minutes. 8. Press the START/STOP button to initiate preheating. 9. Once preheated, place the muffin molds in the Ninja Foodi Smart XL Grill. 10. Cover the hood and allow the grill to cook. 11. Serve, when done.

Serving Suggestion: Allow to cool completely then serve.
Variation Tip: None
Nutritional Information per Serving: Calories 189 | Fat 9.9g |Sodium 165mg | Carbs 21.9g | Fiber 1.2g | Sugar 7.1g | Protein 3.3g

Marshmallow Banana Boat

Prep time: 19 minutes | Cook Time: 6 minutes|Servings: 4

Ingredients

4 ripe bananas
1 cup mini marshmallows

½ cup of chocolate chips
½ cup peanut butter chips

Directions:

1. Slice a banana lengthwise, keeping its peel. 2. Use your hands to open banana peel like a book, revealing the inside of a banana. 3. Divide marshmallow, chocolate chips, peanut butter among bananas, stuffing them inside. 4. Select the "Grill" function, adjust temperature to "MED" and set the timer to 6 minutes and preheat Ninja Foodi Smart XL Grill. 5. Let it preheat until you hear a beep. 6. Transfer banana to Grill Grate and lock lid, cook for 4-6 minutes until chocolate melts and bananas are toasted.

Serving Suggestion: Serve and enjoy.
Variation Tip: use nuts for crunch.
Nutritional Information per Serving: Calories: 505| Fat: 18 g| Carbohydrates: 82| Fiber: 6 g| Sodium: 103 mg| Protein: 10 g

Strawberry Cobbler

Prep time: 10 minutes | Cook Time: 45 minutes | Serves: 6

Ingredients:

2 cups strawberries, diced
1 cup self-rising flour
1¼ cup sugar

1 teaspoon vanilla
½ cup butter, melted
1 cup milk

Directions:

1. Place the cooking pot in the Ninja Foodi Smart XL Grill. 2. In a bowl, mix flour and one cup sugar. Add milk and whisk until smooth. 3. Add vanilla and butter and mix well. 4. Pour mixture into the baking dish and sprinkle with strawberries and top with remaining sugar. 5. Select the Bake Mode and set the temperature to 350°F/175°C. 6. Use the Arrow keys to set the time to 45 minutes. 7. Press the START/STOP button to initiate preheating. 8. Once preheated, place the baking dish in the Ninja Foodi Smart XL Grill. 9. Cover the hood and allow the grill to cook. 10. Serve, when done.

Serving Suggestion: Allow to cool completely then serve.
Variation Tip: You can also add some fresh chopped raspberries.
Nutritional Information per Serving: Calories 405 | Fat 16.5g |Sodium 129mg | Carbs 63.4g | Fiber 1.5g | Sugar 46g | Protein 4g

Rummy Pineapple Sunday

Prep time: 10 minutes | Cook Time: 8 minutes | Servings: 4

Ingredients

½ cup dark rum
½ cup packed brown sugar

1 pineapple cored and sliced
Vanilla ice cream, for serving

Directions:

1. Take a large-sized bowl and add rum, sugar, cinnamon. 2. Add pineapple slices, arrange them in the layer. Coat mixture then let them soak for 5 minutes, per side. 3. Select the "Grill" function, adjust temperature to "MAX" and set the time to 8 minutes and preheat Ninja Foodie Smart XL Grill. 4. Let it preheat until you hear a beep. 5. Strain extra rum sauce from pineapple. 6. Transfer prepared fruit in grill grate in a single layer, press down fruit and lock lid. 7. Grill for 6-8 minutes without flipping, work in batches if needed. 8. Once done, remove and serve.

Serving Suggestion: top each pineapple ring with a scoop of ice cream, sprinkle cinnamon and serve Enjoy!
Variation Tip: use melted chocolate for taste.
Nutritional Information per Serving: Calories: 240| Fat: 4 g| Carbohydrates: 43 g| Fiber: 3 g| Sodium: 32 mg| Protein: 2 g

Apricots with Brioche

Prep time: 15 minutes | Cook Time: 2 minutes | Serves: 8

Ingredients:

8 ripe apricots
2 tablespoons butter
2 tablespoons sugar

4 slice brioches, diced
2 tablespoons honey
2 cups vanilla ice cream

Directions:

1. Place the cooking pot in the Ninja Foodi Smart XL Grill then place the grill grate in the pot. 2. Toss the apricot halves with butter and sugar. 3. Place brioche slices in the Ninja Foodi Smart XL Grill. 4. Cover the Ninja Foodi Smart XL Grill's Hood, select the Grill mode, set the temperature to LO and grill for 2 minute per side. 5. Now grill the apricots in the same grill for 2 minute per side. 6. Top these slices with apricot slices, honey and a scoop of vanilla ice cream. 7. Serve.

Serving Suggestion: Serve the Apricot Brioche with chocolate or apple sauce.
Variation Tip: Dip the brioche in maple syrup.
Nutritional Information per Serving: Calories 117 | Fat 12g | Sodium 79mg | Carbs 24.8g | Fiber 1.1g | Sugar 18g | Protein 5g

Chocolate Cheesecake

Prep time: 15 minutes | Cook Time: 15 minutes | Servings: 4

Ingredients

2 cups cream cheese, softened
2 eggs
2 tsp cocoa powder

1 tsp pure vanilla extract
½ cup Swerve

Directions:

1. Add in eggs, cocoa powder, vanilla extract, swerve, cream cheese in an immersion blender and blend until smooth. 2. Pour the mixture evenly into mason jars. 3. Put the mason jars in the insert of Ninja Foodi Smart XL Grill and close the lid. 4. Select the "BAKE" function of the Ninja Foodi Smart XL Grill at 360°F/180°C for 15 minutes. 5. Bake the cake for 15 minutes until done. 6. Refrigerate for at least 2 hours.

Serving Suggestion: Serve and enjoy.
Variation Tip: use chopped nuts for garnish.
Nutritional Information per Serving: Calories 244| Total Fat 24 g| Carbohydrates 2.1 g| Fiber 0.1 g| Sodium 204 mg| Protein 4 g

Ninja Foodi Grilled Donut Ice Cream Sandwich

Prep time: 5 minutes | Cook Time: 3 minutes | Serves: 2

Ingredients:

4 scoops vanilla ice cream
½ cup whipped cream

2 glazed donuts, halved
2 cherries

Directions:

1. Press "Grill" button in a Ninja Foodi Smart XL Grill and set the time to 3 minutes. Adjust the temperature to MAX heat. 2. Press START/STOP to begin preheating. 3. Place donuts in it when it shows "Add Food" and cook for 3 minutes. 4. Dish out and fill each donut sandwich with vanilla ice cream. 5. Top with whipped cream and cherries. 6. Serve and enjoy!

Serving Suggestions: Top with chocolate syrup before serving.
Variation Tip: Cherries can be omitted.
Nutritional Information per Serving: Calories: 637 |Fat: 33.3g|Sat Fat: 16.8g|Carbohydrates: 77.6g|Fiber: 2.4g|Sugar: 28g|Protein: 7.5g

Cute Marshmallow and Banana

Prep time: 19 minutes | Cook Time: 6 minutes|Servings: 4

Ingredients

4 ripe bananas

1 cup mini marshmallows

½ cup of chocolate chips

½ cup peanut butter chips

Directions:

1. Slice a banana lengthwise, keeping its peel. Ensure not to cut all the way through. 2. Use your hands to open banana peel like a book, revealing the inside of a banana. 3. Divide marshmallow, chocolate chips, peanut butter among bananas, stuffing them inside. 4. Pre-heat Ninja Foodi Smart XL Grill by selecting the "GRILL" function and setting temperature to "MED" and timer to 6 minutes. 5. Let it pre-heat until you hear a beep. 6. Transfer banana to Grill Grate and lock lid, cook for 4-6 minutes until chocolate melts and bananas are toasted.

Serving Suggestion: Serve and enjoy.

Variation Tip: use chocolate shavings for little crunch.

Nutritional Information per Serving: Calories: 505| Fat: 18 g| Carbohydrates: 82 g| Fiber: 6 g| Sodium: 103 mg| Protein: 10 g

Marshmallow Stuffed Banana

Prep time: 15 minutes | Cook Time: 10 minutes | Serves: 2

Ingredients:

¼ cup of chocolate chips

1 banana

¼ cup mini marshmallows

Directions:

1. Place a peeled banana over a 12 x 12-inch foil sheet. 2. Make a slit in the banana lengthwise and stuff this slit with chocolate chips and marshmallows. 3. Wrap the foil around the banana and seal it. 4. Place the banana in the Ninja Foodi Smart XL Grill. 5. Cover the Ninja Foodi Smart XL Grill's Hood, set the temperature to 375°F/190°C and select the Bake mode for 5 minutes. 6. Unwrap and serve.

Serving Suggestion: Serve the marshmallows with a scoop of vanilla cream on top.

Variation Tip: Add chopped nuts to the marshmallows.

Nutritional Information per Serving: Calories 248 | Fat 16g | Sodium 95mg | Carbs 38.4g | Fiber 0.3g | Sugar 10g | Protein 14.1g

Lemon Mousse

Prep time: 15 minutes | Cook Time: 12 minutes|Servings: 2

Ingredients

4-ounce cream cheese softened

½ cup heavy cream

⅛ cup fresh lemon juice

½ tsp lemon liquid stevia

2 pinches salt

Directions:

1. Take a bowl and mix cream cheese, heavy cream, lemon juice, salt, and stevia. 2. Pour this mixture into the ramekins and transfer the ramekins in the cooking pot of Ninja Foodi Smart XL Grill. 3. Select the "BAKE" function of the Ninja Foodie Smart XL Grill for 12 minutes at temperature setting of 350°F/175°C. 4. Bake the ramekins for 12 minutes until done.

Serving Suggestion: Pour into the serving glasses and refrigerate for at least 3 hours and serve.

Variation Tip: use orange juice for flavor.

Nutritional Information per Serving: Calories: 225| Fat: 17 g| Carbohydrates: 13 g| Fiber: 3 g| Sodium: 284 mg| Protein: 6 g

The Healthy Granola Bites

Prep time: 10 minutes | Cook Time: 15-20 minutes|Servings: 4

Ingredients

Salt and pepper to taste

1 tablespoon coriander

A handful of thyme, diced

¼ cup of coconut milk

3 handful of cooked vegetables, your choice

3 pounces plain granola

Directions:

1. Pre-heat your Ninja Foodi Smart XL Grill to 350°F/175°C in "AIR CRISP" function set a timer to 20 minutes. 2. Take a bowl and add your cooked vegetables, granola. 3. Use an immersion blender to blitz your granola until you have a nice breadcrumb-like consistency. 4. Add coconut milk to the mix and mix until you have a nice firm texture. 5. Use the mixture to make granola balls and transfer them to your Ninja Foodi Smart XL Grill. 6. Cook for 20 minutes. 7. Serve and enjoy!

Serving Suggestion: Serve and enjoy.

Variation Tip: add dates for sweetness.

Nutritional Information per Serving: Calories: 140| Fat: 10 g| Carbohydrates: 14 g| Fiber: 4 g| Sodium: 215 mg| Protein: 2 g

Lovely Rum Sundae

Prep time: 10 minutes | Cook Time: 8 minutes|Servings: 4

Ingredients

Vanilla ice cream for serving

1 pineapple, cored and sliced

1 tsp cinnamon, ground

½ cup brown sugar, packed

½ cup dark rum

Directions:

1. Take a large deep bowl and add sugar, cinnamon, and rum. 2. Add the pineapple in the layer, dredge them properly and make sure that they are coated well. 3. Pre-heat your Ninja Foodi Smart XL Grill in "GRILL" function with "MAX" temperature settings, and timer to 8 minutes. 4. Once you hear the beep, strain any additional rum from the pineapple slices and transfer them to the grill rate of your Ninja Foodi Smart XL Grill. 5. Select them down and grill for 6- 8 minutes. Make sure not to overcrowd the grill grate, Cook in batches if needed.

Serving Suggestion: Serve Top each of the ring with a scoop of your favorite ice cream, sprinkle a bit of cinnamon on top.

Variation Tip: use melted chocolate for extra taste.

Nutritional Information per Serving: Calories: 240| Fat: 4 g| Carbohydrates: 43 g| Fiber: 8 g| Sodium: 85 mg| Protein: 2 g

Ninja Foodi Vanilla Donuts

Prep time: 10 minutes | Cook Time: 3 minutes | Serves: 4

Ingredients:

1 cup powdered sugar

½ teaspoon vanilla extract

2 tablespoons whole milk

1 cup prepared biscuit dough

¼ teaspoon ground cinnamon

Directions:

1. Add milk, vanilla extract and powdered sugar in a bowl. Mix well and set aside. 2. Now, make donuts shape out of the prepared biscuit dough and refrigerate for about 5 minutes. 3. Meanwhile, arrange "Grill Grate" in a Ninja Foodi Smart XL Grill and press the "Grill" button. 4. Adjust the time to 3 minutes and temperature to HI heat. Press START/STOP to begin preheating. 5. Place donuts in it when it shows "Add Food" and cook for about 3 minutes. 6. Take out and sprinkle with cinnamon and vanilla extract mixture. 7. Serve and enjoy!

Serving Suggestions: Put chocolate chips on the top before serving.

Variation Tip: You can omit cinnamon.

Nutritional Information per Serving: Calories: 171 |Fat: 2.4g|Sat Fat: 0.9g|Carbohydrates: 36.7g|Fiber: 0.3g|Sugar: 30.9g|Protein: 1.3g

Banana Muffins

Prep time: 10 minutes | Cook Time: 15 minutes | Serves: 10

Ingredients:

1 egg

¾ cup self-rising flour

⅓ cup olive oil

2 ripe bananas, mashed

1 teaspoon cinnamon

1 teaspoon vanilla

½ cup brown sugar

Directions:

1. Place the cooking pot in the Ninja Foodi Smart XL Grill. 2. In a bowl, mix egg with mashed bananas, oil, vanilla and brown sugar until well combined. 3. Add flour and cinnamon and mix until well combined. 4. Spoon mixture into the silicone muffin molds. 5. Select the Bake Mode and set the temperature to 320°F/160°C. 6. Use the Arrow keys to set the time to 15 minutes. 7. Press the START/STOP button to initiate preheating. 8. Once preheated, place the muffin molds in the Ninja Foodi Smart XL Grill. 9. Cover the hood and allow the grill to cook. 10. Serve.

Serving Suggestion: Allow to cool completely then serve.

Variation Tip: None

Nutritional Information per Serving: Calories 148 | Fat 7.3g |Sodium 9mg | Carbs 19.9g | Fiber 1g | Sugar 10g | Protein 1.8g

● Conclusion ●

Ninja Foodi Smart XL Grill has taken the culinary world by storm. This unique appliance offers the convenience of an indoor grill with the results of an outdoor grill. The secret is in the Smart Cook System, which uses patented Cyclonic Grilling Technology to circulate hot air evenly around food for perfect grilling results every time. Steak, chicken, fish, vegetables, and even fruit can be grilled to perfection with the push of a button. Ninja Foodi Smart XL Grill also includes a large capacity cooking basket that can accommodate enough food for the whole family. And when you're finished grilling, the removable non-stick Grill Grate makes cleanup a breeze. Whether you're a beginner or a grill master, Ninja Foodi Smart XL Grill is sure to take your grilling game to the next level.

This smart Grill is the perfect kitchen gadget for those who love to cook outdoors but don't always have the time or weather to do so. It's a 6-in-1 indoor grill that can air fry, bake, roast, and dehydrate. The Grill has a 4-quart cooking pot and can accommodate up to 6 servings. It also has a built-in smoker box that can be used with wood chips to add flavor to your food. Ninja Foodi Smart XL Grill is a must-have kitchen gadget for those who love cooking and entertaining. Not only will it make your food taste great, but it will also save you time and effort in the kitchen.

● Appendix 1 Measurement Conversion Chart ●

WEIGHT EQUIVALENTS

US STANDARD	METRIC (APPROXIMATE)
1 ounce	28 g
2 ounces	57 g
5 ounces	142 g
10 ounces	284 g
15 ounces	425 g
16 ounces (1 pound)	455 g
1.5 pounds	680 g
2 pounds	907 g

VOLUME EQUIVALENTS (LIQUID)

US STANDARD	US STANDARD (OUNCES)	METRIC (APPROXIMATE)
2 tablespoons	1 fl.oz	30 mL
¼ cup	2 fl.oz	60 mL
½ cup	4 fl.oz	120 mL
1 cup	8 fl.oz	240 mL
1½ cup	12 fl.oz	355 mL
2 cups or 1 pint	16 fl.oz	475 mL
4 cups or 1 quart	32 fl.oz	1 L
1 gallon	128 fl.oz	4 L

VOLUME EQUIVALENTS (DRY)

US STANDARD	METRIC (APPROXIMATE)
⅛ teaspoon	0.5 mL
¼ teaspoon	1 mL
½ teaspoon	2 mL
¾ teaspoon	4 mL
1 teaspoon	5 mL
1 tablespoon	15 mL
¼ cup	59 mL
½ cup	118 mL
¾ cup	177 mL
1 cup	235 mL
2 cups	475 mL
3 cups	700 mL
4 cups	1 L

TEMPERATURES EQUIVALENTS

FAHRENHEIT (F)	CELSIUS(C) (APPROXIMATE)
225 °F	107 °C
250 °F	120 °C
275 °F	135 °C
300 °F	150 °C
325 °F	160 °C
350 °F	180 °C
375 °F	190 °C
400 °F	205 °C
425 °F	220 °C
450 °F	235 °C
475 °F	245 °C
500 °F	260 °C

● Appendix 2 Recipes Index ●

Printed in Great Britain
by Amazon

28064644R00076